GLOBALIZATION AND HIGHER EDUCATION

Jonathan Westover, Editor

GLOBALIZATION AND HIGHER EDUCATION

Jonathan Westover, Editor

COMMON GROUND PUBLISHING 2017

First published in 2017
as part of the *Global Studies* Book Imprint
doi:10.18848/978-1-61229-930-3/CGP (Full Book)

Common Ground Publishing
2001 S. 1st St., Suite 202
University of Illinois Research Park
Champaign, IL
61821

Library of Congress Cataloging-in-Publication Data

Westover, Jonathan.
Globalization and Higher Education / by Jonathan Westover
    p. cm.
ISBN # 978-1-61229-930-3 (pbk: alk. Paper) – ISBN # 978-1-61229-931-0 (hardcover: alk. Paper) – ISBN # 978-1-61229-932-7 (pdf)

Names: Westover, Jonathan H., author.
Title: Globalization and higher education / by Jonathan Westover [editor].
Description: Champaign, IL : Common Ground Publishing, 2017. | Includes bibliographical references.
Identifiers: LCCN 2016049740 (print) | LCCN 2016050596 (ebook) | ISBN 9781612299303 (pbk : alk. paper) | ISBN 9781612299310 (hbk : alk. paper) | ISBN 9781612299327 (pdf)
Subjects: LCSH: Education, Higher. | Education and globalization.
Classification: LCC LA184 .G56 2017 (print) | LCC LA184 (ebook) | DDC 378--dc23
LC record available at https://lccn.loc.gov/2016049740

Cover Photo Credit: Phillip Kalantzis-Cope

Table of Contents

ACKNOWLEDGEMENTS

I want to thank Common Ground Publishing for providing me with a venue for publishing this edited compilation. Additionally, I would like to thank the many individuals who contributed their own research to this edited work. Of course, this book would not be possible without each of their important contributions. Most of all, I would like to publically thank my wife, Jacque, and my six wonderful children (Sara, Amber, Lia, Kaylie, David, and Brayden) for all of their love and support!

Contributor Information

Jonathan H. Westover

Dr. Jonathan H. Westover is an Associate Professor of Organizational Leadership in the Woodbury School of Business and Director of Academic Service Learning at UVU (and previously the Associate Director of the Center for the Study of Ethics). He is also president of the Utah Academy of Sciences, Arts, and Letters and is a human capital leadership and performance management consultant. He was recently a Fulbright Scholar (Minsk, Belarus), a POSCO Fellow at the East-West Center (Honolulu, Hawaii), and visiting scholar at the Wilson Center (Washington, D.C.) and he is a regular visiting faculty member in other international graduate business programs (U.S., U.K., France, Belarus, Poland, and China). Prior to his doctoral studies in the Sociology of Work and Organizations, Comparative International Sociology, and International Political Economy (University of Utah), he received his B.S. in Sociology (Research and Analysis emphasis, Business Management minor, Korean minor) and MPA (emphasis in Human Resource Management) from the Marriott School of Management at Brigham Young University. He also received graduate certificates in demography and higher education teaching during his time at the University of Utah. His ongoing research examines issues of globalization, labor transformation, work quality characteristics, and the determinants of job satisfaction cross-nationally.

Melville Miranda

Melville Miranda is a scholar of law, legal and social policy, legal research, and education, with intensive and extensive experience in teaching and law, as well as extensive practical legal experience India. He has contributed plenty of legal precedents to Indian judiciary on Common Law. He is a prospective solicitor and barrister in Australia from 2019–20.

Ewa Bacon

Ewa K. Bacon, PhD, received her BA in psychology from Stanford University and her doctorate in history from the University of Chicago. She is professor emeritus in the History Department of Lewis University in Romeoville, Illinois. World history is her special teaching interest. She has recently developed a course linking the development of science to world history from 1500 to the present. Her major research interest is in Nazi labor practices in Auschwitz with an emphasis on the work of prisoner physicians in the Buna-Monowitz subcamp. Her book Saving Lives in Auschwitz: The Prisoners Hospital in Buna-Monowitz will be published in 2017 by Purdue University Press.

DENISE EGÉA

Denise Egéa is Professor Emeritus at Louisiana State University, USA, and Professor in the Graduate School of Education at Nazarbayev University, Astana, Kazakhstan. She is a Fellow in the Philosophy of Education Society, a Phi Kappa Phi scholar, and an Officier dans l'Ordre des Palmes Académiques. Across disciplines and borders, her primary areas of scholarship are philosophy of education, curriculum studies, culture and language studies, and philosophy and methodology of research, with a focus on ethics, and on human, cultural, linguistic, and educational rights.

YANG-SEOK YOO

Dr. Yoo, Yang-Seok, Professor of General Education at Kookmin University, earned a BS in Mathematics from Harvey Mudd College, MS in Computer Science from Brown University, MBA from Columbia University, MA (Suma Cum Laude) in Intercultural Leadership from Asia Pacific College and PhD in Education from University of Philippines. Dr. Yoo pursues academic and research interests in globalization and multicultural implications in education, and serves as a member of the board for Center for Asian Pacific Exchange (CAPE). He is the author of the first authoritative English book on Korean tea culture, The Book of Korean Tea – A Guide to the History, Culture and Philosophy of Korean Tea and the Tea Ceremony.

SYLILA MONTEIRO

Sylila Monteiro teaches a wide range of communication and integrated practice papers across UNITEC at the under graduate level which include, critical thinking and sustainability. She previously taught at Zambia Institute of Technology now known as the Copperbelt University. She specialises in business document translation services for French and Portuguese organizations engaged in international communication. She has also provided training for NZ Army personnel in Portuguese and French as preparation for overseas assignments. Sylila's research interests include interdisciplinary integrated practice in education, intercultural communication and sustainability. She has presented her research at several conferences in New Zealand and overseas. Highlights of her research are publications in the International Learning Journal, Global Studies Journal and e-Learning Journal.

RASHIKA SHARMA

Rashika is a lecturer in Integrated Practice at Unitec Institute of Technology in New Zealand specialising in sustainable practice, societal context and generic skills on the Bachelor of Applied Technology. Rashika is currently pursuing a Doctoral Degree in Education from Deakin University in Australia and holds a Master's degree in Education from Unitec Institute of Technology. Rashika's research focus is on education for sustainability and takes keen interest in student centred teaching and learning strategies. Rashika has also taught at the Fiji Institute of Technology in Suva, Fiji.

DEJUN CAO

Dejun Cao received his Ph.D in Business Administration in 2003 in China. He is interested in analysing business issues by means of Networking Theory, He has been teaching international business for over 10 years. He is a member of Academy of Management (AOM), Academy of International Business (AIB) as well as a member of executive board of Global Digital Business Society (GDBS) at IUP. Currently he serves as Director of Foreign Affairs Office of SWUFE and is in charge of international exchange programs of the SWUFE.

JOHN ZHANG

John Zhang is a statistician. He has graduate degrees in mathematics, computer sciences, statistics, and management. His current academic interests include statistics, business, and multidisciplinary issues intersecting sciences and business. He has been teaching at Indiana University of Pennsylvania (IUP) for over 13 years. He was the president of the Allegheny Mountain Section of Mathematics Association of America (MAA), one of the 27 MAA sections. He has also directed the Applied Research Lab for IUP for 5 year. He has provided consulting services for numerous business and government entities. His hobbies include traveling and wine.

SHIXIANG ZUO

KAORI SHIMIZU

Kaori Shimizu is originally from Japan, and taught Japanese at universities in the United States. She is currently a doctoral student at the College of Human Sciences and Education, Louisiana State University. Based on her experience as a foreigner and as a foreign language instructor who attempted to communicate her culture to students, her research interest is to explore the notion of alterity and cultural difference, using the method of narrative inquiry.

HIEN NGUYEN

Hien Nguyen obtained an MBA from Asia International University in Hanoi, and a MA in Educational Leadership at Simon Fraser University in 2009, and is currently working as a Research Assistant at the Faculty of Education. Her research interests include higher education policies, small schools, leadership, globalization and student identities.

MICHELLE NILSON

Dr. Michelle Nilson is the Assistant Professor in Educational Leadership at the Faculty of Education, Simon Fraser University. Her research interests include higher education policies, globalization and higher education funding.

ALLAN MACKINNON

Dr. Allan MacKinnon is the Associate Professor at the Faculty of Education, Simon Fraser University. His research interests include science education and higher education reform in South East Asia.

NORASMAH OTHMAN

Norasmah Othman is an Associate Professor in Business and Entrepreneurship Education at Universiti Kebangsaan Malaysia, Bangi. She obtained her PhD of Entrepreneurship Education and Assessment from the Universiti Putra Malaysia and her Masters in Finance from the University of New Haven, Connecticut. Her Bachelor degree is also in the field of Finance which she obtained from the University of Minnesota, USA. Norasmah's research has been in 16 journals, 2 books, 22 chapters of books, 46 papers at the national and international levels in the area of entrepreneurship education. She also works closely with the Department of Orang Asli Affairs Malaysia for the sake of inculcating entrepreneurial culture especially to the Orang Asli adolescents.

HENRY J. RUTZ

Economic anthropologist with research interests in the cultural nationalism of Pacific Island States, with special reference to Fiji; also research interest in changing culture of the middle class in an era of globalization, with special reference to issues of class and education in Istanbul; Recent publications are Cultural Preservation, in World at Risk: A Global Issues Sourcebook (2002), The Rise and Demise of Islamic Religious Schools: Discourses of Belonging and Denial in the Construction of Turkish Civil Society and Culture, Political and Legal Anthropology Review (1999), and Evaluating the Discourse of Tradition, Pacific Studies (2000); growing interest in the relationship of cultural pluralism, contested commodities, and intellectual property rights at the intersection of cultural anthropology and law.

EROL M. BALKAN

Balkan earned a PhD in economics from the State University of New York at Binghamton and joined the Hamilton faculty in 1987. His current research focuses on the formation of middle classes through education and financial liberalization in developing countries. Balkan has received several awards and grants for his work, including the International Development Research Center Grant in 1996 to study the effects of short term capital flows on the Turkish economy. He teaches economic development, international finance and political economy of the Middle East at Hamilton and has lectured as a visiting professor at Bilkent University in Ankara and Sabanci University in Istanbul, Turkey. Balkan's recent books "Reproducing Class: Education, Neoliberalism, and the Rise of the New Middle Class in Istanbul" (2009) and "The Neoliberal Landscape and the Rise of Islamic Capital in Turkey" (2015) was published by Berghahn Books. He is currently making a documentary film called "The Euphrates: A River Journey." His current research project (with several faculty from New York Six Colleges) entitled "Refugees on the Move: Global Refugee Crisis and Local Refugee Lives" is being funded by the Mellon Foundation.

EVANTHIA KALPAZIDOU SCHMIDT

Dr. Evanthia Kalpazidou Schmidt is Associate Professor, Research Director at Aarhus University, Department of Political Science, the Danish Centre for Studies in Research and Research Policy. She is specialized in higher education policy, European research policy and evaluation, science and society studies, gender equality in research and innovation. Dr. Schmidt is appointed member of the European Commission's Advisory Group for Gender and of the European RTD Evaluation Network. She was member of the ex-ante impact assessment group of the European Research Programme Horizon 2020 in the area of environment and climate change and of the ex-post evaluation group of the 7th Framework Programme for Research and Technological Development (FP7), international cooperation. Dr. Schmidt has been involved in a number of projects funded by the European Commission. She has also been engaged in the evaluations of FP6, FP7 and Horizon 2020 project proposals and has been advisor to national research councils in many European countries. She has been visiting professor at the Université Catholique de Louvain, Belgium, the Centre for National University Finance and Management, National Centre of Sciences of Japan, the International Christian University and the EU Institute in Japan.

NANETTE SVENSON

With over 20 years of experience in international development, Nanette Svenson, Ph.D. directs the Panama programming for Tulane University's Master's of Global Development. She also works as a consultant for the United Nations and other international organizations and sits on the boards of several national and regional non-governmental organizations. Previously, she helped establish the United Nations Development Programme Regional Centre for Latin America and the Caribbean and for four years headed its research and knowledge management efforts. Nanette has worked frequently with public and private entities in Panama to draft national policy documents and recommendations for improved education, research and social development. Her education includes a PhD in International Development from Tulane; an MBA from IESE in Barcelona; and a BA from Stanford. Nanette is based in Panama and teaches, researches and consults on topics related to knowledge and education in developing regions, particularly Latin America and the Caribbean. She recently published the book *The United Nations as a Knowledge System* and is now editing a volume on North-South university research partnerships in Latin America.

VICTOR E. DIKE

Dr. Victor E. Dike, EdD, who is currently the Founder and CEO of the Center for Social Justice and Human Development (CSJHDEV), an NGO in Sacramento that provides educational and skills training services to the underserved groups in the area, was formerly adjunct professor, School of Engineering, Technology and Media, National University (Sacramento Campus), California. He has more than 20 years of experience in education, ranging from high school/adult, career and technical education to the university level.

INTRODUCTION

Given the rapidly changing global higher education landscape, the systematic internationalization of higher education offers the potential for many positive outcomes and benefits for an increasingly interconnected and globalized citizenry, students, faculty, and institutions. Additionally, with more and more competitive pressures being put on institutions of higher education, a continually increasing number of universities and colleges within a variety of national contexts are actively looking at the potential of internationalization. Within the context of these complex global tensions, the internationalization of higher education has emerged as a balanced approach to addressing the rapidly shifting competitive landscape of higher education.

This edited collection will help you answer the following key questions:

- Why is understanding the internationalization of higher education important?
- How is globalization changing the context and shifting the dialogue surrounding the internationalization of higher education?
- Given the ever-increasing importance of contextualization, what are the country and region-specific considerations in internationalizing higher education?

OVERVIEW OF THE FORMAT OF THE BOOK

This edited collection provides a comprehensive introduction to globalization and higher education and explores its increasingly important role within a shifting higher education landscape, presenting a wide range of cross-disciplinary research in an organized, clear, and accessible manner. This book will be informative to higher education scholars and administrators seeking to understand the role and implementation of the internationalization of higher education in response to a shifting higher education landscape and increasingly globalized world.

This book is comprised of 14 chapters, being divided into two main parts: (I) Higher Education and Globalization, and (II) Country and Region-Specific Considerations. Each part starts with a brief overview, outlining the overall theme of the section and specific chapters that it contains.

Chapters 1–6 make up Part I of the book, which provides a general overview of higher education and globalization, including the internationalization of higher education. Chapters 1 and 2 look at the politics of international education and the importance of understanding the context of global education. Chapters 3 and 4 examine the commodification of global education and a proposed multicultural vision for global education. Chapters 5 and 6 explore the importance of sustainability in transnational education programs and the importance of the transnational student experience.

Chapters 7–14 make up Part II of the book, which looks at country and region-specific considerations in examining higher education within the context of globalization. Chapters 7-10 look at global education and the internationalization of higher education specifically in China, Japan, Vietnam, and Malaysia. Chapters 11–13 explore the impact of globalization on education reform in Turkey, Panama, and the Danish higher education systems. Chapter 14 examines the role of human capital development in Nigeria.

PART I

Higher Education and Globalization

PART I:

Higher Education and Globalization—Overview

Chapters 1–6 make up Part I of the book, which provides a general overview of higher education and globalization, including the internationalization of higher education. Chapters 1 and 2 look at the politics of international education and the importance of understanding the context of global education. Chapters 3 and 4 examine the commodification of global education and a proposed multicultural vision for global education. Chapters 5 and 6 explore the importance of sustainability in transnational education programs and the importance of the transnational student experience.

CHAPTER 1

The Politics of International Education

Melville Miranda

INTRODUCTION

The role of international post-secondary educational facilities has moved beyond purely academic. As all institutions take on a more global focus, universities have also looked toward current trends in the world to shape their educational focus. The corporate world has turned to the educational research realm to do their leg work. Research programs are gaining corporate sponsors to do research in specific areas. This is particularly true in the world of technology, biotechnology, and medical research. The deals between the universities and the corporations, as well as the details of the research, the results, and any possible trade secrets, which are involved in the research, need to be kept under strict confidence. According to Philip Altbach, author of "International Issues Higher Education-Expansion" "University-industry relations have become crucial for higher education in many countries. Technical arrangements with regard to patents, confidentiality of research findings, and other fiscal matters have become important."[1]

Along with this, any disputes that arise between the corporate sponsor and the university, or specific researchers is often kept out of court for the sake of privacy and settled through arbitration.

Due to the fact the location and origin or the sponsor and the university are often different; the issue becomes one of international education, which may require international arbitration. According to Stefan Tiessen, "international arbitration offers a private, binding method of dispute resolution not tied to a particular country's national laws or legal system."[2] The growing dependence on arbitration to settle disputes has led to a surge of international arbitration institutions being developed, which include the International Chamber of Commerce (ICC), the London Court of International Arbitration (LCIA), and the American Arbitration Association (AAA). There are two problems which arise from this. The first is that arbitration laws vary greatly from country to country, and what use to be an assumed confidentiality no longer exists. The second problem is that most parties involved create contract agreements assuming there won't be disputes or issues in the future, and they don't

---

[1] Altbach, Philip. (2009). "International Issues Higher Education-Expansion: Hallmark of the Postwar Era, Change and Reform: Trends since the 1960s." http://education.stateuniversity.com/pages/2042/Higher-Education-International-Issues.html. (Lasted Visited Dec. 17, 2009).

[2] Tiessen, Stefan. (2009). International Construction Arbitration: When Cultures Collide." http://www.sgrlaw.com/resources/trust_the_leaders/leaders_issues/ttl1. (Last visited Dec. 17, 2009).

include a confidentiality clause in their agreement, which opens the door for additional problems. The obvious solution is that confidentiality clauses become standard in all international education agreements, and that there is some kind of law or guideline in place, so that the country where the agreement is in dispute is required to uphold the confidentiality portion of the agreement. Another possible solution is to include a confidentiality clause that is all-encompassing, which would be difficult to do, as well as expensive and time-consuming. Finally, a deterrent solution would be for education facilities and potential business partners to take their time when entering into an agreement to understand the goals and expectations of the other party. Although this would avoid issues of oversight or miscommunication, it would not deter all potential disputes.

CONFIDENTIALITY

Within the recent past, various countries, including Sweden, Australia, United States, and England have made rulings regarding the confidentiality in an arbitration agreement. There rulings have been vastly different, which aids in demonstrating the problem facing international education. The first example is the case of *Bulgarian Foreign Trade Bank Ltd. V. AI Trade Finance Inc.* in 2000, [3] which ruled that the implied confidentiality in private arbitrations is not expressed or implied. This was after the arbitration ruling was published in an arbitration publication called Mealey's International Arbitration Report.[4] This ruling set an important precedent in the world of international education as far as private agreements, arbitration, and confidentiality are concerned. Under Swedish law, confidentiality is only enforced if it is included in detail within the contract agreement between the two parties involved. In that particular case, AI Trade Finance Inc. tried to claim that the bank violated the duty of confidentiality under the rules of the United Nations Economic Commission for Europe (UNECE). The Swedish Supreme Court, however, disregarded this claim by ruling that the UNECE upholds the confidentiality of arbitrary proceedings, but not the results.

There were similar rulings in court cases heard in the United States and Australia. In the case of *United States v. Panhandle E. Corp.*,[5] Panhandle attempted to seal the files on arbitration they were involved in with the Algerian state oil company. The U.S. court ruled against them stating that there was no implied confidentiality in their agreement. This case was ruled on by a district court. The U.S. Supreme Court has yet to hear a case involving implied confidentiality in international arbitration. Likewise, in the case of *Esso Australia Res. Ltd. V. Plowman*[6] the Australian High Court ruled that confidentiality was not an "essential attribute" of arbitration. The Australian case was also pivotal in that it defined a difference between "privacy" and "confidentiality." They ruled that the definition of breaching confidentiality is not the same as an invasion of privacy and that corporations do not have implicit rights to

---

[3] Case No. T1881-99 (Swedish Sup. Ct. 27 Oct. 2000).
[4] Sarles, Jeffrey. (2005). "Solving the Arbitral Confidentiality Conundrum in International Arbitration."
[5] 118F.R.D. 346 (D. Del. 1988).
[6] (1995) 128 A.L.R 391, 183 C.L.R. 10 (Austl.).

confidentiality throughout proceedings. [7] These rulings have made it hard for international education facilities and corporations to consider all the possibilities when entering into an agreement. Creating an all-encompassing confidentiality clause would be costly, timely, and potentially impossible since the parties cannot always foresee what the results of a business relationship will be. Fortunately, not all courts have rules in this manner.

Rulings in support of the implied confidentiality of arbitration agreements have been made in England, France, and New Zealand. In England, the court ruled that implied confidentiality is "an essential corollary of the privacy of arbitration proceedings" in the case of *Ali Shipping Corp v. Shipyard Trogir*. [8] England's level of confidentiality applies to the results, transcripts, testimony, and written statements. However, England does maintain that under certain statutes disclosure is permitted only under court order and with the consent of all parties involved when it is reasonably necessary. The French court upheld a similar ruling in favor of implied confidentiality. The court in New Zealand, actually took the implication of confidentiality a step further in 1996 with Section 14 of their Arbitration Act. New Zealand put into law that "parties shall not publish, disclose, or communicate any information relating to arbitral proceedings under the agreement or to an award made in those proceedings" [9] The huge difference in arbitration laws makes some countries more desirable than others to initiate contractual agreements and arbitration for international schools and corporations. However, the overall subjectivity on the matter has created a lack of confidence from all parties when entering into an arbitration agreement.

Of course there are some issues, which seem immune to the debate over confidentiality, and trade secrets are one of those issues. According to the International Chamber of Commerce (ICC), there are many provisions ensuring the exclusion of non-participants from the sharing of sensitive information. [10] These rules also assist in the preparation for arbitrators to aid in the procurement and preservation of trade secrets. This is under the situational structure laid out in order for all parties to keep confidential information in the hands of those who are required to use this information and no one else. This sort of preservation falls under the jurisdiction of confidentiality in international education.

In regards to all other information besides what is deemed trade secrets, lawyers cannot be expected to know firsthand which countries will follow international policies regarding confidentiality and which countries will not. Most international institutions, corporations, and lawyers do not understand the difficulties involved in solving an international confidentiality issue until they are involved in one. "Companies should not have to perform 'due diligence' into multifarious

---

[7] International Chamber of Commerse, Rules of Education, art. 21.3. (effective 1 January 1998). http://www.iccwbo.org/court/english/education/rules.asp. (Last visited Dec. 17, 1009).

[8] All E.R., 1 Lloyd's Rep. 643 (Eng. Ct. App. 1998).

[9] New Zealand Arbitration Act, Sec.14 (1996). http://rangi.knowledge-basket.co.nz/gpacts/public/text/1996/se/099 se14.htmln. (last visited Dec. 17, 2009).

[10] International Chamber of Commerse, Rules of Education, art. 21.3. (effective 1 January 1998). http://www.iccwbo.org/court/english/education/rules.asp. (Last visited Dec. 17, 1009).

confidentiality standards before entering into a contract or agreeing to arbitrate."[11] One potential solution to this problem is to institute one uniform standard of confidentiality. It can be the default expectations in all situations where the parties involved in the agreement did not predetermine their expectations of confidentiality.

The creation of an international standard understanding of the implied confidentiality in arbitration would be impeded by multiple parties, including independent arbitration institutions. Arbitration institutions have found a very profitable niche within the business world. Going through arbitration is very desirable to most institutions and corporations in order to avoid court proceedings. Because of the drastic difference in the understanding of the confidentiality laws, arbitration institutions compete on the basis of how much confidentiality they can guarantee their clients. Each arbitration institution also has its own rule sin regards to how things happen. For example, the ICC, which is the largest arbitration institution, excludes the presences of anyone who is not directly involved in the proceedings to be in the room. [12] The London Court of International Arbitration (LCIA) upholds the view of confidentiality that the English court does that

The parties undertake as a general principle to keep confidential all awards in their arbitration, together with all materials in the proceedings created for the purpose of the arbitration, and all other documents produced by another party in the proceedings not otherwise in the public domain – save and to the extent that disclosure may be required of a party by legal duty, to protect or pursue a legal right or to enforce or challenge an award in bona fide legal proceedings before a state court or other judicial authority. [13]

The China International Economic and Trade Arbitration Commission and the World Intellectual Property Organization provide similar protection over confidentiality.

Despite the possible interference from international arbitration institutions, a universal law regarding the definition of confidentiality would protect corporations and educational institutions internationally against unforeseen outcomes of their business relationships. Sarles supports the proposed default law introduced by Michael Whincop and Mary Keyes in their article, *Putting the "Private" Back into Private International Law: Default Rules and the Proper Law of the Contract*. Their proposed rule is as follows:

> In all arbitrations, the arbitrators shall require at the threshold that the parties agree on the scope of confidentiality, failing which the arbitrators shall enter a protective order on the scope of confidentiality. The parties shall by rule be deemed to have agreed to the terms of that order. Any claim asserting a violation of the parties' confidentiality agreement or protective order accruing during the course of the proceeding shall be resolved by the

---

[11] Sarles, Jeffrey. (2005). "Solving the Arbitral Confidentiality Conundrum in International Arbitration."
[12] International Chamber of Commerse (ICC), Rules of Arbitration, 21.3. (Effective 1 January 1998). http://www.iccwbo.org/court.english/arbitration/rules.asp. (Last visited Dec. 17, 2009).
[13] LCIA Arbitration Rules, art.30.1 (Effective January 1998). http://www.lcia-arbitration.com/lcia/rulecost/english.htm. (Last visited Dec. 17, 2009).

arbitrators. Any violation of the parties' confidentiality agreement or protective order accruing after the proceeding is terminated shall be resolved by arbitration according to the terms set forth in the parties' arbitration agreement. Arbitrators may impose appropriate damages and penalties on parties found to have breached the confidentiality agreement or protective order.

This sort of universal default rule would keep the matter in arbitration and away from the laws and politics of a particular country. Setting it up this way would cover any possible outcome whether or not the parties involved could have predicted it. There would also be a great potential for this law to be supported by the arbitration institutions because it would ensure ongoing business from their clients.

One of the benefits of this proposed rule is the involvement of penalties. Besides the varying degrees of consideration for implied confidentiality in arbitration showed by different countries, there is also the issue of enforcement once the issues goes into litigation. The court systems have a hard time assessing damages when the information disclosed does not have a clear monetary value. It is hard to estimate the potential damage an information leak can cause. "The provision for penalties in the event of a breach of the confidentiality agreement would serve to deter breaches where damages from a breach may be nonexistent or minimal." [14] Although this universal rule has not been tested, it has the potential of solving the issue of confidentiality. This rule will be standard in all arbitration agreements, but would only be effective if the parties did not create their own confidentiality clause within the agreement.

Another possible solution to the issue of international confidentiality is that both the educational institution and the party they are involved with come to a mutual understanding and have it in written at the onset of their relationship. Currently, international education already leans towards the implied confidentiality, but adopting a reformed confidentiality rule would go a long way towards mutual support. If a corporation or government sponsor needs to be concerned, or if an educational facility is unsure of whether or not the details of their research will go public, there will be an overall lack of confidence in the relationship. One of the appealing attributes of a reformed confidentiality law is that it would serve to protect future trade secrets. This is particularly applicable in the computer market, where advancements are happening daily. If information is leaked regarding possibly new technology, that technology can become obsolete before it is ever actually introduced to the public. In order for both parties to enter into an agreement with confidence, there needs to be a shared sense of responsibility regarding the information being exchanged.

It is, of course, possible to create a contractual agreement that is suitable to everyone and made in good faith. Too often, the resulting litigation regarding confidentiality is due to the educational institution and its international sponsor entering into an agreement to quickly. The sponsor wants their research done right away and the educational facility wants funding to continue their mission of educational research, which is essential to their marketing to students internationally.

---

[14] Sarles, Jeffrey. (2005). "Solving the Arbitral Confidentiality Conundrum in International Arbitration."

If educational facilities took a three step approach to entering into an arbitration agreement, many of their problems could be eliminated or dramatically decreased. The first step is to create a vision of what they want out of the relationship. What type of research and recognition is the institution looking for? Once the vision is clear, the institution needs to successfully communicate that vision to the interested party during the initial arbitration. The second step is to enter into open dialogue with the potential sponsor. There should be a mutual sharing of ideas and interests. Finally, once everyone's goals and expectations have been established, it is time to set real goals. This is when their agreement should be written done and reviewed. Although following these three steps would not eliminate future issues or solve the problems related to international law regarding confidentiality, it may work to avoid confidentiality issues all together.

CONCLUSION

In a simpler time there was an underlying understanding that all parties involved in an arbitration agreement on non-divulgence of sensitive information. This included information that was within the parameters of private educational research. However, it is no longer appropriate to make these assumptions. Confidentiality is up in the air in many ways, including concept and approach. There is a growing need for supervision, as education becomes more of a negotiating process involving shifting principles and differing goals and expectations. The international courts, which have rules on the existence of implied confidentiality worked to further confuse the situation.

In order to cover all potential information to be covered by a confidentiality clause and to avoid potential disputes, there needs to be a universal default clause worked into all arbitration agreements. The clause would effectively keep the issue in arbitration and out of the court system, as well as establish and enforce penalties for a breach of contract. This would allow all parties involved to work towards a mutual goal despite their geographic borders. Limiting educational research and partnerships to countries, which maintain implied confidentiality would place serious limitations on international education. It would also work against international schools in countries such as Sweden, Australia, and the U.S. because they would be limited in their ability to recruit international students and professors looking to further their research interests. The decrease in international diversity on campuses would further decrease the international benefits and education supplied to the remaining students.

CHAPTER 2

Creating a Deep Context for Global Education: Eine Neue Weltanschauung

Ewa Bacon

In the 21st century, we are educating students in the humanities under unprecedented conditions. We have more students, we have more diverse students, and we have students who are more motivated toward business careers and practical education than academic pursuits. I find that my students in world history classes have little interest in and less familiarity with the classical history of the west and are searching for a rubric to explain the immediate past and the puzzling future. One goal of a humanistic education is to provide a historical narrative for students to give them both an understanding of the past and a value system for the future.

The great narrative of the 20th century which had separated the world into a Manichaean dichotomy of Cold War adversaries has collapsed into the single narrative of globalization. I will bring a meta-historical perspective to bear on the concept of globalization to create a context in which to understand all those phenomena that are loosely labelled "globalization" today. As educators in the humanities we must search for a new narrative which relies on the evidence which comes from many disciplines: I can no longer reach my students with the stories of Tacitus or with a Biblical allusion, but I can speak to them using evidence from archaeology, from anthropology, from statistics, from sociology, and most definitely from biology. (The sub-text of any evolving new Weltanschauung has to become congruent with socio-biology.) Can we understand and teach globalization from a meta-historical perspective?

When I talk about a meta-historical perspective, I want to present a view from an Olympian height to explain why we are inundated with the term and phenomenon of "globalization." It is being used in economics, in politics, and in the popular press. It is being used to frighten as well as to explain. Competing systems of world economics died away as the Soviet Union and the socialist challenge to capitalism disappeared in 1990. We're back to the historic state of Russia and its neighbours. It's only since the end of the USSR, just twenty-five years ago, that we hear about the absolute triumph of capitalism and even, [says Fukayama] about "the end of history" in the new global world.

I would tell the end-of-history crowd: Not so fast! My perspective is designed to do the following:

1. To view the present in a deep context, the ultra *longue duree.* [15]
2. To frame an argument to allow you to connect the worrisome unknown future with a coherent view of the past.
3. To remind you that you have the power to act as a responsible educator and teach our students about human values.

Globalization is an important event. It does not pay to trivialize what is happening. Economists tell us statistics about world trade [it's growing], and politicians tell us that the nation-state is obsolete [it is: we have trans-national companies wealthier than some countries.] Philosophers and theologians warn us of the plight of the impoverished [it's serious]. Optimists tell us that a bright future is before us while pessimists tell us that the planet is doomed. What can we understand in this phantasmagorical mix of conflicting opinions?

Yes, globalization is not only an important event—I would call it a species-altering event because it impacts culture so deeply that we, as a species, have significantly altered our families, our work, and how we live. We are now experiencing a huge three century long wave of change which originates from one place—Great Britain—and from one event: the Industrial Revolution.

Globalization may have gotten labelled a decade ago, but its roots are deep in the human experience. The mongers of panic and fright want to convince us that something new and threatening has surfaced. The deep historical context shows us that the changes in how we produce and consume is not an unprecedented event and it is most certainly not just a Western event. The origin of the steam engine, the switch from biological/muscle power to mechanical/engine power began in Great Britain, in the West, but that it is "western" is not its most defining characteristic. And, this great transformation is certainly not the first such transformation to impact humanity.

Taking the very long view, we know that as a species, as Homo sapiens sapiens, we've been around some 200,000 years. Hominids, of course, are some million years old. When I teach about the origin of man, I teach about specific, defining human behaviours like language and art as evidence of symbolic thinking. One of the other important characteristic human behaviours is that we migrate, that we are constantly in motion and have migrated from one place—Africa—and covered the globe. Early man moved and settled his hunting and gathering tribes across Europe, across Asia, into Australia, the Polynesian islands of the Pacific, across the Bering Strait into North America—all the way to the tip of Tierra del Fuego. That was the first globalization! [16]

But the critical date for our story is 12,000 years ago when mankind began a significant transformation on a scale that I call species-transforming. This change occurred seven times completely independently: seven times human beings discovered agriculture as a new way of life: in Mesopotamia, in Egypt, on the Indus River, on the Yellow River of China, in Central America, in South America and on

---

[15] Fernand Braudel (see, for instance, *A History of Civilization*) introduced 20th century scholars to the long waves of history which are necessary to explain huge events like globalization.
[16] World history (see, for instance, Howard Spodek's *The World's History*) has replaced "Western Civilization" in many undergraduate programs in the United States.

the Niger in Africa. Human beings abandoned hunting and gathering to become farmers.

The pain of this transition, the assault on the tribal values of hunters and gathers, the hideousness of the new and demanding village life, the disintegration of ancient customs governing men's and women's lives caused atrocious disruption of what was "normal" and "natural". We don't remember any longer how terrific and awesome this transition was.

We are seeing this cultural wrench replayed today as the whole planet is now being pulled into yet another new way of life. The agriculturalists are being replaced by the industrialist and the pain of the transition is once again both terrific and awesome.

Hunters and gatherers were the denizens of the Biblical Eden. Life was good, food was available, social structures were intimate, contained and well understood. But the agricultural world was more efficient, produced more food at the cost of more work, and created both the village and the city. The village and certainly the city brought about huge alterations: complex social hierarchies formed, great wealth as well as abject poverty now became commonplace. Women lost out enormously since this was the age of the warrior who swaggered across the battlefield with lances tipped in bronze or iron. The domain of women, who had once moved confidently in the world, now shrank under the patriarchal confines of the village and town.

Agriculture created a new system of values, of work, of vibrant cities and states that covered the world. It was successful in raising huge empires—the Roman, the Ottoman, the Mongol; the great dynasties of China like the Han and the Ming and the great kingdoms of the Maya, the Inca and the Aztec. The globe was in the hands of farmers. [17]

> Why should societies change?
> Why should "ordinary" life de-stabilize?

That's probably the same question the hunter/gatherer asked the villager: wasn't the old life excellent and fine? We don't know the reply because the townsman ignored this naïve question: he was already busy with new crafts like potting or smithing, excited about buying and selling goods, or searching for entertainment and diversion. And that is exactly what is happening today.

The same process of transformation is altering the globe. Now however, the agricultural world, successful as it had been, is yielding to a new world.

We have to remember the pain of the transition from farming when it occurred in the West a couple of centuries ago. We go to our history classes to read about the English and Scottish farmers who resented the rise of the factory amidst their carefully tended fields. We go to our literature classes and read the poet William Blake's lament about the rise of the "satanic mills" and think how quaint. We re-read Charles Dickens and learn about the diseases and the crowded tenements of the

---

[17] Jared Diamond's *Guns, Germs and Steel* argues that the uneven distribution of wealth on a global scale is the consequence of the uneven distribution of resources across the globe. Those regions which could undertake the transformation to agricultural became dominant states.

medieval English cities trying to cope with the influx of that strange new industrial worker. We vaguely remember the birth pangs of this new class and its early struggles to get decent wages and working conditions. Do we remember the children who worked in the English mines and textile mills of the early 19th century? We clearly remember the revolutions which toppled governments, the world wars which erupted as competition between newly industrial states exploded into conflicts. This, then, is the argument:

The last two centuries are the transition from the agricultural world to the industrial world. As Marx already noted mid-19th century: "The bourgeoisie, by the rapid improvement of all instruments of production, by the immensely facilitated means of communication, draws all, even the most barbarian, nations into civilization."[18] Globalization is the end state of that transition.

The change-over from agriculture to industry did not [like the agricultural revolution] take place multiple times, but only once. It spread so quickly from its origin in England that no competitor arose. That's why it has such a deeply western cast. Western political values, western art, western culture, western consumption patterns—they are an artefact of its origin but not a necessary condition of the great industrial transformation. Only small alterations of historical developments could have produced a first industrial revolution in China[19]. From a historical perspective, the "Rise of the West" or the current dominance of western states is trivial—what counts is that Homo sapiens sapiens has entered into a new period: the replacement of muscle by machine, the end of the values of the agricultural world, the end of its mores and its parochialisms. But the end of the old, of course, produced the shock of the new.[20]

There is no question of the pain we are witnessing as one traditional agricultural society after another is seeing its isolation and its traditional life style disappearing under the impact of technologies which are now not merely the machine but also the computer.

The birth of the virtual reality of a cyber-global village is bloody, frightening, but like every birth, filled with potential for change and growth. Human beings produce ever more complex societies and economies and we are in that stage of the Industrial Revolution in which it is expanding into every economy, every nation, and every culture, melding and fusing world cultures.

It should not surprise us that the highly complex Chinese who created the absolutely highest quality society under the constraints of the available agricultural resources have rapidly adjusted their state and their economy to a global context. China as well as India were dominant states in the agricultural old regime. Their inherent strengths have been obscured in the transition to industrialization, but it's

[18] Karl Marx "The Communist Manifesto" in Lewis Feuer, ed., *Marx and Engels, Basic Writings on Politics and Philosophy,*(New York, Anchor Books, 1959).
[19] The dominance of China is revealed in Andre Frank's *ReOrient: Global Economy in the Asian Age* (Berkeley: U. of California Press, 1998).
[20] The phrase comes from the pen of the eminent art critic Robert Hughes in *The Shock of the New* (NY, Alfred A. Knopf, 1980).

clear that their dominance is re-emerging.[21] Nor should we be surprised that portions of the Islamic world, especially the Arabic world, is not.

The crucial variable is not the Islamic religion. The crucial variable is the durability of ancient tribal organizations in deeply agricultural societies. Saddam Hussein was a clan chieftain. The Taliban are a deeply rural society affronted and panicked by the mores of the new world arriving on radio waves, air waves and cable networks.

One of the consequences of making global connections is that ideas travel not only out from the west, but also back from the Arabic world to us. Forget   about Ronald McDonald and his hideous clown smile. Don't think that globalization can be equated with a universal Coca Cola sign. Those are just the rude manifestations of the surface. They may look like a threat to traditional societies, but thoughtful Arabic intellectuals see far deeper.

The philosopher of Islamic terror, Sayyid Qutb, who was executed by Gamal Abdul Nasser in Egypt in 1966, was not only a learned scholar of the Qur'an, but was also steeped in modern, secular western thought. His was a generation that argued passionately against European imperialism, but I believe his vision for the Arab world was also a profound defense again the secular, sceptical, and open society produced in the wake of economic transformation and, which I have been arguing, is overwhelming the traditional world. Qutb believed that humanity is in an unbearable state of crisis. He spoke of the same anomie that western sociologists were already talking about in the 19th century: social isolation, depression, degenerating morals, rampant sexual promiscuity, the hollow escape of drugs and alcohol. Pessimistic western philosophers like Nietzsche pointed to one villain: an unwarranted belief in the power of reason--an error promulgated since the Greeks. Qutb, from his deep Islamic orientation, instead placed the blame on another critical juncture at the very root of western thought: the first century after the crucifixion of Christ. Qutb claims that the spiritual message of love proclaimed by Jesus was lost during the period of Roman persecutions. In defense, the disciples adopted a Hellenistic formula based on the Greek separation of the spiritual and material life. Christianity, according to Qutb, lost touch with daily life and the material world. Then, with the rise of science in the 16th century [which pre-dates the industrial revolution by two centuries], the material world separated even more from Christian theology. The result is a catastrophe--a West that dominates via science and technology, but exists without a theological foundation. Paul Berman puts it eloquently:

"[For the Arabs] it was the agony of inhabiting a modern world of liberal ideas and achievements while feeling that true life exists somewhere else. [It's] the agony of being pulled this way and that. The present, the past. The secular, the sacred...a life of confusion and madness..." [22]

Western thinkers recognize this malaise--but Qutb's comprehensive answer is to replace Christianity with Islam. Islam, say the terrorists who have read and studied

---

[21] Robert Marks (*The Origins of the Modern World*) presents an elegant summation of current long term analysis of these historical trends.
[22] Paul Berman, "The Philosopher of Islamic Terror," *The New York Times Magazine* (March 23, 2003); p. 29.

Qutb, must fight against the West to defeat the corrosion of the secular state, to resist a fatal separation of church and state. In Islam the church and the state must be one.

Put into the context that I'm presenting here, Qutb's heartfelt cry is an attempt to save his Eden, his ideal--a world unchallenged by the great transformation that is sweeping across humanity. He is defending the traditional agricultural world from the changes inherent in the industrial world.

Is the pain we see confined only to Qutb? Does it exist only on the newest borders of the agricultural and the industrial worlds? Is stress and conflict exclusively housed in the obvious rural enclaves of secluded corners of the world?

As educators in the humanities we know full well that the border of the old and the new exists within ourselves and within our communities as well. We can talk about the stress of change with a great deal of authority ourselves. The great transformation is only some two centuries old and we, too, like Qutb, harbour profound unease about the direction in which this brave new world is heading. Along with globalization on the level of the world economy, we see in our own society the change which is bringing us from modernity [the first response to industrialization] to post-modernity [the next response].

Globalization and post-modern values create a formidable force which is now changing already industrialized societies. Before we trivialize the pain of traditional societies adjusting to modernity, let's remember ourselves the confusion and alarm we experience in our now post-modern state.

If globalization refers to changes inherent in late industrialization, then the coda of post-modernism is our cauldron. In a traditional society, in the agricultural world, the elders knew what the truth was; in the modern world, "experts" were given the job; but in post-modernity we no longer acknowledge that any group holds all the answers.

In the traditional society religion was the revealed word; in modernity religion was attacked by secular sceptics; in post-modernity, religion is reviving but no longer under some great hierarchy of church authority.

In traditional societies the written word was the purview of the scribe; in modernity the printed word exploded access to information; in post-modernity anyone can both write and print in cyberspace.

For the traditional man, nature was a chaotic system of individual events; modern man developed taxonomies, categories, lists and boxes for every group under the sun; post-moderns have shown that those cherished categories are artificial and useless: reality is a continuum.

We used to have distinct categories of male and female; post moderns offer us a bell curve, a distribution of traits which encompass a bewildering set of fluid and changing definitions.

The problems that we meet in our daily lives within our already thoroughly industrial and post industrial world are the same kind of problems that a Taliban meets when confronted with globalization and the end of his traditional life. We are all sharing in the species transforming event of the Industrial Revolution—we are just on different part of the modernization torture rack.[23]

I've said earlier that the transformation started in England, but it could have started [and eventually would have started] elsewhere. Western pre-eminence is quite recent and will probably be brief. In 2000 BCE, Ur in Iraq was the pre-eminent global city; in 500 BCE it was a Persian city; Rome gets the honours for the year 1, but Changan is pre-eminent in 500 CE and Kaifeng in 1000. New York may be seen as the dominant world city in 2000 but it is not likely to hold that position in 2500. [24]

So—does it matter that it is Western thought which is intimately associated with the cultural baggage of globalization?

Yes, it does matter. Industrialization and the eventual global reach of the industrial transformation on, let us say, a Chinese template, would have stressed group harmony, an elite meritocracy, and, of course, chop sticks for all.

The western model carries with it a concept of man and man in society that has proven to have great moral value. The concept of the individual in society and the rights of the individual was articulated by classical Greeks. The value of the individual is reinforced by Christianity. It is the founding idea of Renaissance Humanism. It is the heart of the Enlightenment. It is this western evolving view of the rights of individuals that is our contribution to the global human heritage. Here is my reply to Qutb: in the agricultural world we were confined within the embrace of the group. The western world has learned to value the individual within the group, the autonomy of the self. It is in the West that women have achieved the equality which had been denied to them since the rise of agriculture.

The idea we nurture is the existence of a universal value: human rights are an essential component of globalization as it formed on a western cultural substrate. The belief in the intrinsic value of every person, the resounding affirmation that life is sacred, that torture is evil, that intellectual and artistic freedoms are imperative, that men and women are free—these have become values attractive to all humanity.

Human rights—not the rights of Man, not the rights of Westerners; not the right of the first world; not the rights of the warrior or conqueror, but the rights we understand to belong to humanity—these are the rights that the globe can share. And…this is the essence of humanistic education in a global world and our mandate as teachers in the humanities who must construct a coherent narrative of our history: *eine neue Weltanschauung*.

---

[23] Peter Watson's *The Modern Mind* (London: Weidenfeld & Nicolson, 2000) traces the details of the intellectual transformation of the current era.

[24] Nicholas D. Kristof, "Kaifeng's warning for America" *New York Times*, May 22, 2005.

REFERENCES

Berman, Paul. "The Philosopher of Islamic Terror." *The New York Times Magazine.*
    March 23, 2003, p. 24-30.

Braudel, Fernand. *A History of Civilization.* New York: Penguin Books USA, 1993.

Diamond, Jared. *Guns, Germs and Steel: The Fates of Human Societies.* New York:
    W.W. Norton & Co., 1997.

Frank, Andre Gunder. *ReOrient: Global Economy in the Asian Age.* Berkeley:
    University of California Press, 1998.

Hughes, Robert. *The Shock of the New.* New York: Alfred A. Knopf, 1980.

Kristof, Nicholas D. "Kaifeng's Warning for America." *The New York Times.* May
    22, 2005.

Marks, Robert B. *The Origins of the Modern World: A Global and Ecological
    Narrative.* New York: Rowman & Littlefield, 2002.

Marx, Karl. "The Communist Manifesto" in Feuer, Lewis, ed., *Marx and Engels:
    Basic Writings on Politics and Philosophy.* New York: Anchor Books, 1959.

Spodek, Howard. *The World's History, 3rd edition.* Upper Saddle River, N.J.: Prentice
    Hall, 2006.

Watson, Peter. *The Modern Mind.* London: Weidenfeld & Nicolson, 2000.

CHAPTER 3

The Commodification of Education: Ethico-political Issues in the Global Marketing of Knowledge

Denise Egéa

> *The impact of information technology will even be more radical than the harnessing of steam and electricity in the 19th century...It will prepare the way for a revolutionary leap into a new age that will profoundly transform human culture.*
> – Attali, 1992, p 11

> *Education is the oil of the 21ˢᵗ century.*
> – Taylor, in Traub, 2000, p. 2

They defined the objectives of their instruction, established a timeline, and fixed a price. This is how Plato described the Sophists' approach to education. Hence their pragmatism (i.e., is true only that which is efficient) and their relativism, also denounced by Plato in these words: "The good is no better than its opposite, neither is the just..." (*République* VII 538e).

This same mercantile approach to education is currently being used in the global marketing of knowledge over Internet and falls into what has been called the "industrial metaphor." The description of this commodification of education is the object of the first part of this essay. Then a reading of Michel Serres's works helps understand how the globalization of education can be at one and the same time both a promise and a threat and raises serious ethico-political issues, and how it can affect the very nature of knowledge.

THE COMMODIFICATION OF EDUCATION: THE INDUSTRIAL METAPHOR

In the industrial model, one knows exactly every step to be taken, every fragmentary partial operation and their sequence, all precisely analyzed, assessed, and controlled, toward the manufacture of a totally predictable product. The industrial metaphor reduces education to its immediate and immediately measurable results. In this context, education can become a product for sale, where one can "convert the university into a production house for making knowledge products," be they in the form of courses, degrees, or certificates for example (Nesson, in Traub, 2000, 90). Charles Nesson, a professor at Harvard Law School, was specifically commenting on Internet instruction, and wondering "What happens ... [when] the university starts looking less like a community of scholars and much more like a drug company that has work-for-hire knowledge workers producing proprietary research?" When it becomes "a production house for making knowledge products?" (Nesson, in Traub, 2000, p. 2 and 12).

Indeed, fifteen years ago online teaching was a rapidly growing business, over two billion dollars worth, and predicted to rise by thirty-five percent a year to reach nine billion dollars by 2005, if one was to believe the projections of Gerald Odening, an analyst with Chase Bank (Traub, 2000, p. 2). Both Christina Hooper, a Distinguished Scientist at Apple Computer and an expert on educational technology and James Traub (2000) believed that "Online education [had] the force of inevitability" (p. 2). Online law schools (e.g., Concord LS, established by Kaplan, Inc.), business schools (e.g., UNext.com and the Cardean University), and Ph.D. programs, as well as thousands of individual courses were already "in business." Starting in February 2001, the Global Education Network (GEN)—founded by Mark Taylor, a professor of humanities at Williams College, and Herbert J. Allen Jr., an investment banker and plutocrat—"sold four or five college courses over the Internet" and planned "to offer 25 courses by ... September [2001]" (Traub, 2000, p. 2).

To someone who understands the nature of higher education in the U.S., it should be no surprise that this trend has only grown stronger over the years in that bartering of education through cyberspace. Besides the fact that no other country is as well (Web-) connected as the U.S., it is also where education has long been said to be "a business," in which "schools market" and "students shop" (Traub, 2000, p. 3). The bestselling points have long been the sports facilities, the food "emporia," and now the Internet connections. In a system where the line between education and training is increasingly blurred and a utilitarian approach to education more heavily promoted than ever (e.g., "school-to-work;" accountability of teachers and school systems as well as students; mandatory "performance assessment"; and so on), the Internet seems to be perfectly suited to deliver the desired product. Almost two decades ago, James Duderstadt, in *Dancing with the Devil* (1999), already argued that the university was inadequate in its size and practices... even as it is now. He believed that higher education must be "scalable," which is made possible by Internet. He also suggested that soon, "a small number of academic celebrities, a larger number of 'content providers,' and a still larger number of 'learning facilitators' [would] create 'learningware products' and market 'courseware' for 'an array of for-profit service companies' who in turn [would] sell these products to students." It is now a reality.[25]

---

[25] For example, Learningware (http://www.learningware.in/) is a leader in developing digital education resources for higher education. They advertise: "Our digital library for engineering education contains

As Traub predicted, the marketing of online education could yet be "a much more profound challenge to the university" even more daunting than "rising tuition costs or affirmative-action programs or speech codes – because its promise and its threat are one and the same" (2000, p. 2).

THE GLOBALIZATION OF EDUCATION: SOME ETHICO-POLITICAL ISSUES

When in 1993 Katherine Fulton designed an introductory course to cyberspace called "2001: A Media Odissey" for Duke University, while leading her students to "conquer the Net," she also already saw the necessity of raising their awareness of ethico-political issues related to the use of Internet in the quest for knowledge. Her course syllabus included "discussions of related social and political issues such as privacy, universal access and the role of government regulations" (Rubin, 2001, npn). Precisely because the Web is the first medium which rendered frontiers truly meaningless, this carries ethical implications for issues of privacy, local regulatory environments, and responsibilities for individual users and Internet service providers (ISP).

Equal Voices, Equal Knowledge and Freedom, Equal Power

A May 2000 report to the United Nations by a panel which included government ministers from Africa, Asia, Eastern and Western Europe, Latin America and the Caribbean, and representatives of private businesses and foundations indicated that "less than five percent of the world population" actually benefited from the global technology (United Nations Report, 2000a, p. 4). This report stressed that developing countries were "not being just marginalized," but they also ran the risk of being "completely bypassed" by the global communication network (p. 4). The UN panel of experts called "on all actors to unite in a global initiative to meet the following challenge: provide access to the Internet, especially through community access points, for the world's population presently without such access by the end of 2004" (p. 5). This report was reviewed by the world's seven leading industrialized nations (G7) and Russia when they met at a summit which took place in Okinawa, Japan in July 2000. Chuck Lankester, a UN consultant on information technology, declared that, according to this report, "by the end of 2004 a farmer in Saharan Africa should be

---

30,000+ learning objects across 56 courses and comes with a powerful set of pedagogic tools including animations, simulations, graphical slides and question banks…. These resources significantly enhance teaching-learning outcomes through structured, engaging and interactive content. Colleges and universities can sign up to access Learningware for all their students, teachers and administrators." They offer: teaching-learning resources, pedagogic tools designed to enhance teaching-learning outcomes, including animations and simulations; access to question banks, large banks of multiple-choice and subjective exam questions across different taxonomy and difficulty levels; custom cloud deployment for college; content mapped to multiple global curricula including US, India, UK and many state university standards.

able to get to a point of access, let's say in half a day's walk or riding on a bullock cart;" and by 2005, everyone in the world should have access to Internet even if they had to walk for half a day to the nearest computer or cell phone (United Nations Press Briefing, 2000b). With Michel Serres, one can wonder how realistic these predictions were. Indeed, in 2013, Marceux wrote: "by 2020 the majority of the global population (55.9%) will continue to remain offline, unassisted by a rapidly growing income inequality globally that is creating a wide digital divide across the socioeconomic spectrum, excluding low-income homes from opportunities in the uptake of telecom goods and services" (p. 1).

In *Atlas* (1994), Michel Serres identified several potential consequences of global communication which he called "utopic." He pointed out that we believe Internet has the potential for everyone to hear and be heard: "everyone, attentive to the voice of others, will make his or her own be heard" (p. 131). Is not the Internet claimed to give equal access to all information disseminated in space and time? And that, for the first time in the history of humanity, since the new technologies seem to erase "the complexities which used to render impossible…this equitable and calculable sharing" (p. 131). In this new universe, Serres describes a "harmony" which he compares to that of a choir, where "everything conspires, intersects and interacts, intercepts…, is congruent and consenting" (p. 128). He sees no center and no periphery, the middle being everywhere, and "any-thing, any place, any individual, any group or any phrase occupies, at least by right, a focal site" (p. 128). However, in order to do so, the Universalists, this small number of privileged "citizens of the world" who own the integrality of the resources, must render the local sites indifferent or undefined. But by destroying their singularity, are they not in fact destroying them, taking away what makes each individual, each place, each activity unique and singular?

For example, one of the first online universities founded by UNext, Cardean University, "provides next generation business courses online to companies around the globe." [26] Rosenfield who founded UNext clearly stated that his goal was to make money, not to replace traditional institutions, declaring: "We have no ambition to substitute for physical colleges…. We think they're first best. But for many people and many places, that's just not going to occur" (in Traub, 2000, p. 5). With a number of other believers, Rosenfield was convinced that online education could mean equal access (if for a fee) to knowledge and to people, which might be perceived as leading to more freedom.

Traditionally, one had to go where knowledge was kept. Available anywhere, anytime on the global network, distance learning is supposed to add its "universal" resources to knowledge which used to be available only locally, in libraries, universities, i.e., in "closed ghettos" for privileged youth. However, now, not only does technology make it available everywhere, but in addition, asks Serres, "why could not knowledge come to us instead of—reinforced with much inequality—only a

---

[26] Cardean University was founded in 1999; accredited by DETC (Distance Education and Training Council) in 2000.

[privileged] few can go to it?" (1994, p. 139). Thus, it appears that Internet has the potential to provide freedom from ignorance.

It seems that equal access would also give equal power to everyone, but "All the power to all," is for Serres the "third utopia" (1994, p. 137). By now, we know that there is much disparity among and within the countries in the availability of access to the tools of technology and to the most "globalizing" of these tools. The "Report of the high-level panel of experts on information and communication technology" expressed deep concern over "the gross disparity in the spread of the Internet and thus the economic and social benefits from it" (United Nations Report, 2000a, p. 4). For example, it stressed that

> [t]here are more hosts in New York than in continental Africa; more hosts in Finland than in Latin America and the Caribbean; and notwithstanding the remarkable progress in the application of ICT in India, many of its villages still lack a working telephone. (p. 4)

In *Atlas*, Serres argued how

> the universal accumulation, monopoly, and distribution of all soft data, signs and values, by a small group to whom, moreover, belong the hard networks of circulation, and whom we must call, as a whole, the new capitalism, in fact causes its power to raise like an arrow [fast and straight]. This power is, from now on, equipotent to the universe, not only in its spatial extension, but also by the totalization, in real time, of its available resources; nothing can escape its grip since by logical definition, the universe knows no exception: here is the iniquitous distribution finally accomplished: everything or nothing. (1994, p. 140)

Serres further noted how those who hold this kind of power, acquired through technology and information sciences, cannot even see these numerous "exceptions," the mass of those excluded, because only a rare few own everything. They own the knowledge and the tools; they are the privileged few who are reconstructing the world, redefining it, and who own the means to know it on a so-called global scale. For example, the Cardean University claims that relying on traditionally exclusive institutions, its collaboration with Columbia Business School, Stanford University, The University of Chicago Graduate School of Business, Carnegie Mellon, and the London School of Economics and Political Science allows it to "bring you the best in business e-learning" (Cardean University). As to the underprivileged countries, third world countries—whatever label is attached to those excluded countries—but also the increasing marginal masses excluded from the mainstream society in developed countries, what part do they play in this process? Serres asked: "How could those who construct the universe have the slightest perception of those whom they exclude from the world, since it is precisely their own world which conditions all vision?" (1994, p.

140) The proportion of the destitute, the excluded of this world has reached an all time high. What Serres finds particularly tragic and unique to our time of advanced communication technology and potentially global education is that, for the first time in the history of humanity, the excluded multitude are deprived of all hope. They are "not only deprived of bread and salt, of remedies for any ills, of freedom, of time and of future, of knowledge and of work, but also of this representation of self in the universe which philosophers say constitutes the humanity of humans" (1994, p. 140).

Objectionable Contents and Privacy: Legal and Political Issues

In the early 2000s, a series of legal actions against Yahoo, Inc. (No Name, 2000; Perez, 2006) illustrates the legal and political issue of objectionable contents and privacy, and raises major questions—especially where education is concerned—inherent in the nature of Internet and the space of freedom it represents. Let us briefly recall that the American society Yahoo, Inc. offered an online auction service which featured Nazi artifacts, an activity legal in the U.S. but not in France. Responding to the legal action undertaken on May 22, 2000 by LICRA (*Ligue Internationale Contre le Racisme et l'Antisémitisme*), the UEFJ (*Union des Étudiants Juifs de France*), and the MRAP (*Mouvement Contre le Racisme et pour l'Amitié entre les Peuples*), the French Supreme Court in Paris ordered Yahoo, Inc. to do whatever was necessary to set a block to prevent French users to access these objects for auction on their site. After the two months delay granted by the French judge, Yahoo, Inc. claimed that they did not have the technological capabilities to set such blocks. However, the situation is much more complex.

Indeed, this legal issue concerns two different concepts of freedom of expression, also found at the core of education: whereas the sale of Nazi artifacts is illegal in France (Article R645-1 of the Penal Code), the American concept of freedom of expression guaranteed by the First Amendment to the Constitution considers all attempts at controlling any kind of expression, no matter how extreme, as censorship (e.g., Yahoo, Inc accepted to host a particularly violent Nazi site which had been interdicted in Germany). More complex still, is the possible creation of a dangerous legal precedent, which might open the door to attempts at justifying other claims, and at closing other sites (and portions of knowledge or syllabi) not in agreement with this or that ideological set of beliefs.

Several major questions were and are still raised by this incident: What role do the political, or geographical frontiers still play when erased by technology? (e.g., Can a judge impose the law of his or her country to a foreign company practicing activities which are legal on its own territory? Can an educational system and its ideological tenets cross all borders?). How can the fundamental incompatibility of two ethical or educational philosophies be resolved? Can two opposite codes of ethics be simultaneously respected? Is a consensus possible? Is a "neutral" Internet achievable and even desirable? What educational contents and methods can be controlled and by whom, according to what and whose criteria? Though not new to education (e.g., Egéa-Kuehne, 1997, 1998), such questions are rendered more acute and pressing by the very nature of Internet and online education: its scope as regards to the subjects studied, its geographical reach, and its velocity.

The technical problems are no less major, especially when we realize that where Internet is concerned, technical and political issues are tightly linked. The technical decisions taken today will influence the future development of Internet and online education, and some believe that their potential for the future must be preserved. In the specific example of Yahoo, Inc., the basic technical problem is threefold: identify the contents, identify users who are not authorized to access the offending site, and set specific blocks to access. The difficulties are pretty daunting on all three counts. For example, American and Scandinavian users have a long tradition of anonymity and do not want to be identified. Some companies have been providing such a service for while (e.g., all the many "Anonymizer" sites, such as SmartHide for example), a kind of bridge enabling users to consult Web pages without leaving a trace. In addition, users can now bypass any block, by reaching a connection outside their country for example. As to creating a category and marking it with a label—as in the case of "Nazi," which would not only block the objectionable contents, but also filter the historic sites on World War II—so far it presents rather insurmountable difficulties. A system of signals, which would need to be coherent on a global scale across all Internet users, might seem the ideal solution, and calling upon the users' sense of responsibility might work toward a freer Internet. But then again, how realistic are those on a global scale?

ONLINE INSTRUCTION: A NEW TYPE OF KNOWLEDGE

In *Atlas*, Serres discusses how the network of communication erasing time and distances touches populations across borders, across peoples, across classes, and redefines and reconstructs a new world, a new universe, moving at light speed from local to global, global to local, and encompassing simultaneously both. And in so doing, Serres reminds us, "the humanity constructs the universe by and through constructing itself" (1994, p. 130). The potential of immediate communication with the entire planet carries "consequences for knowledge and for the human community" which in turn transform our lives (Serres, 2000, p. 16).

Subject/Object: The New "Global World-Object" and "Global Humanity-Subject"

We can no longer rely on the traditional concepts of subject and object and on their duality to discuss knowledge. These terms have changed, and so has their relation to each other. For Serres, the meetings in Rio and Kyoto on global warming revealed that a "new collective global subject" is progressively taking form in the face of a "new global natural object" (Serres, 2000, p. 17).[27] This new object goes far beyond the traditional concept per force locally defined. Serres defined the "world-objects" for the first time over forty years ago, in "La Thanatocratie" (1974, p. 101), giving as examples ballistic missiles, satellites, and nuclear wastes, objects whose dimensions, measured by speed and energy, are on a planetary if not universal scale. Internet is another example, measured by both distances and velocity. As such, asks Serres, can they still be called "objects," according to the literal sense of "that which is thrown or which one throws forth"? Serres goes on to describe how, originally, objects had a local dimension in space and in time, and the distance, the gap, between object and subject was used to define them and our environment, and thus to structure our knowledge of that environment. It was then possible to know and define "what we controlled and how" (2000, p. 13). "Held by a subject," Serres explains, "a technical object can act upon [other] objects: all these elements remain in a spatio-temporal sub-ensemble, narrow and relatively stable over time" (2000, p. 13). This notion of stability in space and time helped define the medieval concept of object, "*objectus*, what lies at an average distance before the body and its force to aid in our actions and thoughts" (2000, p. 13). However, nowadays, as this stability is no longer[28] and the quantity of world-objects has increased, a world order of a new and different nature organizes itself through globalization.

As a consequence, Serres suggests that the relation between the subject of knowledge and its object must be re-thought. Traditionally, the former has been assumed to be active, and the latter passive, with the subject taking possession "of the information given...by the object" (2000, p. 23). The significance of the word "*donné*" (given) in a philosophical context indicates that something is given with no expectation of return: "The subject takes everything and gives nothing, whereas the object gives everything and receives nothing" (2000, p. 23). Here, knowledge is free, gratuitous, given away with no compensation. Nowadays, Serres sees this relation subject-object in the quest for knowledge in the process of changing, or rather, it should, it ought to change—from a one-directional taking to a process of exchange: if the subject takes, it must give something in return. Pedagogy then becomes a "balanced and equitable exchange" or a "contract of exchange with its environment" (Serres, 2000, p. 23). In this exchange, the subject becomes the object "of that which we do not even know that they are objects: if we treat the world as an object, we

---

[27] Since 2000, other yearly meetings were held, the last one from November 30 to December 1, 2015, the "2015 United Nations Climate Change Conference, COP 21 or CMP 11" took place in Paris, France. It was the 21st yearly session of the Conference of the Parties (COP) to the 1992 United Nations Framework Convention on Climate Change (UNFCCC), and the 11th session of the Meeting of the Parties to the 1997 Kyoto Protocol. Hence its nicknames COP21 and CMP11.

[28] In Atlas (1994), Serres described his theory of the three stages of development linked to the elements: solid, liquid and gas. The industrial revolution prompted the third one by propagating heat technologies which "accelerated the rise of the local to the global" (2000, 12), heat of course being the result of the agitation and instability of the molecules. At the extreme, atomic energy is released by the ultimate instability, releasing deadly intensity of heat levels, and the potential of global destruction.

condemn ourselves [as part of this world] to become, in turn, objects of this object" (Serres, 2000, p. 22). This is where Serres sees the necessity of a contract, to think this new order, to define both this new global object and the new global subject "which conceptualizes it, acts upon it, whose debates make it visible, whose actions make it react, and whose reactions in turn condition the survival of this same collective group which conceptualizes it and acts upon it" (2000, p. 22).

This exchange between object and subject and this play of action-reaction necessitate a legal step to ensure fairness and a certain amount of justice, a contract to regulate this juridical debate where the world community finally takes notice of this new object, "which for want of a better word we shall continue to call nature" (Serres, 2000, p. 22). The contract, what Serres called the "Natural Contract," is acknowledged and "signed" by gatherings such as those in Rio, Kyoto, and Paris. Such gatherings are prompted by a disequilibrium in the exchange, an abuse, an exploitation by one of the parties. Serres asserts that he is not aware of "any education which does not begin ... by some juridical conditions" (2000, p. 21) (e.g., tests, entrance examinations, degrees, rewards, and so on) and that "any and all pedagogy begins with this Contract" (2000, p. 23).

A New Philosophy for a New World

The legal and ethical issues emerging around the use of global electronic technology to disseminate education point more sharply than ever to an acceleration of science and technology advances, which seems to leave us little time to "evaluate the substantial loss of culture which corresponds to this gain" (Serres, 1992, p. 85). Furthermore, "the problems posed by [such] global changes" as the use of Internet in general and in education in particular, can "cause a considerable revolution in mores and societies, even in our planet and humanity" (Serres, 1994, p. 122).

Science and technology have already "brought profound transformations in the relations they entertained with the world and humanity" (Serres, 1992, p. 29). This problem takes two aspects: on the one hand, Bruno Latour identifies it with the "classic theme of the Sorcerer's apprentice" (in Serres, 1992, p. 249); and on the other hand, it may be summed up by Rabelais's sentence, "Science[29] without conscience is nothing but the ruin of the human soul." In any case, science and the subsequent technological developments seem to have outdistanced both epistemology and ethics which seem unable to keep up with the pace. For Serres, along with many, the explosion of the atomic bomb on Hiroshima brought the realization that, for the first time in human history, scientists had gained the ultimate power and control to destroy the planet and extinguish humanity. It also brought into glaring light the fact that these same scientists (as well as the great majority of people) had been educated (if at all) in a philosophy, ethics, deontology and law which were no longer adapted to, or adequate for, the scientific knowledge now available or the technology it produced.

---

[29] In Rabelais's text, meaning "knowledge" in general.

Indeed, especially since the middle of last century, sciences and the techniques and technology they generated have experienced an unprecedented powerful rise and hegemony in all existing areas, while new ones emerged and grew very rapidly. They seemed to expand the boundaries of our knowledge while pushing back the limits of what we could not control, leading the (mostly Western) world to believe that, perhaps, they could free humanity of all boundaries and limits ... forever. Had they not enabled us for example to organize labor and production (and consumption) as well as communication much more efficiently, while allowing us to control sex and reproduction, aging and youth, illnesses and diseases (to prevent or to propagate) that is life and death, on both individual and collective, local and global levels? But in this "new" world scientists are creating, they continue to think as they did in the "old" one, and "philosophy has not studied yet the reasons nor the consequences" (Serres, 2000, p. 12).

Our decisions, choices, and actions were once guided by the distinction we had learned to make between what we were responsible for, and what we were not responsible for, what we could control, and what we could not control. The traditional notions of object and subject could organize our context, where for the most part they could be located in time and space, and helped define an environment over which a philosophy of mastery, possession and control could be developed. Sciences and techniques have erased these distinctions, and consequently, the necessity of this "wisdom" which, in the past, helped us endure the inevitable hardships then considered a consequence of the limits of our knowledge and an intrinsic part of life, and for which we were not responsible. Serres reminds us that in the past, "wisdom," "morality was a survival technique" which the advances of science, by pushing back the limits of necessity," have rendered superfluous, almost obsolete (Serres, 1992, p. 247). Now we find ourselves "masters of what used to control us" (p. 247), and we hope to eventually gain global control, over literally the totality of the world, even the universe and beyond—including its origin and its end. However, as the conferences in Rio and Kyoto and subsequent meetings glaringly revealed, that is but an illusion, the blinding effect of the lightning speed at which sciences have advanced. Somewhere along the way, we have lost our ability to distinguish between what can be controlled and what cannot. We forget that while sciences seem to hold "all the powers, all the knowledge, all the reason, all the rights too," or perhaps because they do, they also carry "all the problems" and "all the responsibilities" (Serres, 1992, p. 131). While the scientific field expands at an unprecedented rate, questions of ethics become increasingly pressing. Recent legal developments, for example those directed at Yahoo, Inc. both in Europe and in the United States on issues of Internet content, privacy and anonymity, free speech, freedom of expression, liberty of communication, control, and so on, should alert us to the dire necessity of ethical considerations and heightened responsibility, especially when planning online education.

With Serres, we can recognize another striking paradox in the face of the development of sciences and technologies and their prevalence in education, for he declared, "no other moment in history has had so many losers and so few winners as the present time," a time in which, as sciences advance, the number of losers has "exponentially increased," and the "club" of the privileged is more exclusive and inaccessible than ever (Serres, 1992, p. 268-269). Parallel to the apparent triumph of the sciences, we can witness a regression and/or degradation of education and culture, and a proliferation of ignorance, prejudices, illiteracy, and "alternative" beliefs (e.g., see the success of programs and books on "non-rational events," including angels, extra terrestrial occurrences and characters, magic practices, and so on). A solid, coherent, and well-balanced, "harmonious" program of instruction and education, equally open to all and buttressed by a solid theoretical and socio-political reflection is dangerously missing in our time.[30]

Simple, pure scientific rationality and technological savvy are not sufficient insists Serres: "the questions tossed around since the dawn of times by what we call the humanities help rethink those posed today about and because of the sciences" (Serres, 1992, p. 46).[31] However, the humanities and social sciences never include the physical world, and so-called hard sciences never take into account human beings as such. Serres's theory of knowledge advocates the breaking of the barriers between these two fields.[32] In the case of what is needed to face the new responsibilities brought upon us by the unprecedented development in the sciences and technologies, Serres believes that the exploration of the intersection of humanities and science is vital. He writes: "today, we live and think at this intersection," at "this junction where philosophy lives" (Serres, 1992, p. 208).

The sciences and technologies have indeed given us—that is the most privileged—unprecedented power in ways and on a scale never available before. But do we have the knowledge and wisdom to gain power over *our own* actions, judgement, and intentions? Do we have a sufficiently clear concept of what the abundance and scope of objects and events produced by science and its technologies imply for human relations, on a local level, and now on an unprecedented scale, on the global level, through satellites and electronic and wireless networks? Our Western scientific culture finds itself suffering from the "Sorcerer's Apprentice syndrome," where our science, technical and technological advances go way beyond our capacities to manage them and certainly our capacity to understand all their

---

[30] In the U.S., under the pressures of "standardization" and systematic testing to satisfy demands of accountability, and corporative cry for "qualified [not 'educated'] employees," education is being pressured toward what I call the "vo-tech syndrome": more functionalism; schooling to learn a trade; fragmentation of disciplines; reduction of curricula to STEM, and so on. Of course, these limitations may affect only "public education." Those who want a more balanced, or "oriented," education for their children and can afford it (while refusing to pay taxes for public education) have the option of putting their children in privileged private or independent schools.

[31] See also D. Egéa (2005, 2016)

[32] For a discussion of Serres's theory of knowledge, see Egéa-Kuehne (1998).

ramifications. The acceleration of sciences and technical developments has moved us at light speed from the "possible" to the "realized" to the "desirable" to the "necessary" (Serres, 1992, p. 249). Now that sciences and technologies have brought us the potential to control our world, if not the illusion that we can do so, we *have to* learn to manage its power. Yet our mastery is surprisingly limited when it comes to controlling it or our own power and desires, for this power of science moves faster than our reflection on its consequences, and goes "further than our faculties to foresee it, our capacity to manage it, our desire to sway it, our will to make decisions about it, our freedom to direct it" (Serres, 1992, p. 250). We have already passed the point where "the task of philosophy is to re-examine all its former concepts such as subject, objects, knowledge and action" (Serres, 2000, p. 15). The new global "world-objects" cannot be reflected upon with an obsolete local philosophy—that is local until Hiroshima and Chernobyl.

CONCLUSION

In this essay, I discussed Internet education as it begins to cast its net(s) and extend beyond borders, and, drawing on Michel Serres's works, I addressed some ethico-political aspects of the commodification of knowledge. Despite the lure of "free" access to education, present and potential risks of "tailoring/Tayloring" marketable courses and syllabi for profit are immense, locally and globally. They require a new understanding of the nature of knowledge, distinct from training and from its traditional basis on the local concepts of subject and object and their relation. The former necessity which bred "wisdom" as described by Serres, perhaps because of a lack of understanding and undue complacency, was forced to change side. A new imperative now finds itself within what we believed was to give us unqualified freedom: science and technology. There is a dire necessity for choices to be made and decisions to be taken in the domain of online education which will affect the future on both local and global scales, and which call more than ever for higher stakes responsibility and a rethinking of the nature of knowledge. All the more so when we engage into any kind of globalization of education, since it increases our responsibility, not only to ourselves, but also to others, other communities, and tomorrow's humanity.

REFERENCES

Cardean   University.   Last   accessed,   June   12,   2016.
    http://www.trinity.edu/rjensen/000aaa/prest/unext/cardean.htm
Duderstadt J.J. (1999). "Can colleges and universities survive in the Information
    Age?" In Katz, R. N. (ed.). *Dancing with the devil: Information technology
    and the new competition in higher education*. San Francisco, CA: Jossey-
    Bass Inc., Publishers. p. 1-25.
Egéa-Kuehne, D. (1997) "Neutrality in Education and Derrida's Call for 'Double
    Duty'," in *Philosophy of Education* 1996, ed. Frank Margonis. Urbana, IL:
    Philosophy of Education Society. p. 154-163. Last accessed, June 12, 2016.
    file:///C:/Users/Denise/AppData/Local/Temp/2257-8248-1-PB.pdf
Egéa-Kuehne, D. (1998). "Michel Serres's Connections Through the Multiplicity of
    Time: a Metaphor for Curriculum." *JCT: An Interdisciplinary Journal of
    Curriculum Studies* 14(3): p. 8-13.
Egéa-Kuehne, D. (2005) "Right to Humanities: Of Faith and Responsibility." In P.P.
    Trifonas and M. Peters (Eds) *Deconstructing Derrida: Tasks for the New
    Humanities*. London: Palgrave McMillan. p. 37-52
Egéa, D. (2016) "The Philosopher and the Teaching of Philosophy in the Age of
    Cosmopolitanism" In M. Papastephanou (ed.) *Cosmopolitanism:
    Educational, Philosophical, and Historical Perspectives*. The Netherlands:
    Springer International Publishing.
Marceux, P. (2013). *Special Report: The Telecom Consumer in 2020*. Euromonitor
    International (August 7, 2013). Last accessed, June 12, 2016.
    http://blog.euromonitor.com/2013/08/special-report-the-telecom-consumer-
    in-2020.html
No Name (2000) "French Uphold Ruling against Yahoo on Nazi Sites," *The New
    York Times* (November 21, 2000). Last accessed June 12, 2016.
    http://www.nytimes.com/2000/11/21/technology/21YAHO.html
Perez, J.C. (2006) "Yahoo Loses Appeal in Nazi Memorabilia Case," *PCWorld*
    (January 12, 2006). Last accessed, June 12, 2016.
    http://www.pcworld.com/article/124367/article.html
Rubin, J.C. (2001). "2001: a Media Odyssey." *Time* (June 24, 2001). Last accessed,
    June   12,   2016.   npn.
    http://content.time.com/time/magazine/article/0,9171,133810,00.html
Serres, M. (1974). "La Thanatocracie," *Hermès III. La traduction*. Paris: Éditions de
    Minuit.
Serres, M. (1992). *Eclaircissements: Entretiens avec Bruno Latour*. Paris: Editions
    François Bourin.
Serres, M. (1994). *Atlas*. Paris: Julliard.
Serres, M. (2000). *Retour au Contrat naturel*. Paris: Bibliothèque nationale de France.
SmartHide. (n.d.) Last accessed, June 12, 2016. http://www.online-anonymizer.com/

Traub, J. (2000a). "This Campus Is Being Simulated." *The New York Times Magazine*
        (November   19,   2000):   5-12.   Last   accessed,   June   12,   2016.
        http://www.nytimes.com/2000/11/19/magazine/this-campus-is-being-
        simulated.html?pagewanted=1

Traub, J. (2000b). "Online U. How entrepreneurs and academic radicals are breaking
        down the walls of the university." *The New York Times Magazine*.
        (November 19, 2000): 88-93.

United Nations (2000a). "Report of the high-level panel of experts on information and
        communication technology." Document A/55/75-E/2000/55 (May 22, 2000).
        Last   accessed,   June   1,   2016.
        http://www.un.org/documents/ecosoc/docs/2000/e2000-55.pdf

United Nations (2000b). "Press Briefing on Information Technology Panel - June
        2000."   (June   19,   2000).   Last   accessed,   June   1,   2016
        http://www.unites.org/html/news/2000/pb190600.htm

Wallis, C. (2001) "The Learning Revolution." *Time* (June 24, 2001). Last accessed,
        June   12,   2016.
        http://content.time.com/time/magazine/article/0,9171,133809,00.html

CHAPTER 4

Globalization Vision for Multicultural Education

Yang-Seok Yoo

INTRODUCTION

The current forms of formal education which have been widely adopted around world were established in the mid-to late 19th century. By the late 19th century, most European nations began to provide elementary education in reading, writing, and arithmetic (Farrell, 2007). The forms of primary education further expanded into secondary education. The forms of education were built on standard curriculums, typically defined by national governments. From its development and by its very nature, education has always been considered a national good; that is, a good that is intrinsically national in origin and which can only be provided by national institutions (Hugonnler, 2007).

The contemporary world of the 21st century represents a significantly different world than that of the 19th century. There are far more complex interdependencies and integrations of people, societies and nations around the globe. These increasing interdependencies and integrations are due to the effects of globalization in the 21st century.

Globalization represents an ongoing process of intensifying economic, social, and cultural exchanges. It symbolizes an increasing integration and coordination of markets, of production, and of consumption. In addition, the globalization of economic forces is stimulating the migration of people. With increasing interaction and migration of people across the globe, globalization fosters a constant exchange of cultures. The cultural exchanges make the old cultural boundaries as well as the aspired cultural coherence and homogeneity of the nation-state, increasingly untenable. These new global realities of heterogeneity and multicultural societies are challenging schools everywhere an in multiple ways (Suarez-Orozco & Sattin, 2007).

Importantly, global changes in culture deeply affect educational policies, practices and institutions. For instance, the question of 'multiculturalism' takes on a special meaning in a global context. How should the citizens learn to live with others with mutual tolerance and respect across national and cultural boundaries? In contrast to previous educational models which were more focused on the needs and development of the individual, with an eye toward helping the person fit into a community defined by relative proximity, homogeneity and familiarity, modern educational paradigms broaden the outline of 'community' beyond the nation or region (Burbules and Torres, 2000). Future generations will have to learn to live in new cultural, social, economic, and linguistic contexts. Educational systems must evolve and go beyond local frameworks.

Currently the majority of educational systems around the world are largely unprepared for the challenges of globalization. Most school curriculums do not take into consideration that today's youths are learning, interacting and living in an environment that is connected (with varying degrees of intensity) to different values, cultures, language groups, levels of economic development and educational systems different than their own local cultures. To meet this challenge, educational systems must adapt and expand their priorities to account for this new context of multicultural social setting and teach students with intercultural skills that can go beyond the local context and to help them think globally (Süssmuth, 2007). Multicultural education represents a category of education that aims to broaden cultural understanding and knowledge; develop intercultural skills and adaptability for plural and heterogeneous societies.

EARLY APPROACHES TO MULTI-CULTURAL EDUCATION

One of the early implementations of multicultural education began in the United States. Multicultural education was initiated in the 1960s to transform the existing educational structure in order to provide equal access, representation and outcomes for all students. Multicultural education was to address civic and economic equality and cultural discrimination based on students' race, ethnicity, gender, sexual orientation, or disability. By framing multicultural education in terms of equal representation of traditionally underrepresented groups, the early approach focused on school policies and practices on social-structural equality and the promotion of cultural pluralism. Programs such as 'celebrating diversity' were organized as an acceptable way of providing multicultural education (Lei and Grant, 2001). Another early implementer of multicultural education, Canada focused its multicultural education on information and observable items and practices that could be identified and communicated. And as a result, much of the focus was on expressions of culture in terms of food, costumes, art, dance, religious symbols and practices (James, 2001).

These early approaches to multicultural education, which are still prevalent today, tend to focus too much on teaching facts about other cultures and there exists too little focus on understanding basic patterns underlying cultural practices or belief systems. It is being recognized that providing students primarily with information or facts is a superficial form of education. What is more important is to be able to help students to create knowledge by teaching them how to interpret and evaluate information, which is a much deeper form of education. Specifically, multicultural education must address the difficulty in perceiving the patterns of other cultures. Since these patterns do not fit those of one's own culture, people often experience them as 'strange', 'odd; or simply foreign (Gärdenfors, 2007).

Using UNESCO's general definition, culture should be regarded as "the set of distinctive spiritual, material, intellectual and emotional features of a society or a social group, and which encompasses, in addition to art and literature, lifestyles, ways of living together, value systems, traditions and beliefs." Multicultural education should be an opportunity to develop an appreciation and the capabilities to approach, interpret and understand various cultures and cultural values.

MULTICULTURAL EDUCATION VISION FOR GLOBALIZATION

Today's multicultural education is not as simple as conducting cultural-festivals or facilitating assimilation and accommodation of minorities to learn the codes of the majority society. Much more is needed in the norm of the heterogeneous societies: both minority and majority cultures must learn together. The people of majority cultures will need to master other cultural sensibilities and codes. They will need the cultural sophistication to empathize with their peers, who will likely be of different racial, religious, linguistic and social origins. The people of majority cultures will need to be able to learn with and from minority cultures in order to work collaboratively and to communicate effectively in groups made up of diverse individuals. Education for globalization should aim at nothing more nor less than to educate 'the whole child for the whole world' (Suarez-Orozco, M., and Sattin, 2007).

In the midst of increasing heterogeneity, one's own unique cultural identity and pride are as important as being able to adapt and appreciate the differences in other cultures. Only through an individual's raised understanding of one's own culture can one broaden cultural understanding of others. Greater understanding of culture can lead to a respect for diversity across cultural barriers, specifically differing customs and traditions, differing languages, differing religions, and differing economic status. And as such, the goal of multicultural education should be to develop competence to recognize and respect uniqueness of all cultures - one's own as well as other cultures. Specifically, cultural competence includes the ability to recognize differences as well as similarities (Kramsch, 1993), the ability to de-center and see one's own culture from an outsider's perspective (Byram, 1989), the ability to accept and understand different ways of acting and thinking and finally, the ability to negotiate a range of meaning and interpretations (Byram, 1997).

The vision of multicultural education is to enable students to develop such cultural competences and a better appreciation of one's own and other's cultures and to achieve a greater recognition of shared values and humanity in a larger global context.

MODERN APPROACHES TO MULTICULTURAL EDUCATION

Many nations recognize the importance of globalization and multicultural education and there are varieties of initiatives underway to respond and reflect their implications in the national educational curriculums. These national initiatives provide practical insights into how modern nations deal with multicultural education and their support for the above vision of multicultural education. The following examples reflect recent educational developments in Japan, Korea and China. These nations have been selected for the relatively homogeneous nature of their societies and their initiatives for dealing with multicultural education are relatively recent developments which are expected to evolve over the next few years.

The Japanese example illustrates an approach of expanding international and multicultural understanding while at the same time cultivating an appreciation for one's own identity and culture. The Korean example demonstrates a systemic approach of addressing within the national educational curriculum the importance of global issues and social responsibilities to achieve a greater recognition of shared values and humanity for the global society. The Chinese example emphasizes the importance of communication specifically the language skills in the highly interconnected and multicultural societies.

Japan

Japan recognizes that the structure and aspects of society have been changing on a global scale, and that complexities have emerged which are difficult to cope with given existing organizations and systems (National Commission on Educational Report of Japan, 2000). In recognizing such changes, the Curriculum Council on internationalism proposed educational changes to broaden multi cultural understanding and at the same time strengthen appreciation for its own cultural identity. The Council stated that "the aim of education is to cope with the progress of internationalization to develop the qualities and abilities of understanding other cultures from a wide perspective, not being prejudiced against, but interacting naturally and living with, people who have different cultures of habits. In order to do that, it is important first to have education which cultivates understanding, love and pride in our own country's history, culture and traditions" (Parmenter, 2000).

Japan's restructuring of its national curriculum reflects such an educational aim. The multicultural education is uniquely being emphasized while cultivating appreciation for its own identity and cultures. Social studies and geography are two subjects largely dealing with multicultural education and the contents of multicultural education are progressively introduced from elementary through high school. In the sixth year of elementary school, the understanding of international sphere becomes a significant part of the social studies curriculum. The depth of the coverage increases and at the junior high level the geography section of the social studies curriculum is divided into "regional structure of the world and Japan" "Japan seen through comparisons to the world" and "investigations appropriate to the regional scale." Similar approaches are also applied to the history and civic sections of the junior high school social studies curriculum. (Parmenter, 2000)

Along with multi culture contents, the 'integrated studies' are important attributes of Japan's educational restructuring. The aim of the integrated studies, where students spend seventy to 130 hours per year from the third year of elementary school to the third year of junior high school, is to develop students' ability and competence to respond independently to the changes of society, such as internationalization, by developing their abilities to transcend subject boundaries and think and learn by themselves. (Kyouiku Katei Shingikai, 1998) Along with expanded coverage of multi-culture and internationalization in the educational curriculums, the integrated studies provide unique opportunities to individual students to extend classroom learning to real-life learning, which undoubtedly is a broadening experience both culturally and intellectually. The importance of developing cultural competency for one's own culture, broadening cultural competency for other cultures and promoting individualized experience-based learning are key fabrics of Japan's educational reform for internationalization and multicultural education.

Korea

Korea's approach to multicultural education strives to teach students with the importance of harmonious living with all people based on an improved understanding of practices and customs of other cultures and heritages, the promotion of human rights in democratic societies, social rights and equity and the pursuit of a peaceful world and the development of capabilities for global citizenship. A recent policy task force for 'the development of educational systems in the era of globalization' proposes a five-stranded framework for globalization and multicultural education. The framework has been developed jointly with the APCEIU (Asia Pacific Center of Education for International Understanding under the auspices of UNESCO). The five strands and their educational aims are (Park, Lee, et al, 2008):

1. Multicultural understanding – Be able to understand the heritage and culture of many nations around the world including language, religion, living customs, and through understanding, respect for all cultures and a promotion of interactions and exchanges. Establish identity and pride of one's own culture and practice living together with all people of the world.
2. Globalization Issues – Be able to understand the close interactions with the world nations and dependencies. Understand how to work and live in the global community and understand our identity and role so that we are able to contribute to the world community
3. Respect for Human Rights –Establish a foundation for human rights and equality inclusive of all people including the disabled, immigrants, etc. so that the equity and respect for each other is maintained in the society; Moreover, collectively work to solve human rights issues.
4. Peaceful World – Recognize conflicts and tension and wars around the world and understand the importance of communication, dialogue, cooperation and accommodation and peaceful means for reconciliation and develop the perspectives and approaches for peace
5. Sustained development – Understand the global issues that are being encountered and develop value systems and leadership for the world that can confront these challenges

This five stranded framework describes the progressive multicultural education contents from elementary school to high school. For instance: the elementary level social studies program includes such topics as 'interests in other cultures; understanding and respect for other cultures; and the importance of our own culture.' The high school program discusses 'comprehensive understanding of culture, creation and evolution of culture; co-existence of multi-culture, and cultural asset preservation.' This framework can serve as an important educational framework for Korea and other nations.

China

China's economic achievements are closely associated with its rapid globalization over the last three decades. The impact of globalization has larger implications beyond the growth of its economy as it has affected all aspects of daily life including higher education. Regarding China's school curriculums, the Ministry of Education is advocating the integration of the sciences and humanities to ensure the all-round development of Chinese students; this includes compulsory education in foreign languages and computer science and the training of hands-on practical skills to be increasingly competitive in market-economies (Yang, 2005).

With its growing presence in the global society, the Chinese government recognizes the importance of multicultural education and so it was adopted in the 2002 National Curriculum Standard. The aim of such education is to increase global awareness and international understanding including significant developments in education of foreign languages, especially English. In fact, English education starts earlier in the 3rd grade with an emphasis on communication skills such as listening and speaking. The increased importance of English is being reflected in college admissions and employment requirements as well (Lin, 2002).

The educational contents of multicultural education include multicultural understanding, world cultural heritage protection, sustainable development, peace education, global awareness and international understanding. These educational contents are delivered across various subjects such as History, Geography, English, Politics and Moral Education, and Science (Yu, 2009). With China's continued efforts in educational reform to support its socio-economic transformation and to raise the global-competitiveness of its educational curriculum, the approach to multicultural education is expected to evolve in order to better enable its growing presence and integration into the world community.

SUMMARY AND CONCLUSION

Globalization continues to accelerate the pace of interaction and exchange of people across the globe. Societies are becoming increasingly heterogeneous requiring greater understanding and adaptations across cultural boundaries. In the norm of heterogeneity, there exists an increasing need for improved cultural understanding. Only through proactive education of the youth of today will nations be better equipped for the challenges and complexities of the multicultural and heterogeneity of future societies. The globalization vision for multicultural education is to equip the youth of today with cultural competency to broaden cultural understanding and knowledge; develop intercultural skills and adaptability for plural and heterogeneous societies and enable students to achieve a greater recognition of shared values and humanity across cultural boundaries. The modern educational initiatives of Japan, Korea and China reflect the growing recognition of the importance of multicultural education. And these nations are at various stages of implementing multicultural educational contents in the national educational curriculums. Recognizing a growing list of challenges requiring all people of all nations to collaborate without borders is of greater urgency in order to raise the priority of multicultural education in all nations.

References

Burbules, N.C., and Torres C.A. *Globalization and Education, Critical Perspectives*, Routledge, 2000: 21-22

Byram, M. 1989. *Cultural Studies in Foreign Language Education*, Clevedon, England: Multilingual Matters.

Byram, M. 1997: *Teaching and Assessing Intercultural Commutative Competence*. Clevedon, England: Multilingual Matters.

Farrell, J. Changing Education: *Leadership, Innovation and Development in a Globalizing Asia Pacific*, Springer, 2007:202

Gärdenfors, P. Understanding *Cultural Patterns, Learning in the Global Era, International Perspective on Globalization and Education*, University of California Press, 2007:67-68

Hugonnler, B. "Can the World Meet the Challenge?" *Globalization and Education, Learning in the Global Era, International Perspectives on Globalization and Education*, University of California Press, 2007:137.

James, C. E. "Multiculturalism, Diversity, and Education in the Canadian Context: The Search for an Inclusive Pedagogy," *Global Constructions of Multicultural Education, Theories and Realities*, Lawrence Erlbaum Associates, 2001: 181

Kramsch, C. *Context and Culture in Language Teaching*, Oxford: Oxford University Press, 1993

Kyouiku Katei Shingikai. *National Curriculum Standards Reform for Kindergarten, Elementary School, Lower and Upper Secondary School and Schools for the Visually Disabled, the Hearing Impaired and the Otherwise Disabled*. 1998

Lei, J. L., and Grant, C.A. "Multicultural Education in the United States: A Case of Paradoxical Equality," *Global Constructions Of Multicultural Education, Theories and Realities*, Lawrence Erlbaum Associates, 2001:205-221

Lin, L. "English Education in Present-day China," *Asian/Pacific Book Development*, 2002, Vol. 33. No. 2:8-9

The National Commission on Educational Reform, *Report by the National Commission on Educational Reform, 17 Proposals for Changing Education*, December 22, 2000, www.kantei.go.jp/foreign/education/report/report.html

Park, J. Y., Lee, H. Y., Chung, I. H., and Kim, Y. *Policy Tasks for the Development of Educational System in the Era of Globalization*, Korean Educational Development Institute, 2008:128-137

Parmenter, L. *Internationalization in Japanese Education: Current Issues and Future Prospects, Globalization and Education: Integration and Contestation across Cultures*, Rowman & Littlefield, 2000: 237-249

Suarez-Orozco, M., and Sattin C. "Learning in the Global Era," *International Perspective on Globalization and Education*, University of California Press, 2007: 7-11; 18-19

Süssmuth, R. "On the Need for Teaching Intercultural Skills," *Challenge for Education in a Globalizing World, Learning in the Global Era*, University of California Press, 2007: 210

The National Commission on Educational Reform, *Report by the National Commission on Educational Reform, 17 Proposals for Changing Education*, December 22, 2000 www.kantei.go.jp/foreign/education/report/report.html

UNESCO, *UNESCO's Intangible Cultural Heritage Division*, http://portal.unesco.org/culture/en/

Yang Z. "Globalization and Higher Education Reform in China," Australian Association for Research in Education (AARE) Conference 2005 ISSN 1324-9339, 2005

Yu X. "In-Service Teacher Training on Education for International Understanding in China," *EIU Best Practices Series* 15, 2009

Zhao Z. *Focus on the Issues on the Development of Global Education-Reports from UNESCO in the 1990s,* Educational Science Press, 1999.

CHAPTER 5

Excellence and Equivalence in Curriculum Design for Transnational Programmes: A Focus on Education for Sustainability

Sylila Monteiro and Rashika Sharma

INTRODUCTION

Globalisation and rapid unprecedented technological development requires education to address the shifting paradigms beyond its control. Internationalisation of educational programmes is a response to the current global market. The portability of education and international student exchange brings a variety of challenges, a consequence of differences in industrial expectations and living standards, especially culturally and environmentally. To address these challenges transnational education should strive for equivalence in the curriculum. The UNESCO (2005) Guidelines for Quality Provision in Cross-Border Higher Education suggests that partner institutions should:

> Ensure that the programmes they deliver across borders and in their home country are of comparable quality and that they also take into account the cultural and linguistic sensitivities of the receiving country. It is desirable that a commitment to this effect should be made public. (p.14)

QUALITY ASSURANCE FOR CURRICULUM EQUIVALENCE

Transnational programmes globally attempt to achieve curriculum equivalence, however there are often unforseen impediments faced by educators and learners that only surface during delivery of programmes. Curriculum equivalence is an essential component of quality, validating the parity of the programme and its delivery to the satisfaction of both parties involved. Equivalence does not mean uniformity and programmes cannot be uplifted from the host partner and delivered without customising and contextualising the programme to make it relevant and meaningful for the transnational student. The transnational student experience, learning styles, assessment type, evaluation strategies and cultural expectations should be considered in design and delivery. Local and global contexts are equally critical.

Woodley (2008) states "it is more realistic to expect that programs, while equivalent in terms of learning outcomes, program purpose, evaluation tools, teacher qualifications, facilities and resources, also be relevant and appropriate to the student cohort and the culture in which they are delivered"(p.3). Woodley advocates comparability over equivalence so as to adapt to cultural differences, thus achieving customisation and contextualisation of the curriculum.

According to Greenholtz (2000), merely incorporating "best practice" curricula and the most advanced technology and facilities cannot fulfil objectives of transnational programmes unless cultural sensitivity is fully recognised and successfully addressed. This cultural dimension makes or breaks the success of the programme. Greenholtz (2000) further elaborates that staff designing and delivering this training are to be adequately qualified with an appropriate level of awareness and expertise in intercultural interactions. This intercultural awareness of staff ensures effective functioning in transnational contexts.

Monteiro and Sharma (2012), in their research affirm that cultural adaptation affects class room interaction and response, which in turn can reflect adversely on student performance. For instance, Monteiro and Sharma (2012), ascertain that assertiveness is an essential skill requisite to success in an individualistic and competitive western oriented educational system. Students coming from a collectivist culture where interpersonal harmony is highly prized are self-restrained and less assertive than their western oriented colleagues in the host country. Asian students have been reported to have more acculturative stress than other groups of international students. Further, the passivity can have a negative effect on relationships with their teachers, peers, and advisors (Poyrazli, Arbona, Nora, McPherson, & Pisecco, 2002) in particular at tertiary level. Cultural adaptation is thus the overarching principle to warrant comparability over equivalence for successful customisation and contextualisation of the curriculum. Regardless of discipline, cultural considerations are vital for delivery of transnational programmes. Education for sustainability (EfS) becomes viable through cultural adaptation.

EDUCATION FOR SUSTAINABILITY IN TRANSNATIONAL PROGRAMMES

The United Nations (2002) has declared 2005-2014 the Decade of Education for Sustainable Development (ESD). The objective of the decade of ESD is to ensure curriculum modification to reflect concepts of sustainability (Parliamentary Commission for Environment (PCE), 2004). Education for Sustainability (EfS) or 'sustainability education' includes all educational systems and processes that aspire to promote and increase awareness about sustainability. Sustainability education is defined by Moore (2005) as "education that concentrates on the concept of sustainability in a manner that fits with the values of sustainability" (p. 78) and by the Parliamentary Commission for the Environment (2004) as education that "examines how people and groups in society can learn to live in sustainable ways" (p. 15). The Earth Summit defined education for sustainability as "critical for achieving environmental and ethical awareness, values and attitudes, skills and behaviour consistent with sustainable development and for effective public participation in decision making" (United Nations Department of Economic and Social Affairs, 1992, para 3). Moore (2005) defines education for sustainability as a "process of creating a space for inquiry, dialogue, reflection, and action about the concept and goals of sustainability" (p. 78). Education for sustainability "encompasses a new vision of education that seeks to empower people of all ages to assume responsibility for creating a sustainable future" (Parliamentary Commissioner for the Environment (PCE), 2004, p. 36). Therefore EfS implies educational processes and systems that transform perspectives and encourage sustainable practice in all aspects of life in keeping with the current and future changing technological environment.

TRANSNATIONAL INTER-INSTITUTIONAL PARTNERSHIPS

Inter-institutional partnerships are initiated and implemented by a written agreement, the Memorandum of Understanding (MoU) between two institutes. The MoU entitles transnational students to achieve a tertiary qualification in the host institution by cross crediting from equivalent undergraduate courses achieved at their home institute. For practical cross crediting purposes, when examined, the learning outcomes, in the programme in the home and host country are relatively comparable. However there are some subtleties that impact on student performance in the host institution. These underlying subtleties are explored in this paper from the educator perspective in the course of classroom delivery and evaluation.

As mentioned earlier all levels of education need to embed sustainability education in the curriculum to achieve a desirable global outcome. There are subtle gaps - barely visible on the surface - which hold tremendous implications on teacher as well as student expectations and student performance in general. In New Zealand, the clean green image and awareness on sustainable living is emphasised and promoted more widely than in some countries. Transnational students from some countries entering the New Zealand education system are not necessarily exposed to this focus on sustainability through their curriculum as there are differences in industrial expectations and living standards, culturally and environmentally. For curriculum equivalence transnational programmes should aspire to bridge these subtle gaps created by these differences in education for sustainability.

REFLECTIONS FOR CURRICULUM DEVELOPERS

Classroom dynamics demonstrate the practical impediments encountered by educators and students in meeting the curriculum in education for sustainability. This is a practitioner based evaluation that is invaluable for successful delivery and implementation especially for transnational curriculum developers. These reflections are centred on an existing MoU over the duration of two years.

> This case involves a partnership between a New Zealand polytechnic and a Malaysian automotive technical institute. The institute offers its own Diploma in Automotive Technology...This Memorandum of Understanding (MoU) between the two institutes allows students, who have successfully completed the two-and-a-half year Diploma in Automotive Technology to transfer their study to the New Zealand polytechnic. The MoU requires the

New Zealand polytechnic to acknowledge full recognition of the Malaysian Diploma in Automotive Technology and delegate 180 unspecified credits towards the Bachelor of Applied Technology (Automotive) programme. Under the MoU students are required to study for a minimum of 3 semesters in this New Zealand polytechnic in order to achieve a Bachelors qualification. The Malaysian qualifications are cross credited making them eligible to enroll and give them the opportunity to successfully complete the Bachelor in Automotive Technology degree. (Monteiro & Sharma, in press)

Under this agreement the students enter the programme in year two and as a result forego first year studies in the host country, where foundational generic skills and capabilities are inculcated. The first year of the programme lays the foundation for deeper understanding and for successful progression to the following years. In the first year skills such as academic writing, referencing, critical thinking, self- directed learning and sustainability education are introduced. These students entering the programme in the second year are unfamiliar with these basic capabilities crucial to lifelong learning. This was most evident in the compulsory Sustainable Technologies course offered in the transnational curriculum. The Sustainable Technologies course designed to broaden student awareness on global sustainability is imperative to and aligns with the United Nations Decade of Sustainable Development. If the skill transfer of global sustainability does not occur then the underlying purpose of transnationalism – the portability of education and global application is defeated.

Academic results for the Sustainable Technologies course indicated that the performance of these students was adversely affected in comparison to that of local students who had completed the first year and had the basic capabilities as mentioned earlier. Informal conversations with teachers and students engaged in the Sustainable Technologies course revealed that the absence of these prior skills and this lack of basic knowledge of sustainable practice was a hindrance. It made it difficult for transnational students to integrate, assimilate and process knowledge of sustainability and relate it to technical implications in a New Zealand environment. In addition the application of this knowledge on sustainability was an alien concept unrelated to their home country environment.

If transnational education is meant to give students the opportunity to learn locally yet with global practical application, students must identify with the relevance of sustainability in their everyday life. In New Zealand, the clean green image and awareness on sustainable living is emphasised and promoted more widely than in some countries. "…New Zealanders have gradually developed a sense of intimacy towards the rest of the natural world in this country…majority of New Zealanders today have a growing desire to maintain the quality of the environment they live in" (New Zealand Parliamentary Commission for the Environment, 2004, p. 24). Simple practices such as recycling, energy conservation, reforestation, industrial environmental policies and governance is the acceptable norm in New Zealand society. New Zealand has in place many key plans such as energy efficiency and conservation strategy, biodiversity strategy and waste strategy that aim at enhancing the environmental quality and achieving sustainable development at the regional and national level. Consequently these sustainability concepts are embedded in the curriculum and are part of the social responsibility and consciousness.

One example to illustrate policy strategies incorporated by the New Zealand government whole heartedly supported by most citizens is "the Waste Minimisation Act 2008 which encourages a reduction in the amount of waste generated and disposed of in New Zealand and aims to lessen the environmental harm of waste. This Act also aims to benefit the NZ economy by encouraging better use of materials throughout the product life cycle, promoting domestic reprocessing of recovered materials and providing more employment"(Ministry of Environment, 2008). Through this legislation a civic awareness of environmental well being, as well as economic and social benefits is created, as opposed to that of some countries where economic and social benefits supersede environmental sustainability. Overseas students entering the New Zealand education system are not necessarily exposed to this focus on sustainability through their curriculum as there are cultural and environmental differences in social and industrial expectations as well as living standards in their home country. Parity of approaches and differences in sustainable practices between the participating countries now become apparent to learners and educators. Consequently, ideal assignment design for transnational students should aim to provide an opportunity for students to investigate and think critically about environmental and social issues in New Zealand and in their home country. This acquisition of transformative learning gives transnational students transferable critical thinking capabilities with global application.

ASSESSMENT DESIGN: RELEVANT AND TRANSFERABLE; LOCAL OR GLOBAL.

For curriculum equivalence transnational students need to be given the option to locate the assignment in their home countries if they so wish, so as to relate locally yet applying global sustainability principles. This addresses the learning outcomes in a manner that is meaningful and relevant to their familiar context. In this way the objectives of global sustainability advocated by United Nations Decade of Sustainable Development can be achieved. These acquired skills become transferable skills and global sustainability can be effected.

Assessment for transnational programmes should typically represent global sustainability principles and theory, yet permit flexibility of content and application. In doing so the students are able to make connections and associations, advancing knowledge processing, critical thinking as well as linking prior knowledge and experience to current contexts. Figure 1 that follows is an example of an assignment used as an assessment in the Sustainable Technologies course where 50 percent of the cohort is transnational students. Figure 2 is the marking criteria used to evaluate performance. The relevance to the learning outcomes, especially the focus on the practical application of principles of sustainability can be determined and assessed.

APPT 6113   SUSTAINABLE TECHNOLOGIES

Assignment 2 - A Case Study (70% of the course grade)

Produce an individual report showing the actual or potential application of sustainable technologies within a selected local case study. Conclude your report with recommendations for the further incorporation of effective sustainable technology into the situation you have described.

The final report should be **2,000- 2,500** words in length and be fully and properly referenced. These references MUST include at least one journal article.

Criteria:
- Describe the case you have selected. (What is the problem you are investigating? Explain the issue, its history, the impact it makes locally).

- Identify areas where <u>sustainable technology</u> does/could play a part in the situation you have described. (What technology exists that deals with the problem you've identified above? How is this technology considered a 'sustainable technology'? – Analyse using Quadruple Bottom line)

- Suggest what future impact your case study could make to the overall problem. What are your recommendations?

Figure 1: An example of an assignment for Sustainable Technologies Course

APPT6113: Assignment 2 Marking Schedule						
Name:						
Student ID:						
Case Topic:						
	Application	**Demonstration**	**Understanding**	**Awareness**	**No comprehension**	Marks out of 70
Case Description	Articulates a clear, complete understanding of the case, its history and its impacts	Demonstrates understanding of the case, its history and its impacts	Shows vague, unfocused understanding of the case	Is aware of the case	Case not described appropriately	/15
Role of sustainable technology	Competently identifies role of sustainable technologies in the case. Analytical skills are evident	Good attempt in identifying role of sustainable technologies in the case	Demonstrates understanding of sustainable technologies in the case	Shows only awareness of sustainable technologies in the case with little analysis	Unable to identify role of sustainable technologies in the case	/40
Future Impact	Response draws logical, clear conclusions to the case. Proposed solutions are clearly outlined as future actions.	Response draws some conclusions to the case but may be brief. Future impacts identified.	Future impacts are described briefly	Response draws a general conclusion but it may be sparse or confusing. Future impacts are brief and/or not directly linked to the case.	Future impacts are not outlined.	/15
					TOTAL:	/70
					GRADE:	
Comments:						

Figure 2: An example of the marking criteria for the assignment in Figure 1.

EDUCATOR REFLECTIONS ON EFFECTIVENESS OF THE ASSIGNMENT

The assignment was designed to allow students to self-select case studies. New Zealand students selected New Zealand specific topics such as bio-degradable landfills, water pollution, industrial waste and effluents, methane gas from cattle farms, carbon tax, and wind farm impact on the natural landscape. It was observed that 100 percent of transnational students chose to select cases based in the context of their home country as they could relate the theory more effectively and associate this theory to the practicalities of the application. Some topics students selected were water pollution in China, waste management in East Asia, bio fuels and palm oil in Malaysia, renewable energy in India, e-waste in Taiwan and deforestation in Africa. Figure 3 is an extract of a student assignment focussing on air pollution in Malaysia.

Air pollution problem in Malaysia

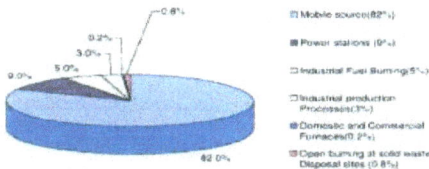

Source from http://www.sciencedirect.com/science/article/pii/S0013935102000592

The graph above shows you the percentage of air pollution in Malaysia. There are three major problems that causes air pollution which is mobile source, stationary source and open burning source. More than five years, the emission for mobile source is increasing and by the meaning of mobile source are personal cars, commercial cars, and motorcycles. The image above shows you that this mobile source causes 82% air pollution in Malaysia. The second problem is power station is Malaysia which contributed 9% harmful air pollution. Industry fuel burning is also another cause of air pollution in Malaysia which only contributes a small amount which is 5%. There was case study, when Malaysia had recession the air pollution in Kuala Lumpur and Selangor grow rapidly because there was too much of carbon oxide.

Figure 3: An extract from transnational student assignment

The same assignment was interpreted contextually and meaningfully by both New Zealand students and transnational students. Therefore it is imperative for assessment design to cleverly integrate this element of duality to establish relevance for national as well as transnational students.

FUTURE TRANSNATIONAL CURRICULUM DEVELOPMENT

In conclusion curriculum developers in future should ensure that programme design incorporates the opportunity to embed culturally and environmentally significant concepts that combine local with global awareness. Curriculum design thus achieves transferability of capabilities and sustainability development is globally disseminated.

Students are now on the pathway to becoming global citizens with a strong awareness of sustainability and contributors to global sustainable development. Globalization, education, and sustainability are intricately linked and global interdependency and interconnectedness ensues.

REFERENCES

Greenholtz, Joe. (2000). Assessing Cross-Cultural Competence in Transnational Education: The Intercultural Development Inventory. *Higher Education in Europe*, 25 (3), 411-416.

Ministry for the Environment. (2008). *Waste Minimisation Act 2008*. Retrieved from http://www.mfe.govt.nz/issues/waste/waste-minimisation.html.

Monteiro, S. & Sharma, R. (2012), Transnational Student Experience: Educational Spaces Created by Globalization. *Global Studies Journal*.

Moore, J. (2005). Is Higher Education Ready for Transfromative Learning?: A Question Explored in the Study of Sustainability. *Journal of Transformative Education*. 3 (1), 76-91.

Parliamentary Commissioner for the Environment (PCE). (2004). S*ee Change: Learning and Education for Sustainability- Background Paper 3: The tertiary education sector*. Retrieved 24 August 2007 from http://www.pce.govt.nz/reports/allreports/1_877274_12_7_tertiary.pdf

Poyrazli, S., Arbona, C., Nora, A., McPherson, R., & Pisecco, S. (2002). Relation between assertiveness, academic self-efficacy, and psychosocial adjustment among international graduate students. *Journal of College Student Development*, 43(5), 632-642.

UNDESA. (1992). *Agenda 21: Promoting Education, Public Awareness and Training*. Retrieved 14 May 2006 from http://www.un.org/esa/sustdev/documents/agenda21/english/agenda21chapter36.htm

UNESCO (2005). *Guidelines for Quality Provision in Cross-border Higher Education*, Paris, UNESCO. Retrieved from http://www.oecd.org/dataoecd/27/51/35779480.pdf

United Nations. (2002). *Plan of Implementation of the World Summit on Sustainable Development*. Retrieved on 27 June 2007 from http://www.un.org/esa/sustdev/documents/WSSD_POI_PD/English/WSSD_PlanImpl.pdf

Woodley, C. (April 2008). *Equivalence and contextualisation in Transnational Education*. Paper presented at the AVETRA 2008, Adelaide. http://www.avetra.org.au/AVETRA%20WORK%2011.04.08/CS4.1%20-%20Carolyn%20Woodley.pdf

PART II

Country and Region Specific Considerations

PART II

Country and Region-Specific Considerations—Overview

Chapters 7–14 make up Part II of the book, which looks at country and region-specific considerations in examining higher education within the context of globalization. Chapters 7–10 look at global education and the internationalization of higher education specifically in China, Japan, Vietnam, and Malaysia. Chapters 11–13 explore the impact of globalization on education reform in Turkey, Panama, and the Danish higher education systems. Chapter 14 examines the role of human capital development in Nigeria.

CHAPTER 6

Globalization, the Shifting Paradigms and Enhancing Transnational Education

Sylila Monteiro and Rashika Sharma

INTRODUCTION

The international knowledge network is constantly affected by developments beyond the control of academic institutions. It is established that education is continually challenged by the process of economic globalisation. Education needs to embrace transformations beyond its control to address the shifting paradigms created in education with globalisation and rapid unprecedented technological development. Programmes of internationalisation are a response to the current demands of globalisation. The portability of education and international student exchange aims at massification and accessibility of programmes to a global market. Education accessibility thus extends global expertise. Students are now global citizens who are no longer limited by geographical boundaries and aspire towards exciting study and research opportunities.

Transnational programmes may be imparted in a variety of delivery formats. Programmes can sometimes be delivered entirely in the host country or sometimes may require students to complete part of their degree with a partner institution. Sometimes the partner institution provides quality assured programmes to the host institution. These programmes are not only designed and moderated by the partner institution but there is ongoing exchange of facilitators creating a transnational community of practice enhancing both the host and partner institution.

INTERNATIONAL INTER-INSTITUTIONAL PARTNERSHIPS

Internationalisation and globalisation exert a dominant influence in tertiary education and the boundaries of education are no longer restricted nationally. Common international trends first emerged in Europe and are now manifested in the Asia Pacific region. Tertiary institutions are at present engaging in inter-institutional partnerships to address the challenge of globalisation. Strengthening agreements between academic institutions within a particular country and across national borders will be central to the mobility of adult students (Guri-Rosenblit, 2006). The above mentioned ideas are encapsulated by Davis, Olsen and Böhm (2000) in their Model of Transnational Education shown in figure 1. This model maps all transnational education provision along two dimensions, a Student Dimension and a Provider Dimension.

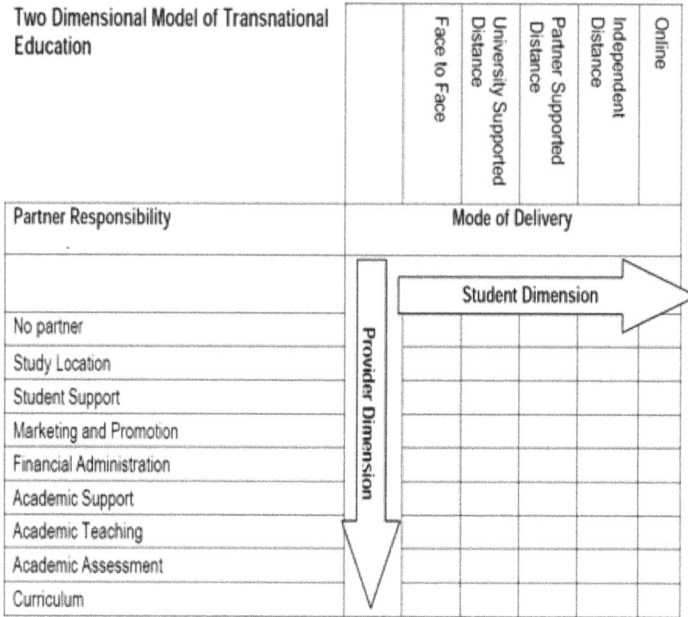

Two Dimensional Model of Transnational Education	Face to Face	University Supported Distance	Partner Supported Distance	Independent Distance	Online
Partner Responsibility	Mode of Delivery				
	Student Dimension				
No partner					
Study Location					
Student Support					
Marketing and Promotion					
Financial Administration					
Academic Support					
Academic Teaching					
Academic Assessment					
Curriculum					

Figure 1.
Source: Davis, Olsen and Böhm, 2000

This two dimensional model identifies five transnational delivery options for student engagement; face to face, university supported distance, partner supported distance, independent and on-line. The provider dimension places emphasis on provider responsibilities. These are specified as no partner, study location, student support, marketing and promotion, financial administration, academic support, academic teaching, academic assessment and curriculum. This spans the transnational educational spaces created.

Several NZ educational providers are already engaged in transnational educational ventures. Olsen (2006) identified China, Malaysia and Vietnam, India and Indonesia as being New Zealand's top five priority countries for transnational education. 8, 413 international students of Asian origin were enrolled in Public Tertiary Education Institutions in 2010 (NZ Ministry of Education, 2008). The majority of international fee-paying students originated from the Asian region (88.9 per cent). South-East Asia was one of the prominent source countries for international students in New Zealand. Malaysia is currently the tenth largest source of international students, the third largest source of university students and second largest source of PhD students in New Zealand. In 2008, 2147 international students came from Malaysia to study in New Zealand which is a 70% increase since 2003 (O'

Sullivan, 2009). This increase is progressive and increases the convergence between countries.

THE CASE STUDY

This case involves a partnership between a New Zealand polytechnic and a Malaysian automotive technical institute. The institute offers its own Diploma in Automotive Technology. A written agreement was signed between the partner institutes specifying in detail how this particular transnational programme will operate. This written agreement, the Memorandum of Understanding (MoU) between the two institutes allows students, who have successfully completed the two-and-a-half year Diploma in Automotive Technology to transfer their study to the New Zealand polytechnic. The MoU requires the New Zealand polytechnic to acknowledge full recognition of the Malaysian Diploma in Automotive Technology and delegate 180 unspecified credits towards the Bachelor of Applied Technology (Automotive) programme. Under the MoU students are required to study for a minimum of 3 semesters in this New Zealand polytechnic in order to achieve a Bachelors qualification. The Malaysian qualifications are cross credited making them eligible to enroll and give them the opportunity to successfully complete the Bachelor in Automotive Technology degree. The overarching objective of this MoU is "to establish an international partnership for providing first class higher education for qualified...candidates through the joint efforts of both parties" (Unitec, 2007).

To assess the success and implications of such an institutional agreement it is imperative to determine student perceptions. Therefore this research explores the extent to which the aims and objectives of the partnership are achieved.

AIMS AND OBJECTIVES

The research was designed to explore barriers overseas transnational students encounter with teaching and learning; and to reflect on the current teaching practices.

METHODOLOGY

Qualitative methodology for this research was based on Creswell's (2007) recommendations that when a complex, detailed understanding of an issue is needed this detail can best be established by directly talking to people and empowering them to share their stories and "allowing them to tell stories unencumbered by what we expect to find or what we have read in the literature" (p. 40). Qualitative study places weight on individual opinions and feelings on issues that directly relate to or affect them. From this perspective the use of quantitative methodology was eliminated.

This qualitative research was a pilot evaluation and hence questionnaires were used as the main form of data collection. Cohen, Manion and Morrison (2007) confirm that "qualitative, less structured, word based and open-ended questionnaires may be more appropriate as they can capture the specificity of a particular situation" (p. 247-248). Cohen, Manion and Morrison (2007) indicate that questionnaires can be administered without the presence of the researcher and are often straightforward to analyse. Through semi-structured questionnaires respondents answered both closed and open qualitative questions. This method of data collection generated insightful spectrum of student opinions and perceptions on their transnational learning experience.

In addition interaction between students and teachers provided anecdotal evidence for this research. Informal conversations between teaching staff also provided valuable data to confirm student responses. Another useful resource was the student's reflections written on their weblogs.

DATA ANALYSIS

The research generated a wide spectrum of feedback from students. The questionnaires were anonymous and were administered by a third party. Sixty five student questionnaires were distributed and forty nine were returned generating a 75% response rate. All students who participated in this research were males aged between 18-40years. In the semester during which this research was conducted the class consisted entirely of males, there were no female students enrolled. However in the earlier semesters there have been female students. The student cohort was multicultural, originating from countries such as New Zealand, Australia, USA, Africa, Eastern Europe, China, Korea, Malaysia, India, Bangladesh, Fiji, Samoa and Tonga.

Eight clear themes emerged from this research on transnational students and the progression of their learning.

1. Culture shock

In their home country respect for a teacher is paramount. Asian students considered questioning and challenging teachers as disrespectful. Many of these students thought it rude when local students interrupted in lectures or asked questions. One student declared "*I lose concentration during lectures when there is a lot interruptions as this does not happen back at home*" Student centred learning approach is a new learning style different from that in their home country. An academic stated that in the home country "*success is teacher's responsibility & parents give them the authority*". Responsibility for and ownership of their own learning was a concept alien to the students.

2. Lack of familiarity with modern tools and equipment.

Teaching in their home institution is mostly at a theoretical level. The use of modern tools and equipment is restricted. The lecturer interviewed remarked that in

> most Asian countries, for example China, students were well taught on a theoretical basis. They don't have many chances to have hands on practice with modern tools and equipment. So some students may quickly grasp the theory but struggle with the practice for some time.

Lack of hands on experience was identified as a major barrier in learning and teaching. Some expensive equipment when used under unsupervised conditions created diffidence and reluctance with the students.

3. Differences in learning and teaching style

Malaysian students found the student -centred learning approach difficult to cope with as they were accustomed to traditional teacher-centred learning approaches in their home country. Limited learning and teaching resources meant that the teacher's role focussed on rote learning. Consequently as the lecturer observed *"They are working hard on taking notes in class, and seldom ask the question "why?"*. The various forms of assessment tools such as reflective logs, portfolios, peer evaluations are a new experience for transnational students as the primary means of assessment in their home countries are written tests or examinations. Asian and in particular Malaysian students are often inactive or passive participants in group discussions. A lecturer further confirmed that, *"There's also not many group assignment/homework in some countries."*

4. Speed of delivery

Malaysian students emphasised the delivery speed of classes as a negative impact. Students found it difficult to follow lectures when the content was covered at a faster rate than in their home countries. One of the lecturers interviewed stated that

> Some overseas students may feel pressured when the speed of delivery of lectures is too fast to handle or too much to absorb especially as their English is not as good as a native speaker, or it's a total new field of study. If there are not many overseas students in the class, the overseas students will suffer more as they may hesitate to talk to the lecturer about his/her problem if most of the other local students are doing ok.

5. Difficulty with English language and accent

English is an additional language for most overseas students hence they have difficulty expressing themselves or understanding the accent used in the partner institute. A student revealed [the] *"First time I had a presentation to do I felt very nervous and did not know how to do it"*. Students have knowledge of the content but are at times unable to explain this to teachers and peers as their accent and language level acts as a barrier to successful communication. The language barrier was evident in the following student remark,*"I know what I am doing but it is difficult to explain it"*.

6. Lack of critical thinking skills

Many students commented on the learning and teaching styles. The teaching styles in their home countries are different with 'prescribed textbook' teaching taking dominance. The research based or student centred learning mode makes it difficult for students to adjust to the new, unfamiliar learning environment. The teacher comment was *"Some students have developed study habits in their home countries to stick to the prescribed textbook to get good results. Here, students are encouraged to do research even though it's a new topic and they were not taught before. Most overseas students lack research skills. They are not good at doing research, using the resources available to learn and develop their opinion".*

7. Lack of confidence and assertiveness

Poor English speaking skills leading to lack of confidence was also identified as a deterrent to their performance. Students explained that they are continuously challenged by their failure to express their knowledge coherently as their vocabulary is limited and they cannot find the correct words to articulate their thoughts and ideas. The lecturer remarked *"when they have some difficulty in their studies, such as cannot understand the lecture, cannot express their ideas in English clearly, failure in the test/exam, or communication gap with other students or don't know how to relieve their pressure, or don't know how to manage their time to make their study more efficient.* In addition it is culturally inappropriate for the student to interrupt or question the teacher; consequently assertiveness is considered discourteous and therefore unacceptable.

8. Use of slang, jargon and technical terminology

Furthermore the use of slang, jargon and technical terminology create additional challenges for overseas students. Their language is generally formal text book language and conversational informal style in spoken English confuses their comprehension.

DISCUSSION

Culture is the overarching principle that links the eight themes of the research findings. It must be emphasised that cultural differences dominated the results.

Culture shock according to Toffler (1970) has two dimensions. It is not simply the imposition of a new culture on an old one but it is also the shock, experienced by the individual when placed in an unfamiliar culture, when the original culture of the individual is no longer there. This causes a breakdown in communication, a misreading of reality and an inability to cope. The processes Toffler (1970) describes are pertinent and applicable to the effects of globalisation and adaptation to change and the implications for education in a worldwide context.

This research affirmed that cultural adaptation affected the class room interaction and response, which in turn affected student performance. Transnational students have to cope with the experience of the cross cultural adjustment. Law and Eckes (2000) established four stages in the transition or settlement process for the students in the new culture. These are: honeymoon, hostility, humour and home. In the initial honeymoon stage all is exciting and novel. However soon reality strikes and leads into the hostility stage where comparisons are made resulting in unhappiness, frustration, anger, anxiety and even depression. Many academic problems arise during this stage and rejection of the new environment may develop. However it is inevitable that the students work towards resolving these issues and enter into the third stage, the humour stage. They begin to feel accustomed to the new environment and look back in humour at the past mistakes and miscommunications. Finally in the home stage they feel at home and comfortable and are able to live successfully in two cultures.

The differences in learning and teaching styles in the home and host countries presented vital challenges that the student found difficult to address. This impacted on their active classroom participation as they were accustomed to being passive learners. In the workshop context as well, their prior theoretical engagement and absence of hands on practice in the home country created diffidence in the new student centred learning environment. In addition, research skills and independent critical thinking were drastically lacking. Theoretical text book and rote learning was the underlying fundamental teaching style that the students were accustomed to in their home learning environment. International students often come from non-Western educational systems in which emphasis is placed on teaching methods that include memorisation, observation and imitation (Roberston, 1992; Grarcha and Russell, 1993; Helms, 1995 as cited in Mu, 2007). The "learning by doing" approach was relatively non- existent in the overseas educational system. Andrade (2006) observed that overseas "students lacked discussion skills and had inadequate listening comprehension for extended lectures. They were accustomed to indirect writing styles and unaccustomed to analysing the strengths and weaknesses of an argument." (p.139)

Consequently critical thinking and research skills are limited as these are traditionally discouraged in the educational environment at home. Analytical skills so desirable in higher education for global application of knowledge are significantly affected. This often adds to sub-standard performance of some of these overseas students and demonstrates conflict between the two diametrically opposed systems.

Semantics and linguistics play a significant role in intercultural understanding and communication and is highlighted in this research. Professors' accents, idiomatic styles, humour and choice of examples in lectures posed problems (Andrade, 2006). Students involved in this research expressed similar concerns. Ramsay, Barker and Jones (1999) found that first-year international students at an Australian university had difficulties understanding lectures in terms of vocabulary and speed, and with tutors who spoke too fast or gave too little input. The use of slang, jargon and technical terminology proved problematic. "Many English language learners often express frustration at not being able to follow the slang, jargon, colloquialisms and idioms ubiquitous in the conversations of native English speakers"(Lieb, n.d.) Difficulty understanding colloquial language has been ranked highly among the problems cited by international students (Robertson, Line, Jones & Thomas, 2000).

Students for whom English is a second language are often reluctant to speak out in class or seek help because they lack confidence in their ability to communicate and are fearful of causing embarrassment for themselves or their teachers (Ramburuth & Birkett, 2000). As in the study by Robertson et al., (2000), the students surveyed in this study reported that difficulties with the language, anxiety and lack of confidence restricted effective participation. International students with low English fluency lacked confidence in interacting with people and were ill at ease in class discussions (Yeh & Inose, 2003) and show lower level of assertiveness and consequently display poor academic performance. Assertiveness is an essential skill requisite to success in an individualistic and competitive Western oriented educational system. Students coming from a collectivist culture where interpersonal harmony is highly prized, are self-restrained and less assertive than their New Zealand colleagues in the host country. Asian students have been reported to have more acculturative stress than other groups of international students. Further, the passivity can have a negative effect on relationships with their teachers, peers, and advisors (Poyrazli, Arbona, Nora, McPherson, & Pisecco, 2002) in particular at tertiary level.

CONCLUSION

This research is indicative of the challenges the transnational students experience in the exchange of educational spaces with the portability of programmes. Cultural adaptation to the host country's classroom dynamics posed the major drawback. In light of globalisation, and internationalisation in tertiary education this paper demonstrates the ever-emerging cultural impact on education. This study gives insights on student and teacher perspectives which can be useful in facilitating and promoting transnational education. Designing programmes should involve collaboration between curriculum developers from both host and home institutions. These developers should be fully aware of the cultural challenges students encounter during the transition process through these transnational educational spaces. Strategies can now be developed to nurture student experiences in the host country. Teaching strategies to extend classroom success include creating settings that are collaborative and culturally relevant to all ethnicities. In the context of growing numbers of transnational students in New Zealand, commitment to embrace cultural diversity and ethnicity is imperative to continuously assess the polytechnic's ability to form and deliver on partnerships, which will ensure the polytechnic remains a first-choice education destination (Fourie, 2010).

REFERENCES

Andrade, M.S. (2006). International students in English-speaking universities: Adjustment factors. *Journal of Research in International Education.* 5(2), 131–154. DOI: 10.1177/1475240906065589

Cohen, L., Manion, L & Morrison, K. (2007). *Research Methods in Education* (sixth edition). Great Britain: TJ International Ltd.

Creswell, J. (2007). *Qualitative Inquiry and Research Design: Choosing Among Five Approaches.* Second Edition. USA: Sage Publications, Inc.

Davis, D., A. Olsen, & A. Böhm. (2000). *Transnational Education: Providers, Partners and Policy. A research study.* Brisbane: IDP Education Australia

Fourie, L. (2010, November 15). International Portability of Education – Destination China [Web log post]. Retrieved on 12 April 2011 from http://www.unitec.ac.nz/unitec/wordpress/?p=140

Guri-Rosenblit, S. (2006). *Access and Equity in Higher Education: Historical and Cultural Context.* An internal paper, Fulbright New Century Scholars Program.

Law, B., & Eckes, M. (2000). *The More Than Just Surviving Handbook: ESL for Every Classroom Teacher.* Winnipeg, Canada: Portage & Main Press.

Lieb, J. (n.d.). *Slang: Breathing Life Into English.* Retrieved on 7 April 2011 from http://www.tht-japan.org/proceedings/2009/56-64_j_lieb.pdf

Ministry of Education. (2008). International Student Enrolments in New Zealand 2002 – 2008. Retrieved on 24 March 2011 from http://www.educationcounts.govt.nz/publications/series/15260/53402/1

Mu, C. (2007). Marketing academic library resources and information services to international students from Asia. *Reference Services Review, 35*(4), 571-583. doi: 10.1108/00907320710838390

O'Sullivan, F. (2009, October 28). Malaysia the key to unlock other doors. *The New Zealand Herald.* Retrieved from http://www.nzherald.co.nz

Olsen, A. (2006). *New Zealand's Export Education Innovation Program: The Opportunity Offshore.* Retrieved on 26 March 2011 from http://www.educationnz.org.nz/indust/eeip/TheOpportunityOshoreAOlsen.pdf

Poyrazli, S., Arbona, C., Nora, A., McPherson, R., & Pisecco, S. (2002). Relation between assertiveness, academic self-efficacy, and psychosocial adjustment among international graduate students. *Journal of College Student Development, 43*(5), 632-642.

Ramburuth, P. and Birkett, W.P. (2000), "Language, learning and diversity project", Report for the (former) Faculty of Commerce and Economics, UNSW, Sydney.

Ramsay, S., Barker, M. and Jones, E. (1999) 'Academic adjustment and learning processes: A comparison of international and local students in first-year university'. Higher Education Research & Development 18(1): 129–44.

Robertson, M., Line, M., Jones, S. & Thomas, S. (2000). International students, learning environments and perceptions: A case study using the Delphi technique. *Higher Education Research and Development, 19*(1), 89-102.

Toffler, A. (1970). *Future Shock*, New York: Bantam Books.

Unitec. (2007). Articulation Agreement. Auckland, NZ: Author.

Yeh, C. J., & Inose, M. (2003). International students' reported English fluency, social support satisfaction, and social connectedness as predictors of acculturative stress. *Counseling Psychology Quarterly, 16*(1), 15-28.

CHAPTER 7

An Analysis of Education Globalization and the Chinese Education Trade Imbalance: An International Student Flow and Service Trade Perspective

Dejun Cao, John Zhang, and Shixiang Zuo

INTRODUCTION

Economic globalization is an irreversible trend. It has been driven by advances in IT and communication technologies and aided by the reduction of trade tariffs and the implementation of trade friendly policies by many governments. The laws of economics dictate that companies are motivated to be global; globalization provides avenues to achieve lower production costs and higher profit margins. It was not long ago that businesses were mostly segmented geographically. Now, many companies, small and large alike, have supply chains and sales channels that reach multiple continents.

Under this backdrop of economic globalization, an increasing global student movement in education has also unfolded. Similar to the economic system prior to globalization, education systems were mostly segmented and primarily serviced local, state, and national interests. Following the foot–steps of the economic globalization that started in the 1980s, education has slowly globalized and this process is currently accelerating, signaled by the following three factors which we define as education globalization: the increasing number and importance of foreign students for education institutions; the change in academic curricula to adapt a more global view, and the policy changes that lower admission barriers for foreign students.

At the macro level, motivations for education globalization include commercial advantage, knowledge and language acquisition, an enhancement of curriculum with international content, and many others (Philip G. Altbach & Jane Knight, 2007). At the micro level, these factors, which influence international student flow, are diversified.

This paper focuses on the factors driving the increase in international student flow in education globalization from a service trade perspective. In our view, international student flow interacts with education curricula and polices and is the single most important factor that fosters education globalization. With increasing demand and financial incentives from foreign students, curricula and policy changes have adapted. At the same time, the curricula and policy changes have stimulated the international student flow. In many occasions in this paper, "education globalization" refers to the increasing international student flow.

Section 2 surveys the current state of education globalization from the international student flow perspective. Underlying factors that are driving the increase are also outlined. In section 3, the phenomenon of the Chinese education trade imbalance is studied. Section 4 gives concluding remarks.

THE EDUCATION GLOBALIZATION

As the world economic landscape becomes flatter, the education market also globalizes. This globalization is symbolized by the increasing international student flow world–wide. A study of retrospective data has revealed that an increasing number of students from developing countries are studying in developed countries. The major factors driving this educational globalization are postulated to be advances in technology, a shift in economic paradigm, and the increasing interdependence between nations.

The Flow of International Students

In an era of economic globalization, the cross–border mobility of international students has become an important form of service trade. International student flow can be viewed as a market–driven activity and as a tradable service product under the General Agreement on Trade in Services (GATS) negotiations (Knight, 2002). Marginson's (2006) model outlines a trend in this commercial market

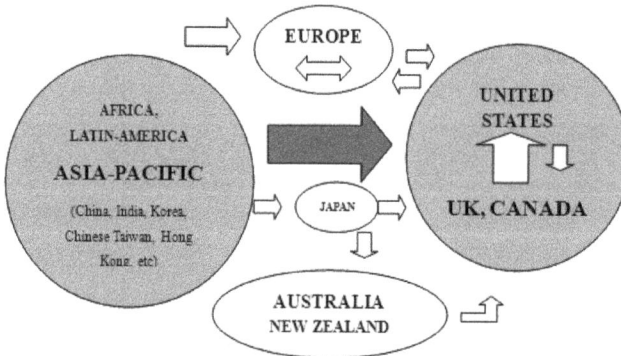

Figure 1: Student Flows in the Worldwide Environment of Higher Education
Source: Simon Marginson, (2006), Dynamics of National and Global Competition in Higher Education, Higher Education (2006) 52: 1–39

From the service trade perspective, this model suggests that those in English–speaking countries such as the United States, Britain and other "developed" countries are the major exporters of international education, while the developing countries in Asia and Africa are the major importers. Developed countries have an education export surplus and the developing countries are in a deficit condition. Take the United States for example. The money paid by international students, including tuition fees, textbooks, living expenses, and insurance expenses, has been rising. Data from United

States Department of Commerce showed that higher education was the fifth largest service export of the country (IIE, 2008). According to the US IIE data published in November 2008, the United States had a total enrollment of 623,805 foreign students in the 2007–2008 school year, a 3% increase from 2006–2007, and a 7% increase from 2002–2003. International students brought in $15.5 billion in revenue. The United States has a surplus in education service trade and is the biggest beneficiary of the education service export.

According to OECD statistics, Asia was the largest exporter of international students in 2006. There were 1,416,262 students who studied abroad and this accounted for more than 50% of the international students in the world. The students studying abroad from Europe, Africa, Asia, North America, South America, and Oceania were 27%, 13%, 50%, 3%, 6%, and 1%, respectively. Asia and Africa, which are mainly composed of developing countries, were the major exporters of international students.

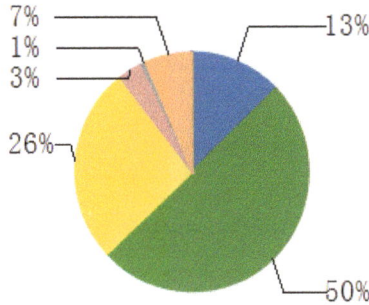

■ Africa ■ Asia ■ Europe ■ North America ■ Oceania ■ South America
Figure 2: Number of International Students by Continent of Origin and Market Shares in International Education (2006, Unit: Person),
Source: Data from the Organization for Economic Cooperation and Development (OECD) "Education at a Glance 2008"

Table 1: Number of International Students by Continent of Origin and Market Shares in International Education (2006, Unit: Person)

Continent	Number	Percent
Africa	361,191	12.80%
Asia	1,416,262	50.20%
Europe	745,755	26.50%
North America	94,351	3.30%
Oceania	18,755	0.70%
South America	182,260	6.50%
Total	2,818,574	100%

OECD statistics (2006) also indicated that Europe, the United States and other developed countries were the favored destinations for international students. A total number of 2,440,657 students went to these countries, accounting for 83% of the international students worldwide. In contrast, the number of students who went to China, Russia, Brazil and other non–OECD countries was only 484,022, about 17% of the total. The United States was the most preferred nation and attracted 584,817 students, 20% of all the international students. Britain, Germany, France, Australia, Canada and Japan combined absorbed more than 1 million students, taking a 64% of the international student share.

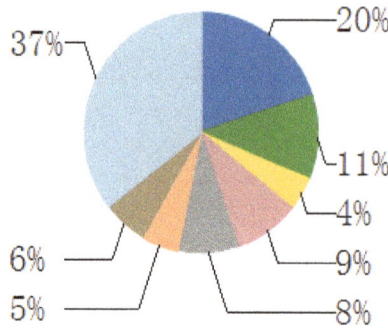

Figure 3: Market share of International Students by Country of Destination (2006, Unit: Person), Source: Data from the Organization for Economic Cooperation and Development (OECD) "Education at a Glance 2008"

Table 2: Number of International Students by Country of Destination and Market Shares in International Education (2006, Unit: Person)

Country	Number	Percent
United States	584817	20%
United Kingdom	330078	11.30%
Japan	130124	4.40%
Germany	261363	8.90%
France	247510	8.50%
Canada	148164	5.10%
Australia	184710	6.30%
Other	1037913	35.50%
Total	2924679	100%

Factors Driving the Education Globalization

Three major factors are responsible for driving education globalization. These factors are not only important in economic globalization but also critical in education globalization.

The Advancement of Technology

The advancement of IT and communication technologies, which has stimulated economic glob- alization, has also made international education more accessible for a larger group of students. Thanks to these technologies, the opportunity of studying abroad, which was previously singularly available to the elite few, is available to many more students. For example, IT technology, college application materials and school information are now online and easily accessible; communications are now made easy by emails; and the admission requirements for foreign students and selection criteria are now more transparent.

Although decreasing in importance, many students in developed countries seeking higher education in the west see it as a ticket to have a better life. The advances of technologies have better informed these students of the living standards, freedoms and social structure in these developed countries. Technology has enabled comparisons in every facet of society and made this information available to a vast majority of people. This information has acted as a catalyst for the flow of international students from developing countries to developed ones.

Technologies have also made the consumption of education from distance possible and affordable. More and more courses have moved online and students can enroll from all over the world. Technologies have broken an important barrier in the delivery of contents in education. Education no longer requires students to be at certain place and at certain time. It is now ubiquitous.

The Shift of Economic Paradigm

Economic globalization has improved the living standards of many developing countries. In BRICS (Brazil, Russia, India, China and South Africa) countries, for example, the middle class has been growing fast. With this new found money, many families are increasing their investment in their children's education. The higher–education quality disparity between developed and developing nations has made colleges and universities in North America and Europe attractive to many of these families.

Due to the decline in international competitiveness in manufacturing and other areas, the role of service trade in developed economies is gaining importance. The industrialization of education has become an inevitable result of this trend. To increase revenue, western educational institutions have placed more importance on their foreign paying customers.

The current financial difficulties in Europe and budgetary cuts in the USA have resulted in significant funding cuts in higher education. Colleges and universities in these countries have been more active in recruiting foreign students to make–up for this shortfall. Both supply and demand favor this transnational student flow, and as a result, the inflow of foreign students to the developed countries has accelerated.

As BRICS countries gain advantages in land area, population, manufacturing, and economic output, the flow of students to these counties also increases. Multinational companies have supply chain management and market expansion interests in these countries. To succeed, they need well educated employees who are familiar with the local culture. These employment opportunities motivate the inflow of foreign students to the BRICS countries. The shift of economic paradigm has changed the old structure of the transnational flow of students.

The Interdependence of Nations

A consequence of economic globalization and proficiency in IT technologies is the increasing interdependence of nations. This interdependence is more than an economical reliance and sense of responsibility between nations. It is also in politics, ecology, and cultural areas. A functional interdependency requires profound mutual understanding, correct calculations, and closer collaborations. The interdependency of nations motivates education globalization, and education globalization lays a foundation for a more efficient interdependence. As the interdependence of nations deepens, the trend of transnational student flow will continue and gain importance.

China's Education Service Trade Imbalance

The Chinese international education service trade is in an imbalanced state. China has a significant current education service trade deficit. This imbalance is not healthy for both China and other nations. Though China is the world's second largest economic power in terms of GDP, China is not well understood by the rest of the world. This misunderstanding may have a serious impact on the growth and stability of the global economy, and has the potential to change the current trend of the interdependence of nations. Increasing China's education export will have the benefit of reducing misunderstandings of China and increasing collaboration between China and other countries.

The Outflow of Chinese Students

As the OECD data in Table 1 has demonstrated, there were a total of 2,924,679 international students in 2006. Among them, 451,526 were Chinese students who accounted for 15.4% of the world's total. China has been the world's largest international student source for education service trade for many years.

Chinese students who study abroad can be categorized as either government–funded or self–financed. The ratio is approximately 1:9. There were few Chinese students who studied abroad until 1978 when China initiated economic reforms and started an "open" policy. Since the 21st century, the number of Chinese foreign students has increased substantially. For instance, in the year 2000, there were 38,989 Chinese students   studying abroad. This figure more than quadrupled in 2008, rising to 179,800. Among the 450,000 Chinese students studying abroad in 2006, 88% went to the USA, Japan, Australia and other OECD countries (Figure 4). Only 16% went to non–OECD countries. The USA was the favored destination and received 21% of the Chinese students, followed by Japan, Britain, Australia, Canada, and Germany, respectively.

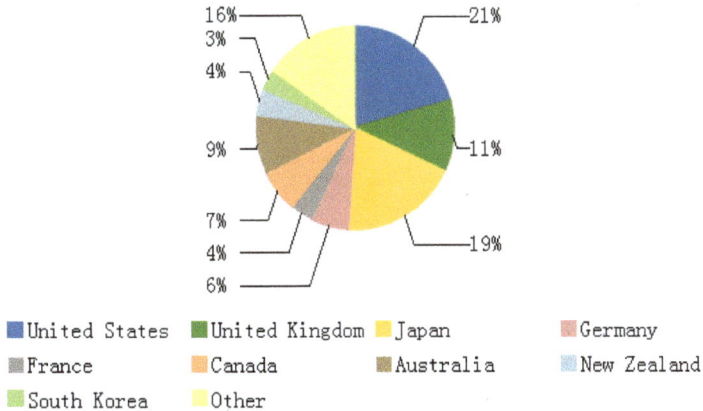

Figure 4: Chinese Students by Country of Destination (2006, Unit: Person),
Source: Data from the Organization for Economic Cooperation and Development (OECD)
"Education at a Glance 2008"

Table 3: Number of Chinese Students by Country of Destination (2006, Unit: Person)

Country	Number	Percent
United States	93672	20.80%
United Kingdom	50753	11.20%
Japan	86378	19.10%
Germany	27390	6.10%
France	17132	3.80%
Canada	30906	6.80%
Australia	42008	9.30%
New Zealand	18791	4.20%
South Korea	15288	3.40%
Other	69208	15.30%
Total	451526	100%

What motivates Chinese students to study abroad? We conducted a survey of students who intend to study abroad in the Southwestern University of Finance and Economics (SWUFE) in order to find the influencing factors. According to the survey results (Appendix I), 34.17% of the students wanted to experience a different culture while 31.67% of the students opted for foreign advanced teaching and research. These two factors accounted for more than half of the total. It is also noteworthy that 10% of the students are motivated by their parents. This illustrates the importance of culture and family values on education globalization.

The Inflow of Students to China

In recent years, the number of foreign students studying in China has exceeded that of Chinese students studying abroad. But interestingly, this does not change China's deficit position in international education service trade. In 2007, for example, there were 195,503 international students from 188 countries and regions who studied in China, 141,689 of which were from Asia, accounting for 72.47% of the total. China may have been in international education service trade surplus if all of them were money paying students.

Table 4: The Inflow of International Students to China

Year	Number
2000	52150
2001	61869
2002	85800
2003	77715
2004	110844
2005	141087
2006	162695
2007	195503
2008	220000
Total	1107663

The Computation of Education Service Trade in China

We compute the education service trade in China in comparison to developed countries in two different ways: by the number of students and by the total monetary volume. These two methods lead to a consistent conclusion.

Chinese International Service Trade in Number of International Students

China's deficit in international education service trade is relative to developed countries. Data quoted from the Ministry of Education of China, OECD, the United States, Japan, France, Britain, Germany and Australia agrees with this assertion.

The data format from the Ministry of Education of China (MEC) is measured in yearly flow (flow data) and the OECD data is measured in current number of students (stock data). For comparison purpose, we needed to transform the data into the same form. We first accumulated the flow data provided by the MEC from 2000–2006 to estimate the corresponding stock data. Then, we converted the OECD data into flow data assuming the average number of study years is four for a typical foreign student.

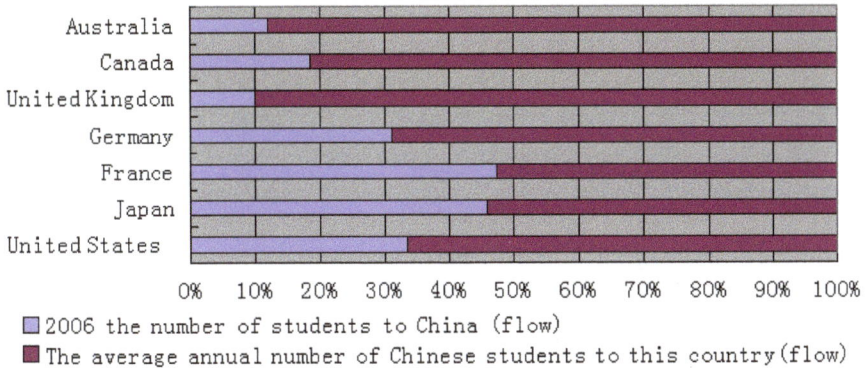

□ 2006 the number of students to China (flow)

■ The average annual number of Chinese students to this country (flow)

Figure 6: The Flow of International Students between China and Developed Countries (2006),

Source: Data from 2001–2007, "China Education Statistical Yearbook" and the OECD "Education at a Glance 2008"

Table 5: The Flow of International Students between China and Developed Countries

	2000–2006 the Number of Students to China (Stock)	2006 the Number of Chinese Students in this Country (Stock)	2006 the Number of Students to China (Flow)	The Average Annual Number of Chinese Students to this Country (Flow)
United States	51393	93672	11784	23418
Japan	113559	86378	18363	21595
France	13166	17132	3857	4283
Germany	13110	27390	3090	6848
United Kingdom	6868	50753	1399	12688
Canada	6902	30906	1766	7727
Australia	7736	42008	1420	10502

Source: Data from 2001–2007, "China Education Statistical Yearbook" and the OECD "Education at a glance 2008"

These results show that the United States had a total number of 51,393 students who studied in China during 2000–2006. In contrary, in the year of 2006, the number of Chinese students who studied in the United States amounted to 93,672. In terms of flow data, in 2006, the number of students from the United States to China was 11,794, while the number of students from China to the United States was 23,418. The number of Chinese students going to the US was much greater than that of the US students coming to China. The same was true between China and other developed countries. China had an education trade deficit with developed countries in terms of the number of international students.

Chinese International Service Trade in Monetary Volume

The economic benefits gained from international students, from a service trade perspective, consist mainly of the revenue from tuition fees and living expenses. We use the formulas developed by Chen Gang (2005) to perform the economic benefit computation:

$$EE = \sum_{j=1}^{4}\sum_{i=1}^{n} T_{ij} \times Q_{ij} + \sum_{j=1}^{4}\sum_{i=1}^{n} L_{ij} \times Q_{ij} \qquad (1)$$

$$IE = \sum_{k=1}^{m}\sum_{j=1}^{4}\sum_{i=1}^{n} T_{ijk} \times Q_{ijk} + \sum_{k=1}^{m}\sum_{j=1}^{4}\sum_{i=1}^{n} L_{ijk} \times Q_{ijk} \qquad (2)$$

In these formulas, EE (Exports of Education) represents the total income of a country's education service export in one year; IE (imports of Education) stands for the annual total expenditure of a country's education service import. T indicates tuition; L stands for the costs of living; i represents the index of students; j stands for the level of study; k is used for different countries; n and m represent the corresponding total number of students and countries, respectively; Q stands for the total number of international students within one year. EE–IE <0 indicates an educational service trade deficit.

Building on the 2006 data, we calculated the annual cost per foreign student in China and the result was used as a benchmark for China's educational service trade. Data for international students in China and Chinese overseas students was taken from the "China Education Statistical Yearbook 2007"; tuition fees and living expenses for students in China were taken from the "Fees for Self–Financed Foreign Students in China 1997." Combined with the data on the structure of foreign students educated in China published by the "China Education Statistical Yearbook" each year, we calculated the weighted average for the annual total cost of one foreign student in China to be 46,974.68 RMB. As for Chinese students studying abroad, we used data published online by the destination countries on tuition fees and living expenses. In accordance with the continent distribution of Chinese students revealed by the "China Education Statistical Yearbook," we calculated that the weighted average of the annual cost of studying abroad for a Chinese student to be 184,773.48 RMB. Taking these numbers into formula (1) and (2), we see that the Chinese education service trade deficit in 2006 was 17.117 billion RMB. Using the same method, we estimate China's education service trade data from 2000 to 2008 as follows.

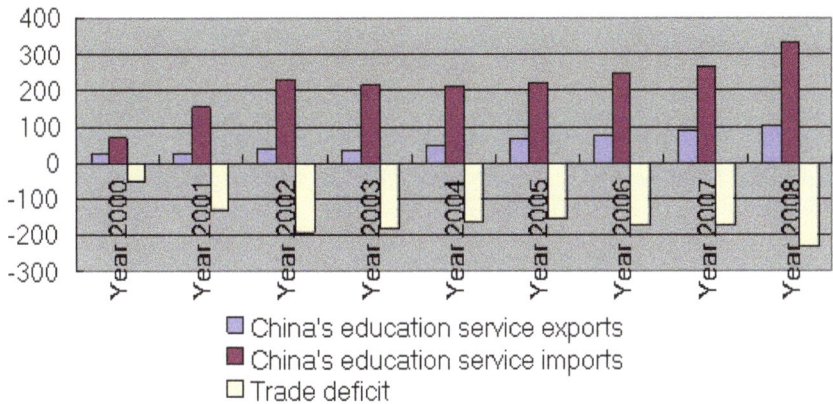

Figure 7: 2000–2008 China's Education Service Trade Estimates (Unit: 0.1 Billion Yuan)

Source: Data from the "China Education Statistical Yearbook," "Fees for Foreign Students at their Own Expense" and other Online Data

Table 6: 2000–2008 China's Education Service Trade Estimates (Unit: 100 million Yuan)

Year	China's Education Service Exports	China's Education Service Imports	Trade Deficit
2000	24.5	72	47.5
2001	29.1	155.2	126.1
2002	40.3	231.2	190.1
2003	36.5	216.8	180.2
2004	52.1	211.9	159.8
2005	66.3	219	152.7
2006	76.4	247.6	171.2
2007	91.8	266.1	174.2
2008	103.3	332.2	228.9
Total	520.3	1952	1430.7

The aforementioned analysis shows that, in nine years, China had an accumulative educational trade deficit of 143 billion RMB. Although the ratio of the number of students from developing countries to China and Chinese students to these countries is 15:1, the corresponding ratio for developed countries to China is 1:4. China charges foreign students tuition only slightly higher than the indigenous Chinese students, and the living expenses in China are low. In addition, the Chinese government grants more than ten thousand international student scholarships every year, and more than 70% of the funds are used for students from developing countries from Asia and Africa. We estimate that if China had an education service trade surplus relative to the developing countries, it would be small.

Ways to Improve China's Education Service Trade Imbalance–A Core Competency Approach

According to economic theory, a trade deficit is usually a result of poor competitiveness in the international market. This is also true in the international education trade. China's long term deficit indicates that Chinese universities are undesirable in terms of their competiveness. If a country is always in deficit in educational service trade, there will be a significant outflow of national wealth and brain power, as well as a cultural unilateralism. This situation is neither desirable for China, nor in terms of sustainable global economic growth, for the efficiency of the interdependence of nations.

To improve the current education trade deficit, Chinese universities must cultivate their competitiveness by developing core competencies. The idea of core competency was developed by Barney (1991), Prahalad, and Hamel (1990). They believed that a competency must meet three conditions: it must be hard–to–imitate, leveraged to different products and markets, and benefit the end user. From a resource perspective, core competency can be evaluated from Value, Rareness, Imitability, and Substitutability considerations.

To build core competency, we believe that Chinese higher education institutions should incorporate local culture and economic/industry experience into their course content and curricula; promote a teacher/scholar model and employ instructors with backgrounds of Chinese culture, international education experiences, and international teaching experience; and create an effective communication system to promote Chinese education institutions to foreign students.

Hard–to–imitate

The institutional structure of higher education in China is similar to that of developed countries. By incorporating Chinese culture with appropriate course content and curricula, Chinese students and foreign students alike can gain a better understanding of the local heritage in which the university is located. This will enhance a student's local living experience and add value to his or her education. For management and engineering students, for instance, the incorporation of interactions, communications, and workshops with local companies would be invaluable.

The employment of faculty with Chinese cultural backgrounds, international education, and teaching experiences, will elevate the communication and teaching quality for all students, foreign students in particular.

The resources built by the foresaid changes clearly pass the Value, Rareness, Imitability, and Sustainability criteria.

Leverage

To increase competitiveness and attract more foreign students, Chinese universities must place priority on teaching. A teacher–scholar model is a model which places importance on both teaching and scholarly activities. Emphases on teaching should improve the Chinese faculty's teaching ability and offer a better education to students. Students come to universities for an education with the objective of having a better life in the future. Only when Chinese higher education institutions deliver these values to their students, will they attract a larger number of foreign students.

The incorporation of local culture and industry with course content and curricula and the adaptation of the teaching–scholar model can be implemented by different departments in a university and by different universities nationwide in China.

End–user Benefit

The foresaid changes in curricula and education philosophy will benefit students and deliver better value for their tuitions. With this increased end–user value, Chinese education institutions will be more attractive to foreign students. It is important to note that these improvements must be made known to the customers in order to have any effect. Therefore, Chinese education institutions must create an effective communication system to promote their educational offerings.

CONCLUDING REMARKS

The law of comparative advantage provides an explanation for the reasons that developing countries are able to attract foreign students. Despite the fact that there are no absolute advantages in developing countries relative to developed ones in the area of education service trade, both parties will still gain by trading, as long as they have different relative efficiencies. Because of the current education quality disparity between developed and developing countries, developing countries have significant disadvantages. The trend of increasing international student flow from developing to developed countries will continue in the near future.

To compete effectively in the international market, developing countries must find ways to develop their core competencies. The increase in comparative advantages in international education for developing countries should drive the future of the education globalization and change the balance of the international education service trade.

There will be a gradual increase in the inflow of students to BRICS countries. The education capacity and throughput in terms of the number of students entering into and graduating from higher education institutions in the BRICS countries will increase. By building up quantity, cost, and core competency advantages, the BRICS countries should eventually reverse the flow of the international students.

REFERENCES

Barney, J. "Firm resources and sustained competitive advantage." *Journal of Management* 17 (1991): 99–120.

Chen Gang. "Statistical Study and Numerical Analysis of China's Educational Trade." *Journal of Public Finance and Trade* 5 (2005): 71–76.

China Education Statistical Yearbook. URL: http://www.moe.edu.cn

"Education at a glance 2008" OECD. 2008. URL:http://www.oecd.org/document/9/0,3343,en_2649_39263238_41266761_1_1_1_1,00.html

Philip G. Altbach, Jane Knight. "The Internationalization of Higher Education: Motivations and Realities." *Journal of Studies in International Education* 1, nos. 3–4 (2007): 290–305.

Prahalad, C. K. & Gary Hamel. "The Core Competence of the Corporation." *Harward Business Review* (1990): 79–91.

Simon Marginson. "Dynamics of national and global competition in higher education." *Higher Education* 52 (2006): 1–39.

APPENDIX I

Questionnaire Topics	# of Respondents	%	Questionnaire Topics	# of Respondents	%
1. The time to study abroad:			**7. The current preparation is:**		
The first year after graduated	92	76.67%	Language learning	44	33.67%
Before graduation	12	10.00%	Information gathering	67	55.83%
After a few years' work	9	7.50%	To raise funds	9	7.50%
Unclear	7	5.83%	Other	0	0.00%
2. The final degree wish to study:			**8. The main reason to go abroad is:**		
Bachelor's Degree	3	2.50%	To accept foreign advanced teaching and research	38	31.67%
Master's Degree	98	81.67%	Experience a different culture	41	34.17%
Doctor's Degree	19	15.83%	Enhance the employability	17	14.17%
			Arranged by parents	12	10.00%
			To seek development in foreign countries	18	15.00%
3. The country you plan to study abroad in:			**9. Subsidize the cost of studying source:**		
United States	62	51.67%	Entirely by the home to support	42	35.00%
Canada	7	5.83%	Apply for scholarship	13	10.83%
France	5	4.17%	Entirely through the work to earn money	14	11.67%
Australia	15	12.50%	Home support, work-study, scholarships	51	42.50%
Britain	31	25.83%			
Other	0	0.00%			
4. The reason of choosing this country:			**10. Your attitude towards your future:**		
No language barrier	13	10.83%	Optimistic	61	50.83%
Policy is attractive, low entrance fees, scholarships	14	11.67%	Confused	39	32.50%
Beautiful environment	10	8.33%	Does not matter	20	16.67%
Brand-name institutions	78	65.00%			
5. The primary factor in the choice of schools is:			**11. Career plan after study abroad:**		
The visibility of the school	47	39.17%	In foreign countries	33	27.50%
School specialty rankings	44	36.67%	Return	81	67.50%
Tuition and scholarship level	12	10.00%	Uncertain	6	5.00%
Country development	17	14.17%			
6. The major barrier for study abroad is:			**12. Your biggest worry is:**		
Science and engineering, the humanities	27	22.50%	Homesickness	17	14.17%
Business	90	75.00%	Cost	34	28.33%
Other	3	2.50%			
Cultural conflict	22	18.33%			
Language barriers	11	9.17%			
The failure of development	21	17.50%			
Discrimination by foreigners	15	2.50%			

Survey Results of SWUFE Students who Intent to Study Abroad

CHAPTER 8

The Direction of Moral Education in Japanese Schools in a Global and Multicultural World

Kaori Shimizu

INTRODUCTION

I am originally from Japan, but I came to the United States thirteen years ago to teach Japanese at a state university in the South. Since all my education up to undergraduate level took place in Japan, the American college culture was quite new to me. I found both the academic and social aspects very intriguing. I was particularly impressed with the students' fervor for football games, particularly when it comes to singing the American national anthem and paying respect to the American national flag as a ritual before the game. Watching this, I wondered how each of those individuals felt about these national symbols, especially since honoring them was voluntary. In Japan, there has been an ongoing controversy over the use of the national flag *Hinomaru* and the national anthem *Kimigayo*. Since 1999, when the Japanese government passed legislation which made the Hinomaru the official national flag and *Kimigayo* the official national anthem, the Ministry of Education [33]has required school personnel, teachers, and students honoring these symbols at all official school ceremonies and events. The Ministry claimed that these national symbols foster a sense of national identity, which allows children to be aware and proud of their identity as Japanese. However, some school teachers refuse to salute the national flag and the national anthem, both of which were used to glorify the emperor under the imperial government and are strongly associated with Japan's nationalistic and militaristic past. Many teachers have been punished every year because they do not stand up while *Kimigayo* is sung at school ceremonies (Otsu 2008, 85).

The teachers' defiance is an only example of the larger struggle occurring within the Japanese culture over moral education in the schools. Moral education in Japan has been included in the school curriculum ever since a modern school system was established in 1872. Moral education was initially called *Shūshin*, (control of self),

---

[33] The Ministry of Education was renamed as the Ministry of Education, Culture, Sports, Science and Technology in 2001. The author uses The Ministry of Education throughout the text for the sake of consistency

which continued until 1945, when Japan's surrender to the Allied Forces brought an end to World War II. After the end of the war, *Shūshin* was suppressed by the Allied Forces because of the importance it gave to nationalistic and militaristic ideology in pre-war Japan (Lanham 1979, 4). At its core, *Shūshin* held extreme patriotism based on absolute loyalty to the emperor, which was not compatible with democracy, the idea brought by the Allied Forces as the foundation for rebuilding Japan. After the San Francisco Peace Treaty (1951), however, the Ministry of Education reintroduced moral education in 1958. The goal of the new moral education was to nurture moral sentiment, judgment, commitment and attitude throughout school activities, with one class hour per week set aside for *Dōtoku* (ethics or moral education) throughout compulsory education in order to "supplement, deepen, and synthesize desirable moral practice, feelings, and judgments" (Khan 1997, 105).

Reintroduction of moral education met strong opposition from university faculty and the Japan Teachers Union (JTU) (Wray 1991, 462), who feared that *Dōtoku* could be a scheme for reviving *Shūshin*. Their fear was rooted in the recognition that Shūshin was used as an instrument for national indoctrination. In order for *Dōtoku* to not invite the revival of *Shūshin, Dōtoku* needed to be developed based on the principle of democracy in formulating its purpose and content. However, an examination of a series of educational reform proposals in postwar years has revealed that, while the idea of democracy has been recognized as an underlying principle of *Dōtoku* curriculum, cultivating national consciousness - nurturing an awareness of being Japanese - has also been included as yet another principle. This inclusion created a sharp controversy; opponents were concerned that the intent of nurturing national consciousness would essentially be the same as the intent of *Shūshin*, which had led to ultranationalism. This concern was strengthened because of the emphasis the Ministry of Education was placing upon tradition, culture and patriotism in school education after the 1990s. The concern continued to grow because of the reinforcement of *Dōtoku* in the curriculum. The concern became even more prominent in 2006 because of the revision of the Fundamental Law of Education, originally enacted in 1947, which emphasized "the dual roots of postwar Japanese idealism, its democratic and pacifistic values" (Horio 1988, 108). In this revision, the cultivation of an attitude to respect tradition, culture and to love the national homeland was clearly articulated. Opponents have since held serious concerns that this would lead to the "return to the prewar and wartime state intervention in education" (Takayama 2008, 131).

Does Japan's current emphasis on national identity in school education adequately prepare children to live in a world that is increasingly interconnected and globalized, in which diverse cultures coexist side by side? In order to explore this issue, I will first review how the pre-war and post-war moral education curricula in Japan were designed. Then reflecting on my own experience of being exposed to the culture of the other, I will consider the implication of the recent tendency of looking inward into culture by drawing on Derrida's notion of an affirmation of otherness.

HISTORICAL DEVELOPMENT OF MORAL EDUCATION IN JAPAN

Before being defeated in World War II, Japan officially referred to itself as the Empire of Great Japan, and more commonly as Imperial Japan (1868-1945). It was founded after the feudal Tokugawa shogunate was modernized into the Meiji government and the Constitution of the Empire of Japan was signed. Imperial Japan established a form of constitutional monarchy, in which the emperor of Japan was an active ruler who wielded political power shared with an elected Diet.

For Imperial Japan, this modernization was urgently crucial. The policy of isolationism existent during the feudal regime ended with the arrival of U.S. Commodore Matthew Perry in 1853, which led to the opening of Japan. As soon as its eyes were opened to Western civilization, Japan realized that it needed to gather information on Western social systems in order to achieve its modernization. Beginning in the 1870s, Western-style social institutions were established in all aspects of Japanese life, including the foundation of a modern school system that closely followed the French model. Under this system, the curricula of all primary and secondary schools included *Shūshin* (control of self), which offered moral education in Imperial Japan.

According to Klaus Luhmer (1990), *Shūshin* rests on three pillars: (1) State Shinto; (2) Confucianism; and (3) modern political and social ethics. Shinto is an indigenous religion in Japan which dates back to the pre-historic period. Its recorded history includes a mythology surrounding the origin and the status of the Imperial Family. The ideals and rituals of Shinto were used by the imperial government to promote the divinity of the emperor and the uniqueness of Japan, which later came to be known as State Shinto. With State Shinto, the legitimacy of emperor worship was established. Confucianism placed individuals within a communal order and prescribed the norms and propriety within which each person should properly act. Specifically emphasized in *Shūshin* was the concept of jin-gi-chū-kō (benevolence, justice, loyalty and filial piety). Children were taught to respect their parents and ancestors in the home. This concept of family was extended to the nation with Japan being seen as the family state with the emperor as its familial head. According to the Imperial Rescript on Education (1890), which served as the guiding principle for the education and morality in the prewar period, the imperial ancestors founded the nation and planted the seed of virtue. Having the emperor as "the living representative of a divine imperial line" (Gluck 1985, 142), children were taught that as subjects of the empire, they should repay the emperor's benevolence with the spirit of loyalty and patriotism.

Shūshin as a curriculum was therefore carefully designed by the Imperial Government to achieve the Western model of modernization. In the event of exposing the country to totally new and different Western ideas, the leaders thought that the cultivation of national unity and cultural identity was critically important. Confucius's teachings and all practices of State Shinto were used to nurture intense and exclusive loyalty to the emperor and to the nation, which supported the rise of militarism and ultranationalism; *Shūshin,* the moral education, was therefore used "as a major instrument for national indoctrination" (Luhmer 1990).

The political system of imperial Japan supported by the emperor system and established for the achievement of modernization was overturned in 1945. After the two U.S. atomic bombs were dropped on Hiroshima and Nagasaki, Japan's unconditional surrender brought an end to World War II. Following the Potsdam Declaration, the Allied powers set the goal of their occupation policy to transform Japan from a militaristic, ultranationalistic, imperial state into a peace-seeking democratic nation (Passin 1990, 124). Under the supervision of the Allied powers, the Japanese Diet passed the new Constitution of Japan in 1946. The emperor maintained a symbolic status, yet, was deprived of all political power. The sovereignty of the people was declared, with power being exercised through the Diet whose members were elected by the people. Human rights were stated as inalienable and the new Constitution renounced war and the use of military force. The Allied powers viewed Japan's prewar education as "one of the most effective agents for nurturing nationalism in the minds of youth" (Shimahara 1979, 63), and the supreme commander General MacArthur immediately issued orders to repudiate "ultranationalistic and militaristic educational ideologies and their influences" (Horio 1988, 131), which included the suppression of *Shūshin* instruction.

The educational system in Japan needed to be drastically reorganized based on the principle of democracy. A U.S. Education Mission was dispatched to Japan in 1946, and their report set the course for the democratization of post-war Japanese education. Inspired by this report, the Fundamental Law of Education was adopted in 1947. Its preamble states that:

> Having established the Constitution of Japan, we have shown our resolution to contribute to the peace of the world and welfare of the humanity by building a democratic and cultural state. The realization of this idea shall depend fundamentally on the power of education (official translation, cited in Horio 1988, 400).

Despite the fact that democratic and pacifistic values were clearly declared in the Fundamental Law of Education, according to Okada (2002), the Japanese education system "passed through a so-called 'reverse course,' or reassessment of Occupation policies" (429). Under this ideological influence, the Ministry of Education issued two directives in 1958: 1) moral education should be taught through all school activities; 2) in order to support this educational initiative, a special hour should be assigned for *Dōtoku* (ethics or moral education). University professors and the Japan Teachers Union (JTU) strongly protested against the reintroduction of moral education, fearing the possibility that it would mirror the role of *Shūshin* and be used as an instrument for the state to control freedom of thought. But their protest did not change the decision of the Ministry of Education. Shimahara (1979) argues that this reintroduction of moral education meant "a victory for the ministry, since it constituted an extension of state power into the control of education" (70).

Dōtoku was added to the official curriculum; however, it was not included as a regular subject, and thus, its outlines were not binding and the subject matter was described only vaguely. A rationale for the philosophy underlying moral education was needed. A special advisory committee prepared a report, and the final report was submitted to the Ministry of Education in 1966. This report was titled Kitai sareru ningenzō (The Desirable Image of Man). Besides stating the necessity of the cultivation of capacity and morality, the report reads that Japan is a democratic country, which requires Japanese people to strive to establish a healthy democracy without disregarding the traditional virtue of communal order. It also reads that the current international situation requires Japanese people to realize that Japan has been opened to the world community without disregarding its national identity. It even refers to the emperor and states that the act of highly respecting the emperor, who maintains a symbolic status, is tightly linked to the act of loving what is symbolized by the emperor, Japan. The report received fierce opposition from JTU, calling it a revival of nationalism and imperialism in education.

These nationalistic and utilitarian educational objectives laid the ground for subsequent educational policies (Okada 2002, 431), which were reflected in The Basic Outlines for an Overall Reform of School Education (1971) and the final report of the Ad hoc Committee on Education (1987). After the 1990s, the emphasis on the cultivation of national identity and the appreciation of tradition and culture "reached another stage" (Ide 2009, 447), and the reinforcement of *Dōtoku* was implemented along that line. In 1997, the Ministry of Education started a program called Kokoro no Kyōiku (Education for the Heart), whose main feature is the reinforcement of rigorous disciplining of children in response to an alleged decline in children's moral behavior. In March 2000, The Education Reform National Conference (ERNC) was set up as a private advisory body to the then Prime Minister Obuchi Keizō. The ERNC's final report issued in December 2000 suggested the revision of the Fundamental Law of Education as well as an increased emphasis on moral education. Since around the time when the educational system took the "reverse course" in the 1950s, the revision of the Fundamental Law of Education had been actively sought by the Liberal Democratic Party (LDP), which has served as the ruling party almost continuously since its foundation in 1955. According to Okada (2002), the LDP's advocacy of the revision of the Law had derived from concerns that the Law was "doing considerable damage to Japanese traditional values as a result of too much emphasis being placed on 'individuality'" and "lacking in assertion of the importance of Japanese 'traditional' morality and values such as pledging people's loyalty to the State, filial piety, family obligation, etc." (429).

In 2002, the Ministry of Education started distributing a guidebook for moral education for teachers, students, and parents titled *Kokoro no Nōto* (The Notebook for the Heart). This Notebook was destined to all elementary and secondary schools in Japan without its having to go through the textbook authorization system. This invited criticism that the Notebook was a national *Dōtoku* textbook, "[l]ike the state authored, state distributed *Shūshin* textbooks" (Higashi 2008, 45). Moreover, the Notebook was criticized because its basic direction is "looking inward into the culture ... even with a tendency towards nationalism" (Saito and Imai 2004, 589).

In December 2006, the revision of the Fundamental Law of Education passed the Diet. Takayama (2008) argues that the most controversial point of this revision was "the inclusion of the expression 'cultivating an attitude that respects tradition and culture and love of the national homeland that has fostered them' (Japan Times 2006)" (131). Takayama summarizes the argument of the opponents of the revision which is "seeing it as a retrogressive conservative move to return to the prewar and wartime state intervention in education, often analogising the proposed revision with the 1890 Imperial Rescript, which played a central role in the dissemination of wartime ultra-nationalism" (131). The debate is ongoing.

THE DIRECTION OF MORAL EDUCATION IN JAPAN

As a Japanese individual who worked in the U.S. college classroom setting, I realize that the Japanese classroom and the U.S. classroom are not physically that different, but they are different cultural sites. Like every teacher, I think that communication with students is important and I listened closely to every student who had a situation. I made every professional decision after giving careful thought to that situation; however, I found that my decisions were occasionally challenged by students, who brought the issue to the Department by whom I was told to modify my decision.

One such instance concerned whether a student was allowed to take a make-up final examination against the class make-up policy. Students were supposed to take the final examination according to the schedule determined by the University. As an instructor, I stated on the course syllabus that "Make-up for the final examination is allowed only with a valid and documented excuse." Nevertheless, there was this case where a student did not show up for the scheduled final examination without prior notice. It was not until a few days later that the student contacted me via email, stating that he did not show up on the final examination because he had lost the paper on which he jotted down the schedule. He asked me "When can I take the make-up exam?"

Losing a paper on which the schedule was jotted down was not a valid excuse. I was a bit surprised by this naïve excuse, but what surprised me more was the fact that the student did not seem to understand the seriousness of the situation in which he was involved. The tone of his email message was extremely casual and the fact that he asked for the make-up examination as if he were entitled to do so indicated that he did not seem to understand the rules and regulations regarding the final examination. I believed that knowing these rules and regulations and following them was critical for students to complete the course successfully. Furthermore, it was each student's responsibility to understand these rules and regulations. This was not the first case that a student failed to show up on the scheduled final examination, but this case was different because of the student's total lack of understanding of his responsibility. I could not find any reason for the student to be excused from the make-up policy, and informed the student that there would be no make-up examination.

Immediately after learning my decision, the student, accompanied by his father, directly went to see the Chair of the department. I was called by the Chair and told that I should give him a make-up final examination because the final examination is too important an exam not to be given a chance to take. I understood that the decision was based on the consideration that the student's "one mistake" should not jeopardize his entire academic plan at the university, and I found it reasonable on its own terms. However, I thought that the very importance of the examination was what he had not essentially understood. Because the exam is important for every student, it must be administered fairly and consistently. In order to achieve this, rules and regulations are set, and the exam is administered accordingly. If a student is excused from the rules, the student should have a valid reason; otherwise, the fairness of the exam would not be maintained. For this reason, although I knew that I had to follow the decision of the department and give the student a make-up exam, I still hesitated to say so to the Chair because it would, to me, jeopardize the integrity of the examination. The Chair was very understanding of my hesitation, and suggested that I could give him a penalty, which I thought was a reasonable solution within the context. The Chair devised a solution which showed respect for the values that I embrace.

This is one of my experiences which made me realize that the Japanese classroom and the U.S. classroom are two different cultural sites. I made the decision about examination requirements based on my understanding on how classroom order should be established, and on what the norms of conduct are for faculty members and students. This understanding was established through my school experiences as a student in Japan. When I started teaching in the U.S. college classroom, I brought in the understandings I had established in Japan into a different context – the U.S. cultural context. Unconsciously and naively, I believed that considering both sites as educational institutions meant that they would both work based on comparable principles and norms of behavior. Therefore, I was shocked when I learned that the student who did not comply with the class make-up policy should be given a chance to take the make-up final examination. Judging from the norms of conduct in which I had believed, Japan's norms of conduct, the U.S. student's actions were totally irresponsible. Under this assumption, the student's excuse should not have been accepted by the authority of an educational institution. However, I learned that what I believed in was neither the norm of conduct nor the norm of the administrative principles in an educational institution in the United States.

What I came to realize – what previously I had failed to notice - was not only this difference in norms and principles of two different cultural contexts, but also the very presence of norms and principles in themselves. More essentially, I came to realize that I had a certain value and belief system which legitimizes these norms and principles. I was not consciously aware of this value and belief system because I think I took it for granted in my native cultural context. My value and belief system seemed to be established primarily by linking what I learned as moral values at home, school, and in the community with what I observed of how things work in Japan. I seemed to have accepted what I had observed rather uncritically as being how things should work universally. The system seemed to be working to a certain extent in the Japanese cultural context, which seemed to help solidify the system to a level that became unconscious; I just took it for granted. However, encountering instances where this system was challenged, my unconscious became conscious, and I realized that I had been deeply embracing my Japanese value and belief system.

Accepting the fact that my Japanese value and belief system does not necessarily work effectively in a new cultural context was a confusing and angst-ridden process. At the same time, it was a process which allowed me to encounter, initially somewhat reluctantly, the culture of the other. Being exposed to a cultural context in which my value system was challenged, I encountered both my inner cultural resources and the culture of the other as stated by the French philosopher, Jacques Derrida:

> There is no culture or cultural identity without this difference with itself ... This can be said, inversely or reciprocally, of all identity or all identification: there is no self-relation, no relation to oneself, no identification with oneself, without culture, but a culture of oneself as a culture of the other, a culture of the double genitive and of the difference to oneself (1992a 9-10, original emphasis).

From my experience of encountering the culture of the other, I am concerned about the persistent inclination of moral education in Japan toward the cultivation of national identity through nurturing the sense of respect for Japanese tradition and culture.

According to Derrida (1992b), it is at the very moment at which the intensification of international exchanges takes place that "national consciousness, search for identity, affirmation or even national demands show up more clearly, or even become exasperated and tense up into nationalism" (6). For Derrida, every nationality takes the form of a philosophy:

> When a nation says: "We are German," for instance, this does not mean that we are simply a particular people among others. Being German means being responsible for humanity, being the best philosophers, having to bear the burden of being witnesses, being responsible for the totality of humanity (1992c 182, original emphasis).

Nationality discourse is philosophically structured, demonstrating the nation's exemplarity. At the same time, Derrida argues that all the concepts and the languages of humanity are tied to national idioms. Pointing out that the current hegemonic status of the English language has necessitated a large number of people to speak their own language plus English, Derrida maintains that under these circumstances, if one claims that he or she has his or her own language and does not want to give up the language, it is already a form of affirming a subtle nationalism:

> When I say "I speak French," it is not simply a constative utterance; it is not simply a description. It is a way of committing myself. As soon as you reaffirm your own language, your own idiom, ... there is the beginning of some nationalistic affirmation. A language is not simply content with describing a situation, but it tries to commit itself, to affirm, to say it is "good" to sign and to countersign (1992c 183).

I want to think about the term "commitment" here. Under the foreign (the U.S.) cultural context, I knew that I had to culturally adjust myself and tried to do so most notably by speaking English. At the same time, as seen by my class administrative decision-making as an instructor, I unconsciously continued to commit myself to the values and beliefs established in Japan. I realized my unconscious commitment when these values and beliefs were challenged. When that happened, I found myself immediately defending them, seeking ways to justify them. This would be "the beginning of some nationalistic affirmation." Indeed, through this process, I realized that I had been deeply embracing these values and beliefs. This occurred through my intrinsic commitment to these values and beliefs, not through being taught to embrace them. Had my respect for Japanese tradition and culture been obtained through being taught, it would have resided as conscious knowledge in my mind.

If commitment in terms of language and tradition is already the beginning of some nationalistic affirmation, Derrida (1992c) asks "how is it possible to reaffirm singularity, minority, specific idioms, natural languages, without giving rise to what we call nationalism in its violent and imperialistic form?" (183). His own response could be found in his text, *The Other Heading* (1992a), in which he discusses European cultural identity. While affirming that the Enlightenment is the European cultural heritage, Derrida argues that this cultural heritage should not be taken for granted; it is necessary to question the values it has given to European people. The imperative remains, as summarized by Nass (1992) in his introduction to *The Other Heading*,

> — to return to these names and discourses precisely because they have given our language – our language of responsibility, of giving, and of the example. The imperative remains, therefore, to question the exemplarity of this language and this heritage in order to encounter or experience what remains necessarily absent and unthought, necessarily without example, in them. (xlviii)

In reviewing the history of moral education in Japan, it seems that moral education is heading in the opposite direction from what is suggested above. History has shown that the underlying principles of *Shūshin* were the exclusive affirmation of nationality and cultural tradition, which led the rise of ultranationalism in prewar Japan. Without giving critical examination to this historical development, *Dōtoku* inherited the spirit of this self-affirmation, in which the cultivation of national identity through nurturing the sense of respect for Japanese tradition and culture has been positively sought.

From my experience of being exposed to the culture of the other, this direction in Japanese moral education seems undesirable. I learned that I have been deeply committed to my value and belief system that was nurtured by the Japanese cultural context, which is already a nationalistic affirmation. Derrida (1992c) cautions that this affirmation should not develop into "'bad' forms of nationalism – aggressiveness, xenophobia, exclusion of the other" (183). The explicit program of cultivation of national consciousness on top of the already nationalistic affirmation – people's commitment to the Japanese language and Japanese cultural tradition - resulted in the rise of bad forms of nationalism in prewar Japan. This should not be repeated. Moreover, I learned that there are occasions when the value and belief system to which I am committed must be negotiated in the face of being exposed to the culture of the other. In such instances, my embracement of my cultural tradition did not help since it does not serve as a guide to dealing with this angst-ridden process. The cultural friction that is expected in the process of encountering the culture of the other could not be creatively solved by simply affirming one's own cultural heritage.

CONCLUSION

Teaching Japanese children simply to affirm their own cultural tradition does not seem to prepare them to live in an increasingly interconnected and globalized world where diverse cultures coexist side by side. Instead, we should be informed by Derrida's insights, and design a moral education curriculum which critically examines the values that our cultural heritage has given us in order to explore what has been absent from, and unthought in, our cultural heritage. This recognition and affirmation of otherness is an imperative that allows us to see "a culture of oneself as a culture of the other," which would be the first step for us to establish and affirm our cultural identity without giving rise to 'bad' forms of nationalism. An affirmation of otherness is needed.

REFERENCES

Derrida, Jacques. 1992a. *The Other Heading: Reflections on Today's Europe.* Translated by Pascale-Anne Brault and Michael B. Nass. Bloomington and Indianapolis: Indiana University Press.

———. 1992b. Onto-Theology of National Humanism. *The Oxford Literary Review* 14: 3-23.

———. 1992c. Talking Liberties: Jacques Derrida's Interview with Alan Montefiore. In *Derrida & Education*, edited by Gert J. J. Biesta and Denise Egéa-Kuehne, 176-85. New York: Routledge.

Gluck, Carol. 1985. *Japan's Modern Myths: Ideology in the Late Meiji Period.* Princeton, New Jersey: Princeton University Press.

Higashi, Julie. 2008. The Kokoro Education: Landscaping the Minds and Hearts of Japanese. In *Social Education in Asia: Critical Issues and Multiple Perspective*, edited by David L. Grossman and Joe Tin-Yau Lo, 39-56. Charlotte, N.C.: IAP-Information Age Publishing Inc.

Horio, Teruhisa. 1988. *Educational Thought and Ideology in Modern Japan: State Authority and Intellectual Freedom.* Tokyo: University of Tokyo Press.

Ide, Kanako. 2009. The Debate on Patriotic Education in Post-World War II Japan. *Educational Philosophy and Theory* 41 (4): 441- 52

Khan, Yoshimitsu. 1997. *Japanese Moral Education Past and Present.* Madison, New Jersey: Fairleigh Dickinson University Press.

Lanham, Betty. B. 1979. Ethics and Moral Precepts Taught in Schools of Japan and the United States. *Ethos* 7 (1): 1-18.

Luhmer, Klaus. 1990. Moral Education in Japan. *Journal of Moral Education* 19 (3): 172-82. http://ccbs.ntu.edu.tw/FULLTEXT/JR-ADM/lumer.htm.

Nass, Michael. B. 1992. Introduction to *The Other Heading: Reflections on Today's Europe.* Bloomington and Indianapolis: Indiana University Press.

Okada, Akito. 2002. Education of Whom, for Whom, by Whom? Revising the Fundamental Law of Education in Japan. *Japan Forum* 14(3): 425-441.

Otsu, Kazuo. 2008. Citizenship Education Curriculum in Japan. In *Citizenship Curriculum in Asia and the Pacific*, edited by David L. Grossman, Wing On Lee, and Kerry J. Kennedy, 75-94. Dordrecht: Springer/Hong Kong: University of Hong Kong Comparative Education Research Centre.

Passin, Herbert. 1990. The Occupation: Some Reflections. *Daedalus* 119 (3): 107-29.

Saito, Naoko and Imai, Yasuo. 2004. In Search of the Public and the Private: Philosophy of Education in Post-War Japan." *Comparative Education* 40 (4): 583-594

Shimahara, Nobuo K. 1979. *Adaptation and Education in Japan.* New York: Praeger Publishers.

Takayama, Keita. 2008. Japan's Ministry of Education "Becoming the Right": Neo-liberal Restructuring and the Ministry's Struggles for Political Legitimacy. Globalisation, *Societies and Education* 6 (2): 131-146.

Wray, Harry.   1991.   Change and Continuity in Modern Japanese Educational
     History: Allied Occupational Reforms Forty Years Later.   *Comparative
     Education Review* 35 (3): 447-75.

CHAPTER 9

Marketization of Higher Education in Vietnam in the Era of Neoliberal Globalization: The Institutional Practice at Vietnam National University, Hanoi

Hien Nguyen, Michelle Nilson, and Allan MacKinnon

INTRODUCTION

Growing up in Vietnam, where education is highly regarded but opportunities to study in university are scarce, many would spend a childhood dreaming of being able to attain university entrance. For generations, a long history of feudalism, colonialism, war, and poverty made higher education in Vietnam just a dream—an unreachable goal for many generations of Vietnamese 'commoners' and working class citizens. Under feudal and colonial regimes, higher education was a symbol of privilege, social status and power. Under the communist regime, even though higher education was "for the people" and a route to social stability, only a small number of citizens could gain entry due to the rigorous entrance exams.

However, over the past two decades, Vietnam's higher education system has undergone a major transformation, changing the institutional framework in which higher education institutions (HEIs) operate. This transformation has been fuelled by two main forces. First, economic reform has increased demand for knowledge workers within the country. Second, rapid technological development has fostered the growth of cross-border academic programmes offered through both conventional and online delivery.

Although it continues to be a communist country, Vietnam has enthusiastically embraced a capitalist neo-liberal free-market policy framework in its higher education system. While market mechanisms may boost production and efficient management of bureaucratic higher education systems in a way similar to a manufacturing enterprise, the question remains as to whether it is wise to match access for the masses with limited resources, or to generally infuse a western experience of market freedom in a culture and society like that of Vietnam. What is the perception of these federal policies by institutional administrators? How are these policies impacting institutions and institutional operations?

This paper reports on a study of higher education policies and their impacts on one institution in Vietnam over the past decade. It presents an illustration of the complexity of national policies in higher education in Vietnam, drawing from institutional documents and interviews with key informants at the Vietnam National University in Hanoi. The study involved an in-depth examination of an institution within a communist country that is faced with human capital, capacity, and market demands in an ever more competitive global market economy making a compelling case for further research into the local impacts of national policies.

NEO-LIBERALISM AND THE MARKETIZATION POLICY FRAMEWORK

In the era of neoliberal globalization, higher education is predominantly viewed as a private commodity and rarely as a public good (Altbach, 2002; Giroux, 2002; Lynch, 2006). It is as though education has become a tradable commodity to be purchased by a consumer, a product to be bought and sold by academic institutions, which have transmogrified themselves into businesses. Within this, marketization can be understood as the use of the market or market-oriented mechanisms with the aim of improving the public sector's activities. It is a term used as part of the vocabulary of New Public Management (NPM) that arose in 1980s (Bevir, Rhodes & Weller, 2003; Christensen, Laegreid, & Wise, 2002; Gray & Jenkins, 1995; Hood, 1995). New Public Management is associated with discourses of neoliberalism (Olssen & Peters, 2005), and is understood as a recipe for correcting the perceived failings of traditional public bureaucracies for efficiency, quality, customer responsiveness and effective leadership (Bevir, et. al., 2003; Hood, 1995; Jackson, 2001). A typical policy instrument of NPM is marketization, which is promoted through the privatization of public enterprises, deregulation, liberalization and competition (Mok & Lo, 2002; Salminen, 2003).

Marketization in higher education commonly refers to several revenue generating strategies that universities have adopted. These strategies include tuition fees, massification of higher education, privatization, commercialization of research, commodification of knowledge, and entrepreneurialism (Clark, 1998; Johnstone, Arora & Experton, 1998; Marginson & Considine, 2000; Slaughter & Leslie, 1997). Universities and colleges operating under the context of marketization policies exhibit at least some of the following principles: (1) self-financing; (2) adopting market discourse and the use of the economic market as a model for managerial practices; (3) focusing on efficiency, economy and effectiveness; (4) revenue generation and cost-effectiveness; (5) competition; (6) accountability; (7) institutional autonomy; (8) quality assurance (Dill, 2003; Hanson, 1992; Johnstone, 1998; Robertson & Dale, 2000; Welch, 1998).

Studies in educational reform find that strong market forces and the ideas of corporate management have significantly affected the development and reform of education in many countries (Jones, 1998; Welch, 1998). The use of market mechanisms have resulted in a dramatic increase in demand for higher education graduates, thus the higher education institutions responded to this notion of marketization by the "massification" of numbers of student intakes or, in other words, by widening access to HEIs (Fox, 2002; Theisens, 2004; Tilak, 2005a & 2005b). The increased numbers of students meant more funding was needed, thus leading to large state budgets and high taxation (Johnstone, 1998; Theisens, 2004; Tilak, 2005a). However, large budgets and high taxation are contradictive to the neoliberal 'free market' ideology, and are perceived as causes of economic problems. This has led to a policy of cutbacks on state budgets for social services, including the budget for higher education, especially in Western European and North American countries (Johnstone, 1998; Theisens, 2004; Tilak, 2005a). Ultimately, per student expenditures have diminished over years, as student enrolments increased faster than governments could increase their budgets (Barr, 1993; Tilak, 2005a). In order for governments to keep expenditures constant and for HEIs to admit more students, HEIs that are primarily dependent on public funds have been forced to mobilize other sources of income by increasing or introducing tuition fees, contracting out research services, marketing educational services, and increasing private funding through privatization of the institution (Currie & Newson, 1998; Johnstone, 1999 & 2003; Johnstone et al., 1998; Rhoades & Slaughter, 2006; Slaughter & Leslie, 1997; Theisens, 2004; Tilak, 2005a).

Given these changes in national policies, what have been the institutional responses to these reforms? Are the responses within a single institutional case study in Vietnam consistent with previous literature that indicates responses to marketization in other jurisdictions? The term "marketization" is still new and controversial to Vietnamese policy-makers and scholars, because it undermines the characteristics of a socialist country. However, since the commencement of the economic reform (đổi mới) in 1986, the Government of Vietnam has introduced a number of changes in the higher education system that reflect characteristics similar to marketization policies.

METHODOLOGY

Yin (1994) suggests that case study methodology is appropriate when a complex social phenomenon is being studied, when there are multiple sources of data, and when there are theoretical suppositions that guide the data collection. In jurisdictions where higher education institutions and national governments are tightly coupled, it is possible to discern a direct link between national policy and the resultant institutional behaviours. This research uses Vietnam National University in Hanoi (VNU-Hanoi) as a case study to examine how national reform policies have been implemented and influenced the practice of a higher education institution. This descriptive case study is based on the analysis of national policy documents, post-secondary institutional documents and website information, as well as information collected from semi-structured interviews (Creswell, 2005; Silverman, 2005). Finally, consistent with Yin's (1994) recommendation, this case is testing the theoretical suppositions posited by earlier literature to determine if the indicators of marketization hold in a new context—Vietnam.

The selection of the VNU – Hanoi as the site for the case study was based on identification of a comprehensive public university where reform policies have been implemented. Interviewees were chosen due to the nature of their positions and their work being directly and/ or closely related to the development of Vietnamese higher education policies, and their understanding of the current issues in higher education.

The student interviewee was selected randomly from the International School of VNU-Hanoi, because the school represents the most recent adoption of the new policies. Interview questions focused on national reform policies and their impacts on the institution's governance, management, financing, and curriculum changes.

Interviewees included a board/ executive member, a Rector of a constituent college, a senior administrator, a Dean of graduate studies, a lecturer, and a student. All interviews were audio-recorded, except for the senior administrator who answered interview questions by email. There were 10 main structured questions; follow up questions or informal questions were inserted during the interviews to clarify the interviewees' intention, to elicit more information, and/ or to direct interviewees back to the main question. All interviews were transcribed and the data were manually analyzed according to marketization themes identified from the literature. Specifically, the themes were: (1) self-financing (charging tuition fees); (2) adopting market discourse and the use of the economic market as a model for managerial practices; (3) focusing on efficiency, economy and effectiveness; (4) revenue generation and cost-effectiveness; (5) competition; (6) accountability; (7) institutional autonomy; (8) quality assurance (Dill, 2003; Hanson, 1992; Johnstone, 1998; Robertson & Dale, 2000; Welch, 1998).

The documents selected for this research were the university brochures, the university website, and legislative policy documents directly related to higher education policy, that were passed from 1995 to 2006. These documents were analyzed using thematic correspondence between the text and the marketization themes from the literature as identified above.

VIETNAM NATIONAL UNIVERSITY-HANOI

Vietnam National University- Hanoi (VNU-Hanoi) was established in December 1993 by merging three leading mono-disciplinary universities in Hanoi: University of Hanoi, Hanoi Teachers' Training College No. 1 and Hanoi Foreign Language Teachers' Training College. The merged university continued to use the constituent campuses; however, construction of a new university compound started in 2003 in the newly developed suburban area of Hoà Lạc in Hanoi.

Despite being one of Vietnam's younger universities, the VNU-Hanoi inherited the legacy of the French colonial University of Indochina that was built in 1906, and of the original member universities that were founded after Vietnam became independent in 1945. The university was established in response to the needs for manpower brought about by the national economic reforms that started in the late 1980s.

As of January 2007, the University had 49,921 students in total; 18,716 full-time "official" undergraduates; 23,296 part-time undergraduates; 5,275 post-graduates; 2,303 gifted high school students; along with 217 foreign students. In June 2008, the number of teaching staff was only 1466, of which 39 were full professors; 232 were associate professors; 566 had a PhD; and the rest only possessed a masters' or undergraduate degree.

THE NATIONAL POLICIES

Although the proportion of the national budget for education in Vietnam has increased gradually, from 7.7% in 1992 to 15.7% in 2003, with an estimated increase to 20% in 2010 (IMF, 1999; 2003; MOET, 2001), there has been a shift away from relying solely on the state budget for financial provision of higher education to multiple sources of funding. The Ministry of Education and Training (MOET) started to allow public higher education institutions (HEIs) to admit fee-paying students in 1987, outside of the centrally planned quota for which scholarships and grants were available (UNESCO, 2006). The number of fee-paying students grew quickly compared with the number of students sponsored by the State. Furthermore, the government also lifted or loosened many regulations that previously restricted the role of the private sector in education (Pham & Fry, 2002; Tran, 2005).

The Vietnamese government promulgated Resolution Number 90/CP on 21 August 1997 on "the orientations and policy of socialization of activities in education, healthcare and culture", calling for a broader participation of the people and the whole society into the development of education (GOV, 1997). The Resolution defined "socialization" of education as "to broaden the sources of investment" and "to exploit the potential in human, material and financial resources in the society". Some measures to "socialize" activities of education and training included: (1) consolidating public educational institutions to help them maintain their leading role and serve as the core; (2) diversifying forms of education (full-time, part-time, continuing education), and types of educational institutions (public, semi-public, private and people-sponsored, distance education); (3) diversifying sources of income for HEIs from tuition fees, contributions from students' parents, production and business services; (4) raising tuition fees at HEIs; (5) and allowing all foreign and domestic agencies, organizations and individuals to take part in the development of education.

In the quest to speed-up the "socialization" process, the government issued two more documents to clarify some key points that would help attract more participants. The first document, Decree Number 73/1999/ND-CP on the encouragement of socialization of activities in education, healthcare, culture and sports, dated 19 August 1999, offered tax incentives for participants in the development of education and provided guidelines in financial management and state management for non-public institutions (GOV, 1999).

The second document, Government Resolution Number 05/2005/NQ-CP on stepping up the socialization of activities in education, healthcare, culture and sports was issued 18 April 2005. In this resolution, the government vowed to continue: (1) reforming State management; (2) strengthening policies; (3) increasing investment resources; (4) shifting public institutions from bureaucratic mechanisms to autonomous, not-for-profit mechanisms, having full autonomy in organization and management; (5) developing and maintaining only two forms of non-public institutions (people-sponsored and private), and gradually abolishing the semi-public establishments; (6) creating an conductive environment for development and competition in order to make both public and non-public institutions commit to quality assurance and broaden their operation scales. The Government also encouraged the establishment of non-public institutions, under the models of not-for-profit or for-profit; and considered converting some public HEIs into non-public institutions to be autonomously managed by collectives or individuals and refund the capital to the State (GOV, 2005; National Assembly, 2005).

The Government also indicated that it would continue: (a) to increase the percentage of budget expenditure on education and training, ensuring funding for general education and key areas of study and research; (b) to give priority to investments in less populated and mountainous areas; (c) to attract investment and resources from all levels of society, and strengthen links between educational institutions with families and society; (d) to fundamentally reform policy on tuition fees, making sure that tuition fees are enough to cover institutions' teaching and learning expenses; (e) and to encourage cooperation between Vietnamese educational institutions with high-quality foreign educational institutions, or the establishment of 100% foreign-invested educational institutions in Vietnam (GOV, 2005).

Taking a further step to associate training and scientific research with actual production, to accelerate the prompt application of scientific and technological research results to production, and to partly supply resources for training as well as scientific research in order to raise the training and research quality, the Prime Minister issued Decision Number 68/1998/QD-TTg on 27 March 1998 allowing the experimental establishment of state enterprises in some public HEIs (universities, colleges and research institutions). Under this Decision, State enterprises established within the public universities are allowed to manufacture and trade in products resulting from the technological research and application, or scientific and technological products and services that are closely associated with the functions and professional tasks of the HEIs.

After eight years of implementation of Decision Number 68/1998/QD-TTg, and aiming to reduce the burden on the state budget, the government issued Decree No. 43/2006/ND-CP on 25 April 2006 to: (1) allow non-business public institutions more autonomy and self-governance in their operations, including organizational structure and financial management; (2) encourage public higher education institutions to convert their operations into the model of enterprises or non-public organizations (Article 4).

We now turn to examine each of the mechanisms of marketization and the resultant impact of these policies on the institution.

INSTITUTIONAL IMPACTS: MARKETIZATION

Diversified University Income Strategies

Given the specific "socialization" language of Resolution Number 90/CP, it should come as no surprise that there were significant impacts on postsecondary institutions and their funding levels. At VNU-Hanoi, according to its Vice President, the proportion funded by the state dropped from 100% of the total income in the early 1980s to the present day figure of 50%, even though the funding in absolute dollars has significantly increased. As demonstrated in the policies above, the State allowed privatization of public HEIs through diversification of their sources of income outside of the state funding. Privatization is traditionally understood by Vietnamese scholars and policy-makers as having private shareholders of public institutions' assets and/ or capital; however, within the literature of neo-liberal policies, privatization means the increased involvement of private sector and any form of private funding, including tuition fees, commercialization of research and knowledge, and entrepreneurial partnerships (Johnstone, 1998). VNU-Hanoi was no exception to the new policy, thus the University has adopted income strategies that are discussed in the following sections.

Tuition Fees

Like many other public HEIs that have started charging tuition fees since 1987, VNU-Hanoi has charged tuition fees since its establishment. Despite tuition fees having steadily increased since their introduction, they only account for 10% of the actual costs of education nationally as of 2009 . At VNU-Hanoi, this source of income accounts for approximately 20% of the total revenue (Vice President, interview 21/1/2008). With a new tuition policy in place starting in the 2010-2011 academic year, students at VNU-Hanoi will pay a 50% increase from the previous rate. While this increase has drawn criticism from the wider society and may cause many students of lower socio-economic groups to drop out of higher education, it only covers a fraction of the total running costs of the University.

Massification

The dramatic expansion in postsecondary student numbers since the late 1980s has been described by Theisens (2004) as "massification". There are three primary ways in which VNU-Hanoi has expanded its numbers: expanded programme offerings, collaboration, and course modularity. First, it has offered several forms of training programmes, including full-time, part-time, in-service and continuing studies. Since fees charged for part-time and in-service programmes are not regulated by the government, they may be set at full cost-recovery.

To broaden access and opportunities for students, VNU-Hanoi has collaborated with foreign HEIs to offer joint programmes. The University also set up an International School that mainly offers cross-border education to students who can afford full tuition fees. A student noted:

> The cross-border educational programmes offered by institutions like this give students, who had failed entrance exams to public universities, an opportunity to undertake higher education studies and to gain a degree from an overseas institution without having to travel abroad and pay higher tuition fees and expenses.

The International School is not eligible for any government funding and its revenue solely comes from tuition fees, because it is considered a private not-for-profit organization operating on a cost-recovery basis within a public institution.

Finally, although many scholars and the University's officials are reluctant to refer to students as "customers" or "consumers", VNU-Hanoi has demonstrated various "customer oriented" practices. For example, the University adopted the credit system, rather than a cohort system, which allows students more flexibility with their study time and choices of programmes. The pedagogy has moved from teacher-centred to student-centred. The curriculum has moved from being theoretically based toward being more practically oriented and industry-related. These practices aim to satisfy "customers", whether they are employers in the market or students.

Commercialization of Research and Services

As a part of the institutional income strategy, VNU-Hanoi has promoted scientific research as another source of income generation. Aiming to become a leading comprehensive and research institution, the University currently has three nationally recognized research institutes, focusing on advanced technology (such as nanotechnology) and providing scientific research service to society. This service comes under the forms of government assignments and/ or contracted research projects from private organizations. These research activities and services aim to help the University not only reach its goals/ missions and boost its reputation within society, but also generate income that, as of 2008, accounted for approximately 30% of the University's total revenue (Vice President, Interview 21/1/2008).

Entrepreneurial Culture

VNU-Hanoi responded to Government Resolution Number 05/2005/NQ-CP, which specified changes in management culture, in various ways that fostered the notion of "market" mechanisms. The University has increasingly operated like a business enterprise, adopting corporate culture and managerial practices such as strategic plans, a mission statement, entrepreneurial structure, institutional autonomy and competition. The following sections explore specific organizational changes at VNU-Hanoi, specifically with regards to structure, accountability, and competition.

Autonomous Decision-making Structure

The managerial structure is certainly one of the most important features of an organization. The highest level of management at VNU-Hanoi is the Board, which is comprised of the President, the Secretary of the Communist Party of Vietnam (CPV) and Vice Presidents of VNU-Hanoi, Rectors of constituent colleges and Directors of constituent research institutes as permanent members. The President of VNU-Hanoi is the chair of the Board, and can make the final decision on the appointment and removal of permanent members, elected members and the secretary of the Board based on the votes of permanent members.

Despite having constraints in some areas of decision-making, the Board and the President of the University have a great deal of autonomy in deciding matters relating to the University's finance, operational strategies, personnel and public relations. For example, rather than having to follow the government's quota for student admissions, the Board can determine the number based on the University's capacity and market demand and then make a proposal to the Ministry Of Education and Training (MOET) for approval. The Board also decides on the University's financial strategies and programmes it can offer. While the University still has to follow MOET's curriculum framework that imposes certain subjects and credit hours in every programme; the Board and the President can decide the content of professional subjects.

It is worth noting that the title President is no longer referred to as Hiệu Trưởng (Rector) but as Giám Đốc (President/ Director) in Vietnamese, which is commonly used for the head of a corporate rather than the head of an academic institution. The President can serve a maximum of two consecutive five-year terms, and is entitled to a high level of autonomy in management and decision-making compared to the same position at other public HEIs. The current president shares some power in decision-making that used to be solely a Minister's prerogative, such as in matters regarding personnel, academic schemes, curriculum, finance, institutional development and student recruitment.

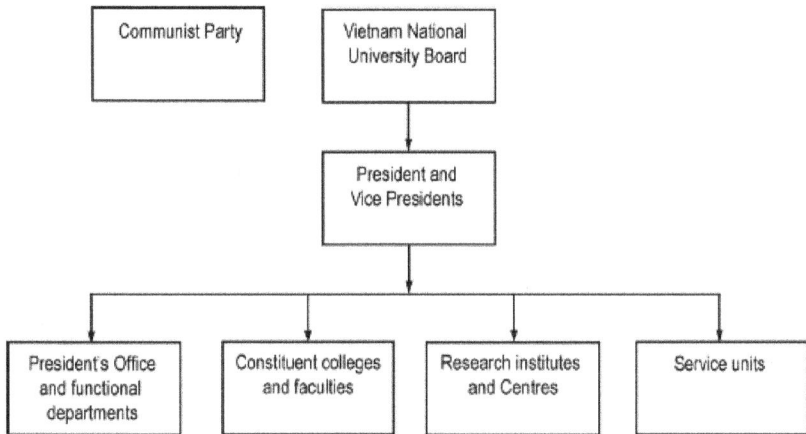

Figure 1: Organizational Chart of VNU-Hanoi
Source: Vietnam National University website http://www.vnu.edu.vn/en/

Through observation, one may come to the conclusion that VNU-Hanoi has a transparent organizational structure and culture of a corporation even though it does not have absolute autonomy. More autonomy could mean more accountability since the managerial role of the State in university governance has increasingly diminished, and the University is responsible to more stakeholders than before.

Accountability

The historic role of HEIs in Vietnam has not been to question authority, but to constitute it. Under the colonial system, the relationship between the University and the State and its political elites was a tight-knit one. The University was held accountable by the State and a small population of the political and intellectual elite. The involvement of the State in the University's decision-making has gradually diminished; therefore, an effective way for it to exert influence is through the use of performance-related funding mechanisms, holding HEIs accountable for the allocated funds. Public HEIs, like VNU-Hanoi, that receive money from the State budget have to comply with quality assessment standards set by MOET.

It was under these circumstances that VNU-Hanoi directed its strategic plans for 2006-2010, toward "quality", "efficiency", and "cost effectiveness", aiming to achieve its mission statement that sets "prestige" as a goal in a timely manner. In terms of "quality", the University is committed to training high-quality students, recruiting highly qualified teaching staff, and improving the quality of student services. In terms of "efficiency" and "cost effectiveness", the University is committed to efficient management, effective mobilization and utilization of financial resources. These commitments are demonstrated through the engagement in various types of quality assurance and accreditation that include internal and external evaluation of the university governance, staff, students, teaching and learning, research, facilities, finance, consultancy and technology transfer, and international relations. These nine areas of assessment were developed by VNU-Hanoi's Centre for Education Quality Assurance and Research Development (CEQARD) in 1995, approved by the Government and agreed upon by universities throughout Vietnam, setting standards for public HEIs to meet expectations of the Government. The University was evaluated for its performance in the 2006-2007 academic year; three out of six colleges were classified as to have met "first class" standards while the three others met "second class" standards.

Certainly, "quality" enables the University to receive government funding as well as to get recognition from the business sector, but "accountability" means more than just guaranteeing "quality". The various stakeholders have competing priorities, which are often at cross-purposes. On one hand, there is a need to train a workforce; while on the other, there are pressures on the system to maintain high standards. The full impact of this "accountability" pressure has forced the University to compete in order to obtain prestige and recognition.

Competition

VNU-Hanoi faces competition on three main fronts: student enrolments, faculty retention, and private sector institutions. Many departments of VNU-Hanoi still see themselves as part of one of the most prestigious institutions in Vietnam and therefore facing little or no competition. In interviews, officials noted that VNU-Hanoi, like other postsecondary institutions, is facing intensifying competition from domestic institutions as well as trans-national institutions. VNU-Hanoi is facing more competition from similar public HEIs than from private HEIs. In pursuit of institutional prestige, being able to recruit good students certainly plays a vital role. In addition to direct competition for students, VNU-Hanoi has been experiencing a "domestic brain drain" and a "brain gain" at the same time. With much better financial compensation, private HEIs are attracting high-quality teaching staff from public HEIs, including those of VNU-Hanoi. VNU-Hanoi is also attracting teaching staff from other public universities due to its resources and standing in the prestige hierarchy. Staff appraisal and rewards aim to promote "excellence", "accountability" and "performance", and at the same time encourage internal competition among faculties and departments. Professional press management and public relations are a vital part of this process. There is clearly an integrated corporate culture that has been adopted by and nurtured at the VNU-Hanoi.

CONCLUSION

This study found that Vietnam's national marketization policies have been accepted and implemented thoroughly at VNU-Hanoi. The market strategies employed by the University were not only to explore additional non-state financial resources but also to improve performance and effectiveness of the University. Some common characteristics of marketization were displayed clearly at the University, including diversified income strategies, cost-effective operations, institutional autonomy and a corporate culture.

In the context of reform, VNU-Hanoi has changed from a bureaucratic environment to an autonomous organization with a strong and expedient central decision-making body able to react to expanding and changing market conditions. This is consistent with the findings of a similar recent study by Mok (2008) that examined the reforms in China and Vietnam. The absence of representatives of other sectors within VNU-Hanoi such as the students' union raises concerns about the balance of power.

In addition, an integrated corporate culture was nurtured at VNU-Hanoi by the use of performance-related measures, by means of incentives and rewards for success, and by appropriate internal and external publicity. The University has become more ambitious, more flexible and needs-driven in order to change its capacities; it has demonstrated a market consciousness by having active units in both mainstream academic and specific fields in order to respond to market needs.

The leaders and administrators of the University are still not comfortable with the term "marketization" or are not aware of what "marketization" really means. Yet the prominence of tuition fees, the commercialization of research activities, the expansion of student enrolment, the consulting services and university-industry partnerships, as well as the adoption of corporate culture have clearly demonstrated that VNU-Hanoi has been experiencing the process of marketization.

Future studies might test Rose's (1991) theory on lesson drawing to examine the process of the development of the higher education policies in Vietnam and across the region. Further study on the impact of these policy and institutional changes on student and parent expectations, faculty life, administration, and organizational behaviour is called for. There are larger geo-political economic implications that need to be examined; as these national marketization policies and resultant implementations are dramatically changing the face—and one might even say the very definition—of communism.

REFERENCES

Altbach, P. (2002). Knowledge and education as international commodities: The collapse of the common good. *International Higher Education*, 28, 2–5.

Bevir, M., Rhodes, R., & Weller, P. (2003). Traditions of governance: Interpreting the changing role of the public sector. *Public Administration*, 81(1), 1-17.

Christensen, T., Laegreid, P., & Wise, L. (2002): Transforming administrative policy. *Public Administration*, 80/1, 153-178.

Clark, B. (1998). *Creating entrepreneurial universities: Organisational pathways of transformations*. Oxford: Pergamon.

Creswell, J. (2005). *Educational Research: Planning, Conducting, and Evaluating Quantitative and Qualitative Research*. Second Edition. New Jersey: Pearson Education International.

Dill, D. (2003). Allowing the market to rule: The case of the United States. *Higher Education Quarterly*, 57(2),136-157.

Fox, C. (2002). The massification of higher education. In D. Hayes and R. Wynyard (Eds.), *The McDonaldization of Higher Education*, pp. 129-142. Westport and London: Bergin & Carvey.

Giroux, H. (2002). Neoliberalism, corporate culture, and the promise of higher education: The university as a democratic public sphere. *Harvard Educational Review*, 72(4), 425-463.

Government of Vietnam (1997). *Government Resolution Number 90/CP dated 21/801997 on orientations and policy of socialization of activities in education, healthcare and culture*. Hanoi: GOV.

Government of Vietnam (1999). *Nghị định của Chính phủ Số 73/1999/N<ETH>-CP ngày 19 thang 8 năm 1999 về chính sách khuyến khích xã hội hoá đối với các hoạt động trong lĩnh vực giáo dục, y tế, văn hóa, thể thao* [Governmental Decree 73/1999 dated 19/8/1999 on Socialization policies of activities in health care, education, culture, sports]. Hanoi: GOV.

Government of Vietnam (2005). *Quyết định của Thủ tướng Chính phủ ngày 17/01/2005 về việc ban hành Quy chế tổ chức và hoạt động của trường đại học tư thục* [Decision 14/2005/QD-TTg by Prime Minister dated 17/01/2005 on the Issuance of regulations on organization and operations of the private universities]. Hanoi: GOV

Gray, A. & Jenkins, B. (1995): From public administration to public management: Reassessing a revolution? *Public Administration*, 73, 75-99.

Hanson, M. E. (1992). Educational marketing and the public schools: policies, practices and problems. *Educational Policy*, 6(1), 19-34.

Hood, C. (1995). The 'new public management' in the 1980s: Variations on a theme. *Accounting, Organizations and Society*, 20(2-3), 93-109.

Jackson, P. (2001): Public sector added value: Can bureaucracy deliver? *Public Administration*, 79(1), 5-28.

Johnstone, D. (1998). Worldwide reforms in the financing and management of higher education. Paper prepared for the UNESCO World Conference on Higher Education. Retrieved on the 20th of December 2008 from:

http://www.gse.buffalo.edu/org/inthigheredfinance/textForSite/ReformsFin
ManHEdWor.pdf

Johnstone, D., Arora, A., & Experton, W. (1998). *The financing and management of higher education: A status report on worldwide reforms.* Washington, DC: World Bank.

Lynch, K. (2006). Neo-liberalism and marketization: the implications for higher education. *European Educational Research Journal*, 5(1), 1-17.

Marginson, S., & Considine, M. (2000). *The enterprise university: Power, governance and reinvention in Australia.* Cambridge: Cambridge University Press.

Mok, K. (2008) .When Socialism Meets Market Capitalism: challenges for privatizing and marketizing education in China and Vietnam, *Policy Futures in Education*, 6(5), 601-615. http://dx.doi.org/10.2304/pfie.2008.6.5.601

Mok, K. & Lo, H. (2002). Marketization and the changing governance in higher education: A comparative study. *Higher Education Management and Policy*, 14(1).

National Assembly of SRV, (2005). *Nghị quyết về giáo dục số 37/2004/QH11* [Decision on Education of the National Assembly No. 37/2004/QH11. Hanoi].

Olssen, M. & Peters, M. (2005). Neoliberalism, higher education and the knowledge economy: from the free market to knowledge capitalism. *Journal of Education Policy*, 20(3), 313-345.

Pham, L. & Fry, G. (2002). The Emergence of Private Higher Education in Vietnam: Challenges and Opportunities. *Educational Research for Policy and Practice*, 1, 127-141

Roberson, R. & Dale, R. (2000). Competitive contractualism: A new social settlement in New Zealand education. In D. Coulby, R. Cowen and C. Jones (Eds.), *World Yearbook of Education 2000: Education in Times of Transition*, pp.116-131. Cheltenham and Northampton, MA: Kogan Page.

Rose, R. (1991). What is lesson-drawing? *Journal of Public Policy*. 11(1), p. 3-30

Salminen, A. (2003). New public management and Finnish public sector organizations: the case of universities. In A. Amaral, V. Lynn Meek and I. M. Larsen (Eds.), *The Higher Education Managerial Revolution?* Dordrecht, Boston, London: Kluwer Academic Publishers, 2003

Silverman, D. (2005). *Doing Qualitative Research.* Second Edition. London: Sage Publications.

Slaughter, S. and Leslie, L. L. (1997). *Academic Capitalism: Politics, Policies, and the Entrepreneurial University.* Baltimore and London: The Johns Hopkins University Press.

Theisens, H. (2004.) *The State of Change. Analysing Policy Change in Dutch and English Higher Education.* Enschede: Center for Higher Education and Policy Studies (CHEPS).

Tilak, J. (2005a). Global Trends in the Funding of Higher Education. *IAU Horizons*, 11(1).

Tilak, J. (2005b). Are we marching toward laissez-faireism in higher education development? *Journal of International Cooperation in Education*, 8(1), 153-165

UNESCO, (2006). *Higher Education in Southeast Asia*. Bangkok: UNESCO.

Welch, A. (1998). The cult of efficiency in education: Comparative reflection on the reality and the rhetoric. *Comparative Education*, 34(2), 157-175.

Yin, R. (1994). *Case Study Research: Design and methods*. Second Edition. Thousand Oaks, CA: Sage Publications.

CHAPTER 10

Does Globalization have an Impact on the Education System in Malaysia?

Norasmah Othman

INTRODUCTION

Education has always been seen as the key towards achieving development in Malaysia. However, globalization has led to changes in education in the last decade of the 20th century [1]. Stromquist argued that globalization fostered considerable demand for higher education throughout the world, as greater levels of remuneration accrue at higher levels of education [2]. Therefore, it is vital to look into how globalization has impacted the education in Malaysia, especially towards higher education.

This paper aims to identify how globalization has impacted education in Malaysia, especially in the field of demand for education, internationalization, lifelong learning, and generic skills, particularly in higher education. Comparisons were made in these four aspects: education demand, internationalization, lifelong learning, and generic skills, before and after globalization, which will indicate how globalization has impacted the education system in Malaysia.

Globalization and Education

Globalization of the education system has become a normal phenomenon, especially in a developing country such as Malaysia. In order to compete in a globally competitive economy, the education system of a nation needs to be able to fulfill the demands of the economic sector, in terms of knowledge and skillful workers. Global forces such as international economies, international political struggles, and global communication systems have affected the institution of higher learning [3]. Therefore, Higher Education Institutions (HEIs) need to respond to the changes of the globalizing world to be able to meet the political, economic, and social demands.

For a country to be globally competitive, the development of human capital is essential. Education can be viewed as a capital good, which is used to developing human resources for economic and social transformation [4]. Globalization forces, especially in the development of technology, have resulted in the increase in the need of knowledge and skillful workers [5]. These have resulted into the transformation of the institutions of higher learning, which are the pillars in producing k-workers for a developing nation, such as Malaysia.

The transformation of institutions of higher education has been revealed through The National Higher Education Strategic Plan Beyond 2020, which provides a framework through which actions can be taken to produce human capital with first class mentality. The strategic plan has identified seven thrusts, through which the process of strengthening and revolutionizing higher education can take place. The seven thrusts are: widening access and increasing equity; improving the quality of teaching and learning; enhancing research and innovation; strengthening higher education institutions; intensifying internationalization; enculturation of lifelong learning; and reinforcing the delivery systems of the Ministry of Higher Education [5]. It is hoped that institutions of higher education can lay the foundation towards improving the nations competitive edge in various aspects, especially in human capital development who are competitive and resilient.

PROBLEM STATEMENT

Malaysia launched its national policy known as Vision 2020 by Dato' Seri Dr. Mahathir Mohammed in 1991, which has been created to aspire Malaysians towards achieving the status of a developed nation by 2020. However, recent global political and economic events have affected the global economy, which has produced some negative impact on this country. These negative impacts have resulted into a slow economic downfall in Malaysia, as well as has increased the competition with other countries in Southeast Asia, especially Vietnam, Singapore, Indonesia, and Thailand. To ensure that Malaysia is resilient in facing the world's economic uncertainties and in facing its competitors, Malaysia needs to revamp its education system to ensure that it is able to produce highly skilled human capital. Malaysia has realized that its education system must be globally competitive, with an emphasis in the quality of producing a workforce, who will be able to lead Malaysia through the threats of globalization. Not only is globalization to be viewed as negative, but it is also to be seen as an opportunity for Malaysia to expand and participate in world's economic events.

Globalization has caused the demand for a "world class human capital" [6]. It is essential to make sure that the institutions of higher education can provide sufficient and quality knowledge as well as the skills needed to enable a Malaysian workforce to be a "world class human capital" [6]. Due to this fact, it is essential to identify how globalization has affected the education in Malaysia, especially the trend in the education demand, internationalization, lifelong learning, and generic skills.

METHODOLOGY

This study aims to identify the trends in the demand for institutions of higher education, internationalization, lifelong learning, and generic skills before and after 1995. The population of this study is administrators from public and private institutions of higher education in Malaysia, whereby they were chosen because of their awareness of the changes in policies in higher education as well as their experience in an administrative role. The population of this study includes Vice Chancellors, Directors, Deans, Deputy Deans, and Heads of Departments. The number of the population identified is 1073 from a total of 20 public and 32 private institutions of higher education. The 31 private institutions of higher education consist of private universities and college universities (26), and five branches of foreign universities from all over Malaysia. The list of private institutions of higher education was obtained from MOHE. A total number of 285 samples were needed, but 288 samples were randomly selected for this study. The number of samples selected was determined by using the Table for determining sample size from a given population by Krejcie & Morgan [7]. The were randomly selected, which is an important requirement to enable that the results obtained can be generalized to its population [7; 8].

This study was conducted by using the survey method, whereby the trend in the demands for higher education, internationalization, lifelong learning, and generic skills before 1995 and after 1995 were surveyed based on the perception of administrators in institutions of higher education. A questionnaire was used as instrument to obtain data. The items in the questionnaire were self-developed by the team of researchers using a document analysis technique. Three important documents, which were used to identify the items in the questionnaire, are [5], [9] and [10]. A pilot test was conducted using 30 samples [7] to test all the items under four aspects, namely for the demand for education, internationalization, lifelong learning, and generic skills. The Cronbach Alpha value obtained was 0.853, which was high [7; 8]. The questionnaires consist of five parts, Part One includes three questions, namely, the type of institutions represented by the respondent, the number of years in service, and the title of the posts held. Part Two consists of 34 items based on four aspects as mentioned earlier. There are nine items for the aspects of the demand of education, ten items for internationalization, seven items for life long learning, and eight items for generic skills.

A total of 600 questionnaires were distributed, but only 288 of the questionnaires can be analyzed, which is sufficient based on the number of samples required. Based on the experience of researchers during the data collection process, "busy" has been the most common reason given by respondents in their lack of response in completing the questionnaires. Questionnaires were distributed using the postal service, and some were personally distributed by the researchers. All of the 34 items were measured using the seven point numerical scale [8] with one being indicated as the least important and seven being indicated as having the most importance. Respondents were asked to indicate the importance of all the items before 1995 and after 1995. The year 1995 has been set as the benchmark for globalization for this study as it was the year Malaysia became a member of the World Trade Organization (WTO). It is an organization, which administers international trade and has 120 members. Verger indicated that countries which became members of WTO agreed upon liberalization of trade by signing up General Agreement of Tariffs and Trade (GATT) [11]. According to Verger, the liberalization of twelve sectors were agreed upon, including education. Even if Malaysia did not participate in the liberalization of the education sector, by signing up GATT and through WTO, Malaysia officially became a member of an organization that promotes globalization through free trade, indicating the era of globalization for Malaysia. Therefore, 1995 is used as the "cutting off point" to measure globalization.

Data obtained were analyzed using the inferential statistics method, a method that uses paired-sample t test, at the significant value of p< 0.05. Each items for all four aspects, which are demand education, internationalization, lifelong learning and generic skills, were compared with two independent variables before and after 1995. Data were processed using SPSS for Windows Version 18.0.

FINDINGS AND DISCUSSIONS

This study aims to find out if globalization affects the trend in the demand for education, internationalization, lifelong learning, and generic skills before and after 1995. 1995 is the year chosen to mark globalization for Malaysia due to its participation in WTO. Findings and discussion will be discusses in accordance to the findings made as presented in Table 1, 2, 3 and 4.

Table 1: Trend in Demand for Education before and after 1995

Education Field	n	mean	df	t	sig.p
Vocational Education before 1995	288	4.91	287	-6.69	0.000*
Vocational Education after 1995	288	5.48			
Technical Education before 1995	288	5.17	287	-10.86	0.000*
Technical Education after 1995	288	5.91			
Computer & ICT Education before 1995	288	4.91	287	-6.91	0.000*
Computer & ICT Education before 1995	288	6.24			
Business & Entrepreneurship Education before 1995	288	4.80	287	-20.00	0.000*
Business & Entrepreneurship Education before 1995	288	6.24			
Biotech/Agrotech Education before 1995	288	4.16			
Biotech/Agrotech Education after 1995	288	6.01	287	-19.63	0.000*
Agriculture Education before 1995	288	5.01	287	-3.80	0.000*
Agriculture Education after 1995	288	5.36			
Professional Education before 1995	288	5.88	287	-10.45	0.000*
Professional Education after 1995	288	6.45			
Teachers' Education before 1995	286	5.65	285	-5.12	0.000*
Teachers' Education after 1995	286	5.98			
Social Sciences Education before 1995	288	4.97	287	-6.01	0.000*
Social Sciences Education after 1995	288	5.44			
Sig at p<0.05					

Table 1 shows the findings made on the trend in the demand for education before and after 1995. Overall, results show that there is an increase in the demand for all fields of education, whereby the significant values for all education fields are p<0.05. The greatest increase can be seen in the demand for business and entrepreneurship education, with t (288) = -20.00, p< 0.005. The increase in the demand for biotechnology and agro-technology education showed a high increase with t (288) = -19.6. These are all in par with efforts made by the government of Malaysia to promote entrepreneurship skills as well as to introduce Malaysia as the next biotech hub [12]. Entrepreneurship education and the development in the field of biotechnology and agro-technology will help the country achieve the status of a developing county by 2020. The nation needs entrepreneurs and scientists, who are resilient to the uncertainty of the global market, as well as a brilliant human capital with new and innovative ideas, which will give the country a competitive edge. The lowest increase can be seen in the demand for agriculture education, which showed a low increase with the mean scores of 5.01 before 1995 to only 5.36 after 1995. Despite the increase, it is not much, which is a concerning factor. Malaysia has traditionally depended on agriculture as one main source of income, but lately, Malaysia has been depending heavily on foreign labors in the agricultural field. Efforts must be made to increase the demand for agriculture education.

Table 2: Internationalization Trend before and after 1995

Internationalization	n	mean	df	t	sig. p
LAN/MQA before 1995	286	4.02	286	-23.85	0.000*
LAN/MQA after 1995	286	6.20			
ISO before 1995	286	4.13	286	-18.21	0.000*
ISO after 1995	286	5.79			
English Language before 1995	287	5.28	286	-13.95	0.000*
English Language before 1995	287	6.38			
International Language before 1995	287	4.59	286	-5.62	0.000*
International Language before 1995	287	5.67			
MOUs before 1995	287	4.45	286		0.000*
MOUs after 1995	287	6.19		-23.23	
Student mobility before 1995	287	4.27	286	-21.59	0.000*
Student mobility after 1995	287	5.99			
Credit transfer before 1995	287	4.25	286	-19.95	0.000*
Credit transfer after 1995	287	5.86			
Research & Development before 1995	287	4.62	286	-21.34	0.000*
Research & Development after 1995	287	6.29			
Foreign student intake before 1995	287	3.89	286	-25.761	0.000*
Foreign student Intake after 1995	287	6.07			
Sig at p<0.05					

Table 2 summarizes the findings made about the trend of internationalization before 1995 and after 1995. Once again, the findings indicate there is great difference in the demand for internationalization after 1995 compared to before 1995. In an increasing interdependent world, with the expansion of communication networks, all these have made international experience necessary [13], especially in the field of higher education. Besides, with the availability of equipments, expertise, research facilities, and infrastructure, as well as the educational mobility involving students, academicians, and scholarships [13], internationalization of education has become unavoidable. The findings indicate that the biggest difference can be seen in the intake of foreign students with t (286) = -25.76, p<0.005. However, this is nothing new. As stated by Bruch and Barty, for centuries students have travelled to other countries to broaden their learning and widen their cultural horizons [13]. Despite this, internationalization has been intensified by globalization, which can be seen in the results of the findings made by this study. The greatest mean increase can be seen in the practice of foreign students' intake in the education system in Malaysia before and after 1995, followed by an emphasis in quality, through the implementation of Malaysian Qualification Accreditation. To attract more foreign students, the element of quality is a competitive edge. The memorandum of understandings with foreign countries' universities and organizations showed a significant increase with t (286) = - 23.23, p<0.005. All this shows that internationalization of HEIs are now being given greater emphasis.

Table 3: Trend in Lifelong Learning before and after 1995

Lifelong Learning	n	mean	df	t	sig.p
Postgraduate education before 1995	288	4.30	287	-25.71	0.000*
Postgraduate education after 1995	288	6.23			
Masters education before 1995	287	4.44	286	-22.71	0.000*
Masters education after 1995	287	6.26			
Doctorate Education before 1995	285	4.26	284	-23.46	0.000*
Doctorate Education before 1995	285	6.24			
Adult students before 1995	287	4.08			0.000*
Adult students before 1995	287	5.74	286	-21.21	
Virtual education before 1995	286	3.43			
Virtual education after 1995	286	5.54	285	-23.23	0.000*
Long distance education before 1995	287	3.96	286	-18.46	0.000*
Long distance education after 1995	287	5.68			
Online education before 1995	288	3.42	287	-23.45	0.000*
Online education after 1995	288	5.74			
Sig at p<0.05					

Table 3 shows the result of the trend on lifelong learning before and after 1995. As expected, overall, there is a high increase for all the elements of lifelong learning after 1995, especially in the trend of postgraduate studies, which shows t (288) = - 25.71. The increase in the demand for masters and doctorate education supports findings made in the increase in postgraduate education. This increase does indicate that globalization has made a difference to the trend of lifelong learning, as indicated by Coulby, who stated that knowledge based economy has become the base of the world economy today [14]. Therefore, to produce human capital for the workforce, lifelong learning has become an important agenda to institutions of higher learning, which can be seen through the increase in the numbers of students enrolling in postgraduate studies. The availability of Information and Communication technology too has encouraged lifelong learning. Moravec wrote that communications technologies have broadened the scope and size of HEIs market reach, and it is replacing face-to-face classroom contact [15]. This is true, as the trend now is virtual and online experience of learning, with the wide use e-learning and mobile learning methods, even the use of Social Networks, such as Twitter and Skype, are being absorbed into HEIs.

Table 4: Trend in Instilling Generic Skills before and after 1995

Generic Skills	n	mean	df	t	sig. p
Effective communication skills before 1995	288	4.77	287	-20.73	0.000*
Effective communication skills after 1995	288	6.33			
Critical Thinking and problem solving skills before 1995	288	4.86	287	-19.91	0.000*
Critical Thinking and problem solving skills after 1995	288	6.40			
Teamwork before 1995	288	4.94	287	-17.78	0.000*
Teamwork before 1995	288	6.34			
Continuous learning and information management skills before 1995	288	4.77		-20.07	0.000*
Continuous learning and information management skills before 1995	288	6.22	287		
Entrepreneurial Skills before 1995	288	4.47	287		
Entrepreneurial Skills after 1995	288	6.22		-21.26	0.000*
Ethical and moral professional skills before 1995	288	5.00	287	-14.44	0.000*
Ethical and moral professional skills after 1995	288	6.15			
Management Skills before 1995	288	4.93	287	-17.13	0.000*
Management Skills after 1995	288	6.19			
Leadership Skill before 1995	260	4.98	259	-14.96	0.000*
Leadership Skills after 1995	260	4.98			
Sig at p<0.05					

Table 4 shows the trend in instilling generic skills before and after 1995. Results show a significance difference in the trend of instilling generic skills before and after 1995, whereby all skills show a significant value of p<0.05. Instilling entrepreneurship skills show the higher increase with t (288) = -21.26, p<0.005. This finding is in par the findings made earlier, whereby there has been an increase in the demand for entrepreneurship and business education, which can be seen in Table 1. Besides that, continuous learning and information management skills show a significant difference before and after 1995, with t (288) = -20.07, p < 0.05. In the era of globalization, lifelong learning skills are essential for individuals to be able to compete with others [12]. Knowledge workers who are creative, innovative, and competitive [5] can be developed by instilling generic skills. The implementation of generic skills is in line with the second thrust of the National Mission, where Malaysia needs to produce human capital with first class mentality in order to face challenges in the knowledge based economy and the innovation field [5].

It can be summarized that globalization has increased the demand for education, internationalization, lifelong learning, and generic skills. All these are important aspects of higher education because institutions of higher education are responsible in developing human capitals that will gear the country towards meeting the challenges of globalization and lead Malaysia towards achieving Vision 2020. Therefore, indirectly, globalization has impacted education in Malaysia, in all four of the aspects mentioned.

CONCLUSION

Based on the results obtained, the realization that education is the key towards becoming a developed country and to produce manpower, who can compete and be resilient towards the challenges of globalization, can be seen clearly. The findings made show an increasing trend in the demand for education, internationalization, lifelong learning, and generic skills after 1995 when compared to before 1995. One of the limitations of this study is the data are gathered from the perspective of administrators in HEIs. To further strengthen the findings, perception of parents or households, as well as perception of students should also viewed. This will allow comparisons to be made. The perception of employers should also be taken into consideration on what they think the current trends in the demand for higher education should be.

REFERENCES

1. Ministry of Education, *Education in Malaysia: A journey to excellence*, Educational Planning and Research Division, 2008.
2. Stromquist, N.P., The impact of globalization on education and gender: an emergent cross-national balance, *Journal Of Education*, Vol 31, 2005, pp. 7–37.
3. Rahmah Ismail & Nor Aini Idris, "Globalisasi dan daya saing global: satu tinjauan. Pembangunan sumber manusia dalam era k-ekonomi" in Pembangunan Sum- ber Manusia dalam Era K-Ekonomi, Rahmah Ismail, Nor Aini Idris, Razak Mohd, Eds. Bangi: Penerbit Univer- siti Kebangsaan, 2007, pp. 17–32.
4. Olaniyan, D.A. & Okemakinde, T., Human capital theory; implication for educational development, *European Journal of Scientific Research.* Vol 24, No 2, pp. 157–162, 2008.
5. Ministry of Higher Education, *The national higher education strategic plan beyond 2020*, MOHE, 2007.
6. Malaysia, *10ᵗʰ Malaysia plan 2011–2015*, Percetakan Nasional, 2011.
7. Chua Y. P., *Kaedah dan statistik penyelidikan: kaedah penyelidikan buku 1*, McGraw Hill Education, 2006.
8. Hair, J.F.Jr., Money, A.H., Samouel, P. & Page, M., *Research methods for business*, John Wiley & Sons Ltd, 2007.
9. Ministry of Higher Education Malaysia, Modul Pembangunan Kemahiran Insaniah (Soft Skills) Untuk Institusi Pengajian Tinggi Malaysia, Serdang: Penerbit UPM, 2006.
10. Ministry of Higher Education, *The statistics of higher education in Malaysia*, MOHE, 2010.
11. Verger, A., The merchants of education: global politics and the uneven education liberalization process within WTO, *Comparative Education Review.* Vol 53, No 3, pp. 379–401, 2009.
12. Malaysia, *9ᵗʰ Malaysia plan 2006–2010*, Percetakan Nasional, 2006.
13. T. Bruch and A.Barty, "Internationalizing British higher education: students and institutions," in The Globalization Of Higher Education, P. Scott, Eds. Buckingham: The Society for Research into Higher Education, pp. 18–31, 2000.
14. D. Coulby, "The knowledge economy: technology and charactersitic," in *Globalization And Nationalism In Eduction*, D. Coulby and E. Zambetta, Eds. Oxon: RoutledgeFalmer, pp. 23–36, 2005.
15. J.W. Moravec,: A new paradigm of knowledge production in higher education," On *The Horizon*, Vol. 16, No 3, 2008, pp. 123–136.

CHAPTER 11

Globalization, Middle-class Formation, and "Quality" Education: Hyper-competition in Istanbul, Turkey

Henry J. Rutz and Erol M. Balkan

> *The social world is accumulated history ... one must reintroduce into it the notion of capital and with it, accumulation and all its effects.*
> – Pierre Bourdieu[1]

When British Prime Minister Tony Blair was asked at a recent press conference about the value of education in today's global economy, he responded gamely, "the more you learn, the more you earn." Middle-class families, especially in globalizing cities around the world, from London to Bombay and New York to Istanbul, have awakened to the belief that the latest round of world capitalist accumulation, termed globalization,2 constitutes a fundamental shift in their ability to provide their children with a comfortable life.

The new knowledge- based industries, along with the general commodification of culture and the increased growth in cultural products and cultural industries, have placed a premium on accumulation of social and cultural capital.[3] Chief among the forms of cultural capital is quality education. This paper identifies the problem of middle-class reproduction in terms of the competition for quality education.[4] It is about competition within the middle class and increasing differentiation between a fraction known as the New Middle Class and the older core middle class of industrial corporate and public administrative managers and other professionals. Rapid increase in the demand for quality education has created hyper-competition over access to the *best* schools among families within and between these fractions.

---

[1] Pierre Bourdieu, "The Forms of Capital," in *Education: Culture, Economy, and Society*, edited by A.H. Halsey, Hugh Lauder, Phillip Brown, and Amy Stuart Wells. New York: Oxford University Press, 1997. 46.

[2] Thomas C. Lewellen, *The Anthropology of Globalization*, Westport, CT: Bergin & Garvey, 2002. 7-8. Lewellen's definition of globalization is "the increasing flow of trade, finance, culture, ideas, and people brought about by the sophisticated technology of communications and travel and by the worldwide spread of neo-liberal capitalism, and it is the local and regional adaptations to and resistances against these flows."

[3] Pierre Bourdieu, 46-48.

[4] Dennis Gilbert, *The American Class Structure*, United States, Thomson-Wadsworth, 2003. 8, refers to class as "groupings of people according to their economic position." A *social* class "becomes a group of people who share the same economically shaped life chances." The economic position of the middle class in a class structure refers to an economic position based *primarily* on expert knowledge and higher education credentials as opposed to possession of capital or manual labor.

While there would appear to be a global trend in economic, social, and cultural differentiation within the middle class, accompanied everywhere by a crisis of access to quality education, the dynamics of middle-class formation can only be understood within local contexts where the contingencies of economic and cultural history can be taken into account.[5] This paper focuses on within-class competition among families in the globalizing city of Istanbul, Turkey.

ECONOMIC LIBERALIZATION AND A CRISIS OF QUALITY EDUCATION

Between 1950 and 1980, an aim of Turkish state economic development policies was protection of fledgling domestic manufacturing industries. By the end of the 1970s, there was a recognizable mass middle class that provided professional, managerial and technical services for the first generation of a national industrial bourgeoisie.[6] Economic policy had shifted away from protectionism to global integration in ways that were sudden and dramatic. After 1980, the state abandoned protectionist policies and ushered in policies that deregulated financial and export markets, initiated privatization of some industries and institutions, and put large numbers of middle-class families at risk by diminishing the role of government in providing public health and education benefits for middle-class families. The new development strategy mainly emphasized production for export. Export-oriented production received special government credits while anti-labor policies kept costs low, allowing export companies to increase their competitiveness in world markets.[7] Lower wages also contributed to the objective of reducing internal consumption to create a surplus of goods for export.

Turkey's liberalization episode, as its experience with economic integration has been called, [8] resulted in profound changes in middle- class welfare and social consciousness. What actually happened? By the end of the first decade of liberalization, and continuing throughout the 1990s, there were clear indications of worsening economic conditions for most of the old or core middle-class fraction, made up primarily of public servants or corporate middle-level managers. This fraction found itself in a serious crisis of falling real income, inflated prices, shaky investments, and added tax burdens.[9] In contrast, a combination of old professional, managerial, and business families along with new economy entrepreneurs were

---

[5] Regardless of whether diversity is defined in terms of human capital that focuses on individual embodied capacity or communal social or cultural capital, the meanings and mechanisms of diversity are shaped through class competition and/or conflict.

[6] See Ayse Bugra, "Late Coming Tycoons in Turkey," *Journal of Economics and Administrative Studies* 1, 1987. Bugra examines the interplay among state, corporation, and family in the rise of a Turkish bourgeoisie.

[7] Erol Balkan and Erinc Yeldan, "Turkey," in Financial Reform in Developing Countries, edited by Jose Fanelli and Rohinton Medhora, New York: St. Martin's Press, 1995. 129-55.

[8] Yilmaz Akyuz, "Financial Liberalization: The Key Issues," in Finance and the Real Economy: Issues and Case Studies, edited by Y. Akyuz and G. Held, Santiago de Chile: United Nations/WIDER/ECLA, 1995. Tosun Aricanli and Dani Rodrik, The Political Economy of Turkey, London and New York: McMillan, 1990. Tevfik Nas and Mehmet Odekon, Liberalization and the Turkish Economy, New York: Greenwood, 1988.

[9] Balkan and Yeldan, see footnote 6.

situated to take advantage of income and wealth-generating opportunities. Some were able to enriched themselves, moving into the capitalist class. Opportunities were especially good in newly emerging sectors such as financial services and investment banking, insurance, media and entertainment, and tourism and advertising. People who had the right education and social connections could find their way into those industries that were most closely associated with Turkey's integration in the emerging global economy.

The process of economic global integration was generating new demand for credentials, especially a degree from one of a handful of Turkey's prestigious universities and/or a degree from a prestigious foreign university. Speaking a foreign language, especially English, became a New Middle Class necessity in the 1980s. The Istanbul Republican upper and upper-middle class had absorbed a cosmopolitan culture partly inherited from its blending of late Ottoman and nineteenth century European elements. Education was a major vehicle for institutionalizing this culture. But global economic integration after 1980 internationalized and valorised domestically the foreign-ness of Turkish elites to a degree that was previously unknown. Large numbers of new aspirants to elite schools that instructed in foreign language underwrote the cultural capital of middle- class families to a point where this education became a part of the consciousness of belonging to a transformed upper middle-class fraction. [10] The vast majority of the older core middle class families desired to emulate this New Middle Class but possessed neither the social capital nor knowledge or credentials to compete for the best jobs being created in the most dynamic sectors of the new economy. These families were losing more than their standard of living. They were becoming déclassé and in danger of losing a hegemon of national culture that was part of the most cherished Republican ideals of equity, national unity, and service demanded of cultural elites since the Founding of the Republic in 1923.

The Turkish Republic's national cultural tradition had viewed public education as the bedrock of reformism and egalitarianism underlying its unification. Education policies of the liberalization period departed from previous policies in three important ways that helped to change middle-class families' aspirations, harden social fault lines among middle- class fractions, and lead to ferocious hyper-competition for quality education that would place their children in the best schools. [11]

First, the state reduced education expenditures. In keeping with the neo-liberal ideology of reducing all social expenditures, there was a reduction over the period 1980-94. Overcrowding, poor teacher training, fewer teachers attracted to the profession, and inadequacy of textbooks are some of the concrete shortcomings that appeared when the reduction of expenditures became cumulative.

---

[10] Leslie Sklair, The Transnational Capitalist Class, Oxford: Blackwell Publishers, 2001. Deniz Kandiyotti and Ayse Saktanber, editors, Fragments of Culture: The Everyday of Modern Turkey, New Brunswick: Rutgers University Press, 2002. "The Emerging Middle Class," Business Week, Special Issue, 21st Century Capitalism, November 18, 1994. 176-192.

[11] Most of the best schools, especially in primary and secondary education, were in Istanbul.

Second, the liberalization policy promoted private investment in education at all levels.[12] As the public system crumbled, middle-class households increasingly came to the realization that private education represented their only viable alternative. The result was an increase in the demand for private education. Paradoxically, state policies subsidized new private schools, creating incentives for education entrepreneurs. Private investment flowed into education at all levels.[13] Deregulating and subsidizing the development of privatized education was welcomed by upper middle-class families, who could afford to shoulder the financial burden of providing quality education. It was received with less enthusiasm by middle-class families who aspired to quality education but found the price prohibitive.

Third, and most importantly for the subject of this paper, the state co-opted the existing school-centered system of selection for places in the best schools by replacing it with selection solely by score on a standardized national test that was controlled and regulated by the state. In effect, the state social engineered, at least in part, the size of the new middle class that was coming into being. Because elite education is the major path to the best jobs and hence to material comfort and social status in Turkish society, it also is constitutive of what it means to be *middle class*.[14]

TEST ENGINEERS AND TEST MACHINES

The education policies of the liberalization episode not only put onto the shoulders of middle-class families a greater financial burden, they also demanded a greater investment of time and effort in the accumulation of human capital. In Turkey, the pivotal point of the system for determining future success was at the end of primary school and the beginning of middle school, when the national tests for selective middle schools, public and private, were given to primary children between the ages of eleven and twelve.[15] Hyper-competition was in large part an artefact of the way in which the State chose to engineer its selective middle school national tests as a selection-out system (rather than a selection-in system) and how families

---

[12] Yakup Kepenek and Nurhan Yenturk, Turkiye Ekonomisi, Istanbul: Remzi Publishers, 1996. 349-350
[13] Kepenek and Yenturk, 349-350. By 1994, nearly a quarter of total education investment in the GDP was private, up from 4% a decade earlier.
[14] Out of a cohort of primary age children totalling about 3,000,000, only 300,000 registered for the national test in 1996. Approximately 1,000,000 high school students take the annual university entrance examination. Of these, only 100,000 gain entrance to university. These figures for success must be tempered by knowledge that Istanbul families would consider only a fraction of these places "quality education."
[15] The presumption of parents is that being educated in the best middle schools increases the later probability of winning a place in the best universities. Based on the 1996 national university entrance examinations results for the top fifteen schools in each type of middle school, Istanbul public middle school entrants comprised 76% (42,239 of 55,277) of the total entrants yet placed less than 5% in universities. In contrast, foreign private middle school entrants had the highest success rate by placing 80% of their entrants in universities. The top Anadolu public schools were also competitive, placing 69% of their students in universities. This performance was followed by that of the top Turk private middle schools instructing in a foreign language, which placed 63% of their entrants in universities. Since the examinations are given in the Turkish language, the poor performance of public high schools is even more glaring.

internalized that system rationality by turning children into test machines during their preparation for what they referred to as *the race*.

There were two separate but similar tests, each with its own student preference and school selection system. One was for public foreign language instruction (Anadolu) schools, the other for private foreign language instruction schools. The State limited the number of school choices for each school type by requiring guardians to register short preference lists. It regulated selection by requiring every private school to establish minimum base points on the test entrance scores and minimum-maximum ranges for every public school. Schools that had the highest minimum base or range points *ipso facto* became known universally as the 'best' schools. Both student scores and school base or range points that reflect student scores were published in national newspapers. Families already know how many places there were in each school they preferred, the minimum or range of scores for each school, their own child's score. From these *objektif* facts they could extrapolate where their child ranked relative to others and the probability of getting into particular schools. It took several months over the summer for the state-regulated 'market' for middle school places to work itself out by the beginning of the next school year.

Families could register a child in one or both tests. In the 1996 national tests, about 300,000 students registered for the national public middle schools test, 30,000 for the private middle schools test. The difference reflected affordability. Almost without exception, Istanbul families preferred selective private foreign schools over all other types, yet the total number of places in these schools, all but one located in Istanbul, were about 1,400, or a probability of 1 in 25. Public selective middle schools had about 30,000 places, or a probability of 1 in 10. The quality of these schools, while preferable to any non-selective public schools, were known to vary widely. There was high agreement on the belief that there were only 5,000 good places in less than 50 schools, lowering the probability of selection to 1 in 100. Because families could register their children for one or both tests, an advantage accrued to middle-class families who could afford private schools, using the best public schools as a safety valve.

State-regulated system rationality was aimed at selection out. The difficulty of State-designed national tests had become well -known to the public and their preparations had become routinized. By 1996 middle-class families had internalized the system rationality of the State. Guardians who registered for the tests considered them *necessary* while at the same time despised them as a system that imposed financial, emotional, and social hardships not only on the test-taker but on every family member, especially the mother. [16] As the number of entrants increased annually, competition intensified. The response to intensification was to move the period for test preparation from the fifth grade back to the fourth grade and, for a growing number of families, to begin preparation in third grade. Most symptomatic, a market emerged for test services that within a few years mushroomed into a test

---

[16] The source for all references to family attitudes, dispositions, and strategies comes from recorded interviews with 26 families, hundreds of informal interviews, and newspaper accounts of this common topic in daily conversation.

industry of tutors, lesson schools, and counselling services which ranged from anxiety management through preference/selection advice to information and management. The high costs of these services relative to average middle-middle class incomes placed core middle-class families at a further disadvantage.

Families were caught between State test engineers and private market entrepreneurs as they became enmeshed in a totalizing standardized system in which children's numerical scores to the third decimal point were converted into a symbolic currency for the reputations of schools, principals, teachers, tutors, and lesson schools—each of which fit into ranked numerical orders of excellence.

The result was that families turned their eleven-year-old children into test machines. *Exam-obsessed mothers* quit their employment or sought leaves of absence to become managers of weekly schedules and routines as mother and child travelled from one education service provider to another. Children became quiet and removed from their playtime and friends to study long hours that included every weekend. Mothers routinely commented that they "took the exam with their child," meaning that they were coerced by teachers, tutors, and lesson teachers to learn all the child's lessons. The engineer and the test machine became one. Families routinely shut their doors to friends, and even to close family members, in violation of all social norms of hospitality, commensality, and sociability. *Winning the test* organized whole families around a single numerical outcome that dominated their daily discourse and social lives.

The whole technology of making a child into a test machine became known as "doping," a pejorative term for rote memorization and the application of technique. Educators and clinical psychologists generally viewed the national tests as a national disaster for child development. The dominant discourse that controlled all conversations of participating agents was an oppositional discourse that pitted the idea of *the test* against the idea of *education*, the former based on technique and memorization, the latter on pedagogy and conceptualization. The contradiction was that all the agents—families, teachers, school administrators, school owners, lesson school teachers, and tutors—came to accept the test as a *fact* and *necessity* even as they embraced the principles of child development and ideals of humane education. The *industry* for producing and managing the test was in the capital of Ankara, separated from the *education* taking place in the schools, but one was very much inside the other. Many poorly paid state school teachers became tutors. Parents extolled the education of the classroom curriculum but paid teachers to favour their child over others and attend to their exam preparation. Status -conscious families worried about other families' preparations, creating an exaggerated importance to market services.

Many families saw the test as a way to maintain or improve class position. Owners of Turk private schools lamented the tests but benefited from them because they were not required to select by the test and could therefore provide a haven for mediocre students from well-off families who could receive special attention or even avoid the tests altogether. These families could acquire the cultural veneer of the upper-middle class that matched their wealth. Tutors preyed on parental anxieties by making exaggerated promises in return for large sums of money when it was not clear who contributed most to the child's preparation.

Modern education has always communicated undercurrents of *improvement* and progressive beliefs as positive values that perform the function of marking individuals and families as morally *worthy*. The education hierarchy in this way reinforced a social hierarchy that gave the middle class its privileged place in the class structure of industrialized society As one dissenting parent with a negative view of the whole process observed, "This race is blown out of proportion, it certainly is not aiming to add anything to a child's education; it is about the competition between husband and wife and one family and another. Children do not keep track of each other's test scores, mothers do, with fathers looking over their shoulder."

CONCLUSION

By 1995, the education crisis of the middle class, among the proximate causes of which economic policies of the liberalization episode figured prominently, had become interiorized as an *examination hell* inside the intimate lives of many Istanbul middle-class families. The examination system, in all its dimensions, had become an objective instrument of struggle between fractions within the middle class, an instrument for drawing increasingly distinct boundaries between a *loser* core middle class and a *winner* new upper middle class. Increasing inequality within the middle-class is only one aspect of cultural conflict in an era of globalization. Issues of social justice and cultural rights generally need to be framed by an awareness of class dynamics.

CHAPTER 12

Higher Education Culture and Changing Framework Conditions

Evanthia Kalpazidou Schmidt

INTRODUCTION

In recent years, higher education has undergone significant changes in a number of European countries. This paper focuses on reforms of the Danish higher education system and a merging process, which have radically changed the legislative and structural framework of higher education with implications on the organisation, autonomy and governance of institutions. Danish higher education is subject to intensive policymaking, as it is perceived in a wider socio-economic context, as an instrument to achieve national objectives responding to globalization challenges.

The most important changes are noticed in the distribution of power among stakeholders in the Danish higher education system with a concentration of power at the top level and a move of power from faculty to other stakeholders. Faculty has lost its influence on decision-making to appointed leaders and external interests. A new higher education culture is emerging, imposed top-down. A key question concerns therefore the effects of the new setting on the higher education culture, the tasks and the working conditions of faculty. Ziman (1991) points out the risks with a model where academia controls the decisions on how to conduct research, but having lost control over the research agenda to external interests. New governance mechanisms and the loss of trust to self-steering ability of faculty - as opposed to strategic decision-making, accountability and assessments - is changing the balance in relation to university leadership and external interests. The balance between the authority of the faculty and the power of leadership is at stake.

Danish faculty has been able, throughout a number of earlier reforms, to keep up this balance and has taken for granted that it is possible to continue "business as usual". The question is whether this is feasible in a completely different set up with appointed leaders and mergers of different types of institutions. Faculty conditions have been radically changed through recent reforms. The pressures on staff are unprecedented and further changes are expected (Kalpazidou Schmidt 2006a).

The Danish Higher Education Framework

The recognition that higher education is a major driver of competitiveness in the global economy has made high quality higher education and research more important than ever. Developing knowledge and building competences for key sectors in the transition to a knowledge-based economy is the subject of intensive policy making and the core of recent higher education reforms in Denmark. Higher education and research policies have primarily focused on efforts to promote quality, efficiency and productivity, as well as links with business, and have been a push for further innovation and increased societal relevance of activities (cf. Kalpazidou Schmidt 2006a).

This development is similar to recent developments in a number of other European countries, where the acknowledgment of higher education's key role in creating the knowledge society - and in the identification and solving of political, socio-economic, environmental and cultural problems - has led to concentrated policy initiatives. However, the Danish case – seen in a comparative European perspective - is the most far-reaching with comprehensive reforms, implemented at a pace never before practised in Europe.

The challenges for Danish higher education in a steadily changing environment are multiple. The legislative framework and thereby the autonomy and governance of universities have been affected in particular with the current University Act. As the state provides lesser amounts of core funding, orienting the financial system towards increased competitive funding, and market pressures are intensifying, the need for a new legislation on the autonomy and governance (in order to ensure an effective and sustainable financial, managerial and capacity building basis) turned out to be more evident (Kalpazidou Schmidt 2006a).

Present governance and management challenges are the result of both internal and external demands. Internal demands have their origin on a rapid growth in the volume of higher education - both in terms of student numbers and complexity of the student population - and research activities. External demands are based on insufficient resources, a complex and highly competitive environment with requirements on rapid responses to a broad range of problems, interests and stakeholders (Kalpazidou Schmidt & Langberg 2007-8).

It is obvious that while in the past public higher education relationships were directed towards the central government, nowadays multiple stakeholders articulate their interests and exert pressure, which results in a complex HE decision-making and governance process. Societal relevance, knowledge management, accountability, efficiency and evaluation have become the new buzzwords. Increased institutional autonomy has resulted in intensive contract management, evaluation and reporting (Kalpazidou Schmidt & Langberg 2007-8).

It has been a first priority for the Danish government to develop a comprehensive and coherent policy for higher education in accordance with national social and economic objectives and to implement it without delay.

The Danish Globalization Strategy and its Implications for the HE System

In 2005, a Globalisation Council was set up by the Government with the aim to prepare the country for further globalization, enabling Denmark to maintain its position as one of the wealthiest countries in the world with strong social cohesion. The Council constituted by 26 members: 5 ministers including the Prime Minister (chairman) and the Minister of Finance (vice chairman) and 21 high level representatives from key sections of the Danish society.

The Globalisation Council presented its strategy, Denmark in the Global Economy, in 2006 (Danish Prime Minister's Office 2006). The strategy contained 350 initiatives which among others entailed extensive reforms of education and training, research and entrepreneurship as well as changes in the framework conditions for growth and innovation in all areas of society.

The Globalisation Strategy has been one of the main driving forces behind a series of reforms within Higher Education and a wide-ranging merging process of institutions. One of the key issues - discussed already in a note presented in 2005 by the Government within the framework of the Globalisation Council - was the fact that the Danish research environments were too small, uncoordinated and dispersed between different institutions and universities. The Danish Research Policy Council had also pointed out the problem based on an OECD evaluation of the universities (cf. The Ministry of Science, Technology and Innovation 2003b).

Another problem pointed out was the size of many of the university research schools, which were considered being too small and hence not equiped to meet the increased international competition. This fact in combination with the - according to the Government - unexploited potential of the research conducted at governmental research institutes (from which not least training of masters- and PhD students could benefit) led to a reform of the entire system.

A number of recommendations in the Globalisation Strategy focus on the nearest future of the university system. In the near future, basic funding of universities will be based on evaluations of the HE institutions' ability to reach objectives given in the development contracts 49 . The quality of HE research will be evaluated by international independent expert panels and a "quality barometer" for research based on internationally acknowledged indicators will be established. HE institutions will be requested to formulate objectives as regards the use of research outcomes in society and more funding will be allocated to strategic research. At the same time 50 percent of public research funding will be competitive by 2010 (as opposed to current 33 percent). The aim is to raise public research and development investments to 1 percent of GDP by 2010 in order to achieve the 3 percent objective of the Lisbon strategy (2 percent is already provided by the industrial sector). Seen in a European perspective, these reforms put Denmark among the countries that are in the forefront in actively using higher education policy to achieve the objectives of the Lisbon strategy.

---

[49]In 1999, development contracts between universities and the Danish Ministry of Science, Technology, and Innovation were introduced. A university development contract is a letter of intent stating strategic areas in which the university intends to focus on. The *first-generation university development contracts* (2000–4) focused on education and research, quality assurance, internationalization, IT-based learning, and innovation. The *second-generation contracts* focus on the strengthening of links with society, national and international cooperation, quality assurance, research, and benchmarking with foreign universities (Ministry of Science, Technology, and Innovation 2004).

From Individual Autonomy and Meritocracy to Institutional Autonomy, Merging and Control

In 2003 the Danish parliament approved a new University Act, which changed the legislation and financial conditions for the universities (Ministry of Science, Technology and Innovation 2003a). With the new Act, universities have gained a higher degree of self-governance and autonomy. Board members are now appointed with a majority representing external interests. Another innovation is the appointment of institutional leaders (rectors, deans and heads of departments), rather than election as it was the case in the past, and the abolition of collegial bodies (Kalpazidou Schmidt 2004, Kalpazidou Schmidt et al 2007).

In addition, the Act extends the role of the universities, incorporating exchange of knowledge and competencies with society, including the private sector. Another innovation stated in the Act is the strategic selection of research and education activities.

Institutional self-governance was introduced in an effort to increase the independence of HE institutions from the Ministry of Science, Technology, and Innovation. The long-term objective is to carry on adding competences and transferring responsibilities to the institutions. However, the institutions continue to be under the control of the minister, who may intervene in the decisions of boards if these do not live up to their responsibilities.

Following the implementation of the new University Act, a merging of universities and government research institutes has also been implemented. The main aim with the mergers was to strengthen education and research, sharpen the profile, and improve the competitive edge of Danish universities.

The mergers between universities and between universities and government research institutes were a top-down initiative, which started in spring 2007 and was concluded almost within a year. Even though the merging policy was imposed by the Ministry of Science, Technology and Innovation, university leaders were given the possibility to choose whether to merge or not and were asked to present their proposals and suggestions on the merging process by outlining a plan on potential partnerships. This initiative, due to the short time span given to the institutions to find partners, negotiate and present their proposals, led to a dynamic but very hectic activity among the boards and management leaders of universities and government research institutes. The merging process resulted in a reduction of the number of universities from 12 to 8 and incorporation of the majority of governmental research institutes into the higher education system (see table 1 (Table 1: Researchers at Danish Universities (UNI) and Government Research Institutes (GRI) in 2006, and the outcome of Mergers in 2007/2008): Source: Langberg & Kalpazidou Schmidt (forthcoming)

Institution 2006	Status UNI/GRI	Research Personnel (full time equivalent) 2006	Institution after the Mergers in 2007/2008
University of Copenhagen	UNI	2523	University of Copenhagen www.ku.dk
The Royal Veterinary and Agricultural University	UNI	950	
The Royal Danish University of Pharmacy	UNI	139	
University of Aarhus	UNI	1687	University of Aarhus www.au.dk
The Aarhus School of Business	UNI	125	
The Danish University of Education	UNI	180	
National Environment Research Institute	GRI	150	
Danish Institute of Agricultural Sciences	GRI	620	
University of Southern Denmark	UNI	841	University of Southern Denmark www.sdu.dk
National Institute of Public Health	GRI	62	
Technical University of Denmark	UNI	1265	Technical University of Denmark www.dtu.dk
Risø National Laboratory	GRI	516	
The Danish Institute of Food Safety and Nutrition Danish Veterinary Laboratory	GRI	233	
Danish Space Research Institute	GRI	65	
Danish Institute for Fisheries Research	GRI	129	
Danish Transport Research Institute	GRI	27	
Aalborg University	UNI	897	Aalborg University www.aau.dk
Danish Building and Urban Research	GRI	66	
Roskilde University	UNI	231	Roskilde University www.ruc.dk
Copenhagen Business School	UNI	280	Copenhagen Business School www.cbs.dk
IT University of Copenhagen	UNI	61	IT University of Copenhagen www.itu.dk
National Research Centre for the Working Environment	GRI	149	National Research Centre for the Working Environment www.ami.dk
The Danish National Centre for Social Research	GRI	82	The Danish National Centre for Social Research www.sfi.dk
Geological Survey of Denmark and Greenland	GRI	125	Geological Survey of Denmark and Greenland www.geus.dk
Statens Serum Institut	GRI	211	Statens Serum Institut www.ssi.dk
Danish Defence Research Establishment	GRI	13	---
Kennedy Center	GRI	15	Kennedy Center www.kennedy.dk

Taking into consideration the short planning and operation time of the mergers, the question which arises is how well-prepared both in organisational, economic and socio-cultural terms the implementation of this political decision was. The other question is how well-equipped the institutions were to meet this challenge as some of the merged institutions were quite large and dissimilar in terms of organisation, mission and culture. The third question relates to the involvement of faculty, researchers and students in the merging process, which was limited and in many cases not existent. The mergers had no negative effects on the employment of staff but in some cases the working conditions and tasks in particular for researchers at government research institutes were changed.

It is worth noticing that no studies of any kind have been conducted in advance in order to assess the potential impact of these radical changes on the HE institutions or the government research institutes.

Institutional and Professional Academic Autonomy

The increasing focus of the Danish reforms on accountability, strategic planning and competitiveness of HE has weakened dramatically the authority of faculty with a significant move of power to appointed leaders at the same time as the professional academic freedom has been under fire. The relationship between accountability and power is discussed by Enders (2006, 12) who states that there is "a certain correlation between accountability and power: those who define the processes and criteria for accountability measurements will have predefined performance and success to a certain extent. The struggle around the setting for evaluations and quality assessments, as well their external and internal use, has thus developed into one of the main arenas of ongoing power games within and around higher education".

In Denmark, the concept of professional academic autonomy has until recently been neglected, while institutional autonomy has been discussed. In addition, the concepts of autonomy of institutions, autonomy of research teams and individual academic freedom have usually being mixed up. In the new context greater attention is given to institutional autonomy, stronger management of processes and control of outputs. Institutional autonomy and academic freedom, often perceived as more or less identical in the past, have become differentiated, which has implications for the faculty (cf. Enders 2006).

Traditionally, faculty at Danish universities had considerably autonomy as regards research and teaching, stemming from their status, intellectual capacity and professional expertise. Danish academics have traditionally valued their autonomy and academic freedom very high, perceiving it as one of the primary values of the profession (Langberg 2003). The radical changes in institutional organisation, governance and management, and the mergers that followed, threaten the core of the academic culture, the autonomy of the faculty and their status as professional experts (cf. Becher & Kogan 1992).

Academic autonomy is a fundamental value of universities, as it affects all aspects of academic activity (Altbach 2001). The shift in authority and power from faculty to appointed leaders, managers and external interests, and the intensification of strategic planning both in education and research, created a gap between faculty and decision makers. As the collegial model has been replaced by professional managers, the number of administrators is increasing while faculty is decentralised in relation to influence of power. The current governance model is a movement away from the importance of faculty in the decision making process as managers take over the means to monitor and control the activities of staff (cf. Sporn 2006). In the new setting, boards represent not only the university, but also the general public and the industrial sector, and have a vital role in formulating strategic targets. The University Act provides boards, rectors, and deans with the necessary authority and instruments to make strategic decisions by concentrating all power at the top and by setting the agenda for faculty activities (Kalpazidou Schmidt & Langberg 2007-8).

The challenge for the boards and management has therefore been to create a university culture where individual academic freedom, institutional autonomy and accountability to external stakeholders can be balanced. However, this process has proved being even more complex with the simultaneous implementation of the mergers.

Mergers and Organisational Culture

Another significant policy intervention in Danish higher education is the mergers, which followed the implementation of the 2003 University Act.

Mergers of higher education institutions as a policy issue have been discussed in a number of publications in HE literature[50] in the last two decades. In particular the post-merger integration has been the point of attention in studies of the factors influencing merger processes. The focus has mainly been on timing, types of mergers and finances, organisational and structural aspects, characteristics of institutions, leadership and management

Little attention has though been paid to the cultural aspects of mergers (cf. Harman 2002). However, there is an increasing interest in using organisational culture theories to mergers in the field of higher education, based on business mergers (Harman 2002; Norgård & Skodvin 2002, cf. Cai 2006).

Studies in business mergers reveal "how cultural differences may create problems in organisational change processes by highlighting such issues as the incompatibility of beliefs and values" (Vaara 2000, p. 83). Harman (2002, p. 99) points out that "...the cultural dimension of mergers is such an important element in helping to ensure integration, creating a sense of loyalty to the new institution and in addressing likely high levels of conflict and stress". The process, according to Harman, involves significant elements including the management of different academic orientations, values and attitudes, the integration of diverse student cultures and the building of a sense of community and loyalty to the merged institution. Buono & Bowditch (1989, p. 142) comment on the potential force of different institutional cultures colliding during the merger process as follows: "...organizations that may appear to be highly

---

[50] See Harman 1986, 1991; McKinnon 1988; Meek 1988, 1991; Goedegebuure 1992; Pritchard 1993; Martin & Samels 1994; Dahllöf & Selander 1996; Wyatt 1998; Skodvin & Stensaker 1998; Skodvin 1999, Eastman & Lang 2001; Kyvik 2002; Lang 2002; Norgård & Skodvin 2002; Harman & Harman 2003; Cai 2006.

compatible on the surface and that seemingly should be able to achieve valuable merger synergies can have underlying cultural differences that seriously threaten their integration. . . Organizational members are usually so embedded in their own culture prior to major organizational changes that they rarely fully realize its influence on their behaviour".

The complexity of higher education with a variety of organisations and objectives, tasks and activities, cultures and norms, implies that mergers of higher education institutions are complex processes of integration. The literature gives though no clear-cut answer to what cultural integration[51] is in mergers of such institutions. According to Cai (2006, p. 217) "Cultural integration in mergers can be generally understood to be the process of adjustment and growing mutual respect and acceptance between different groups of staff from pre-merger institutions. Therefore, cultural integration as an essential part of a post-merger situation can be understood as a process of institutionalisation".

On the other hand, an institutionalised system does not necessarily mean that values and norms in the merged system are all of the same type. Cultural integration can take place to various degrees and each pre-merger unit may maintain its fundamental cultural elements. However, the key task is to develop a common organisational culture that can bind together different research and teaching units and groups (Cai 2006).

The question as regards the Danish case is whether this is feasible within the existing framework of some of the merged institutions. A key problem is the location of the institutions merging into the new universities. An example is the University of Aarhus which after the mergers has campuses all over the country (cf. Norgård & Skodvin 2002). It is obvious that it is difficult to create a common organisational culture that can function as "glue" between the pre-merger institutions (cf. Smircich 1983). The amalgamation of dissimilar institutions makes the task even more difficult. Incorporation of the government research institutes - with a very different setting, culture and tasks - into the universities is another challenging exercise.

Many scholars point out the significance of an effective leadership and management in assuring the success of mergers (cf. Harman 2002). The timing of the Danish higher education merging process could for that reason not be better. The question is though how to smoothly integrate different academic orientations, objectives and values, and achieve the sense of community and loyalty that characterises an organisational culture. Nevertheless, studies[52] reveal that there are no successful mergers without the effective participation and integration of staff.

---

[51]For a discussion of the concept cultural integration see Buono and Bowditch (1989) where they suggest four levels of such integration: a. *cultural pluralism* which allows different partners to operate autonomously; b. *cultural blending* which occurs in mergers of equals; c. *cultural takeover* where the dominant culture takes over, a situation which demands strong, decisive leadership and skilful management of emerging cultural crises; and finally d. *cultural resistance* which occurs where there is a lack of understanding or attention paid to the cultures of the merger partners.

[52] See Currie & Newson 1998; Skodvin, 1999; Eastman & Lang 2001; Curri 2002; Kyvik 2002; Lang 2002; Norgård & Skodvin 2002; Harman & Harman 2003.

It is obvious that the effects of the very recently carried out mergers – in contrast to the effects of the 2003 University Act, which are profound by now - are still to be seen but the process could certainly benefit from studies of policy implementation procedures, organisational cultures and integration practices.

CONCLUDING REMARK

Danish higher educations organisation, role and responsibilities have been substantially changed over the last years due to intensive policy making. A new distribution of power has been established where the faculty has lost its power in decision making to external interest, boards, rectors and deans. Institutions have gained greater autonomy while the autonomy of the faculty has been limited. Accountability, performance contracts and evaluations are adopted as control mechanisms. A merging process between universities, and universities and government research institutes followed. The effects of the implementation of the 2003 University Act are tangible while the effects of the recent mergers in administrative and economic terms on the one side and academic terms on the other are still to be seen.

The transformation taking place within the Danish higher education environment is a unique experiment in Europe. Further studies could be expected to enrich the knowledge reservoir and experience linked to vigorous higher education policies and their impacts.

REFERENCES

Altbach, P.G (2001). Higher Education and the WTO: Globalisation Run Amok. *International Higher Education, no. 18, pp. 2–4.*

Buono, A. R. & Bowditch, J. L. (1989). *The Human Side of Mergers and Acquisitions - Managing Collisions Between People, Cultures, and Organizations.* San Francisco: Jossey-Bass Publishers.

Cai, Y (2006). A case study of academic staff integration in a post-merger Chinese university. *Tertiary Education Management 12, p. 215-226.*

Curri, G. (2002). Reality versus perception: Restructuring tertiary education and institutional organizational change – a case study. *Higher Education, 44, pp. 133–151.*

Currie, J., & Newson, J. A. (1998). *Universities and globalization: Critical perspectives.* Thousand Oaks, CA: Sage Publications.

Dahllöf, U. & Selander, S. (eds.) (1996). *Expanding Colleges and New Universities. Selected Case Studies from Non-metropolitan Areas in Australia, Scotland and Scandinavia.* Uppsala: Department of Education, Uppsala University.

Danish Prime Minister's Office (2006). Progress, Innovation and Cohesion Strategy for Denmark in the Global Economy - Summary. Copenhagen.

Eastman, J., & Lang, D. W. (2001). Mergers in higher education: Lessons from theory and experience. Toronto: University of Toronto.

Enders, J. (2006). The Academic Profession." In Forest and Altbach, ed., International Handbook of Higher Education. Dordrecht: Springer Verlag, vol. 18, pp. 5–21.

Goedegebuure, L. (1992). *Mergers in Higher Education – A Comparative Perspective.* Centre for Higher Education Policy Studies, University of Twente, Enschede.

Harman, G. (1986). Restructuring higher education systems through institutional mergers: the Australian experience 1981–1983, *Higher Education* 15, pp. 567–586.

Harman, G. (1991). Institutional amalgamations and abolition of the binary system in Australian higher education under John Dawkins, *Higher Education Quarterly* 45 (1), pp. 176–198.

Harman, K. (2002). Merging divergent campus cultures into coherent educational communities: Challenges for higher education leaders. *Higher Education 44, pp. 91-144.* Kluwer Academic Publishers, Netherlands.

Harman, G., & Harman, K. (2003). Institutional mergers in higher education: Lessons from international experience. *Tertiary Education and Management 9, pp. 29–44.*

Kalpazidou Schmidt, E. (1996). *Research Environments in a Nordic Perspective. A Comparative study in Ecology and Scientific Productivity.* In Acta Universitatis Upsaliensis. Uppsala Studies in Education 67. Uppsala. Almqvist & Wiksell, Sweden.

Kalpazidou Schmidt, E. (2004). Higher Education and Research in the Nordic Countries - A Comparison of the Nordic Systems. Report no. 3, *The Danish Centre for Studies in Research and Research Policy.*

Kalpazidou Schmidt, E. (2006a). Management of Knowledge and Organizational Changes in Higher Education: The New Danish University Act. *The International Journal of Knowledge, Culture and Change Management, vol. 5, pp. 147–56.*

Kalpazidou Schmidt, E. (2006b). Higher Education in Scandinavia. In Forest and Altbach, (eds) *International Handbook of Higher Education, Dordrecht: Springer Verlag 2006, vol. 18, pp. 517–37.*

Kalpazidou Schmidt, E. (2007): The case of Denmark (chapter 5). In Mora J.-G., Vila L., Psacharopoulos G., Kalpazidou Schmidt E., Vossensteyn H. & Villarreal E., *Rates of return and funding models in Europe, Final report prepared for the European Commission, Directorate-General Education and Culture, January 2007.*

Kalpazidou Schmidt, E.; Graversen, E.K.; & Langberg, K. (2003). Innovation and Dynamics in Public Research Environments in Denmark: A Research Policy Perspective. *Science and Public Policy, vol. 30, no. 2, pp. 107–16.*

Kalpazidou Schmidt, E. & Langberg K. (2007-8). Academic Autonomy in a Rapidly Changing Higher Education Framework - Academia on the Procrustian Bed. The Implications of Competition for the Future of European Higher Education (I). *In European Education, vol. 39, No. 4. M.E. Sharpe.*

Kalpazidou Schmidt, E.; Langberg, K.; & Aagaard, K. (2007). Funding Systems and Their Effects on Higher Education Systems. Country Study Denmark." *In Funding Systems and their Effects on Higher Education Systems. International Report, OECD-IMHE Study.*

Kyvik, S. (2002). The merger of non-university colleges in Norway. *Higher Education, 44, pp. 53–72.*

Lang, D. W. (2002). There are mergers, and there are mergers: The forms of inter-institutional combination. *Higher Education Management and Policy, 1, pp. 11–50.*

Langberg, K. (2003). Changes in Research Management at Danish Universities and Government Research Institutes. Report no. 4. *The Danish Institute for Studies in Research and Research Policy.*

Langberg, K. & Kalpazidou Schmidt, E. (forthcoming). Local Diversity and Identity versus Global Interaction. Changes in the Danish Higher Education System.

Martin, J. & Samels, J. E. (1994). Conclusion: The mutual-growth process – myths and realities, in Martin et al. (eds.), (1994), *Merging Colleges for Mutual Growth: A New Strategy for Managers.* Baltimore: Johns Hopkins Press, pp. 227–238.

McKinnon, K.R. (1988). United we stand . . . the process of amalgamation at Wollongong University, in Harman, Gr. & Meek, V. L. (eds.), *Institutional Amalgamations in Higher Education – Process and Outcome in Five Countries.* Department of Administrative and Higher Education Studies, University of New England, pp. 105–120.

Meek, V. L. (1988). Notes on higher educational mergers in the United Kingdom', in Harman, G. & Meek, V. L. (eds.), *Institutional Amalgamations in Higher Education – Process and Outcome in Five Countries*. Department of Administrative and Higher Education Studies, University of New England, pp. 159–169.

Ministry of Science, Technology and Innovation (2003a) Act on Universities of May 28, 2003 (Translation) Explanatory notes. Copenhagen

Ministry of Science, Technology and Innovation (2003b) Danish universities - at the brink of transition. Background report to the OECD examiners panel. Copenhagen

Norgård, J. D., & Skodvin, O. (2002). The importance of geography and culture in mergers: A Norwegian institutional case study. *Higher Education, 44, pp. 73–90.*

Pritchard, R. (1993). Mergers and linkages in British higher education, *Higher Education Quarterly 47(2), pp. 79–102.*

Skodvin, O. (1999). Mergers in higher education – Success or failure?, *Tertiary Education and Management 5(1), pp. 65–80.*

Skodvin, O. & Stensaker, B. (1998). Innovation through merging?, *Higher Education Management* 10(3), pp. 73–86.

Sporn, B. (2006). Governance and Administration: Organizational and Structural Trends. In Forest and Altbach (eds), *International Handbook of Higher Education. Dordrecht: Springer Verlag 2006, vol. 18, pp. 141–57.*

Smircich, L. (1983). Concept of culture and organizational analysis. *Administrative Science Quarterly, 28, pp. 339–358.*

Vaara, E. (2000). Constructions of cultural differences in post-merger change processes: A sense making perspective on Finnish-Swedish cases. *Management, 3, pp. 81–110.*

Wyatt, J. (1998). A rapid result: the achievement of a merger in higher education, *Higher Education Review 31(1), pp. 15–34.*

Ziman, J. (1991). Academic Science as a System of Markets. *Higher Education Quaterly, no. 1, pp. 57–68.*

CHAPTER 13

Analyzing the Effects of Globalization on University Systems in the Developing World: A Conceptual Framework Applied to the Case of the Republic of Panama

Nanette Svenson

INTRODUCTION

In the past two decades, global political and economic forces have significantly impacted the evolution of university systems around the world and especially in developing countries. The effects of this impact are noticeable in two primary areas: the university regulatory environment, which has been influenced mainly by multilateral and bilateral conventions and interventions, and the university program offer, which has been influenced by the increasing presence of transnational higher education corporations and foreign university programs.

At both international and national levels, influences related to these political—regulation oriented forces—and economic—market driven forces—act simultaneously in different ways to affect the development of the university system in any given country. These forces, in turn, help shape both the national vision being created for university education and the business opportunity associated with it. The existing university system will be a reflection of the specific forces that are strongest in that country.

This chapter presents a conceptual framework designed to isolate key factors of the political and economic influences and use them to analyze effects on the development of the university system in a particular country. By better understanding the inputs that have the greatest impact on the university system, decision-makers at all levels have more complete information to use in the formulation and management of higher education policy, legislation, regulation and incentives.

This is important since many university systems throughout the world have expanded very quickly in recent years, often without the benefit of established quality assurance mechanisms, stringent regulatory environments, or even sufficient research on the phenomenon (World Bank 2000). Scholars estimate there are over 70 million students currently in higher education, with nearly all industrialized countries and most middle-income countries now enrolling over a quarter of the corresponding age cohort (Altbach 2007). Because the growth of new universities has, in many areas, outpaced the growth of either the relevant quality assurance mechanisms or information dissemination systems, there is an increasing need for research and systematic models dedicated to analyzing the university systems that are evolving.

This is especially true for developing countries; most have had nothing more than a handful of public universities for centuries, but in recent years with the proliferation of transnational programs, branch campuses, online learning, university corporations and the like, university growth has often been exponential.

The Republic of Panama, a middle-income country in Central America, is used as an example for how this framework can be applied to a developing country case study as the model was recently incorporated into a research project funded by the Panamanian Secretariat for Science, Technology and Innovation (SENACYT) that sought to study the effects of globalization on the country's university system from1990 to 2007. A summary of the findings is presented here along with concluding ideas for how application of this model might be instrumental for university capacity development efforts in other developing counties.

Global Trends Affecting Higher Education

As background to the framework, it is important to review the major global trends affecting higher education over the past 20 years, most of which—as mentioned— tend to be either politically motivated and regulation oriented or economically related and market driven.

Political Forces

The most important global political trend shaping higher education is the emergence of new international accords to harmonize higher education priorities, systems and services within and between regions. The goals of these tend to include convergence (inter- and intra-regional) of programs; harmonization of curricula; facilitation of student and faculty mobility; implementation of quality assurance mechanisms; and increased attractiveness and competitiveness of programs. Except for North America[54], most regions of the world are currently engaged in discussions aimed at creating more accords toward these ends. The forces driving many of these agreements and declarations of the past two decades are closely linked to the Bologna Process, Europe's ongoing effort to create a unified European Higher Education Area.

The Bologna Process began in the late 1980s and is generally regarded as having led the global movement toward university standard convergence across the world (Charlier and Croche 2004). This movement and the accords generated, in turn, have begun to affect countries' national higher education legislation and regulation.

For Latin America (Panama included), the significance of the Bologna Process is that it spearheaded the Florianopolis Declaration of 2000, which brought the countries of the region together in a similar convergence initiative for the first time.

---

[54] North America has been less active than the rest of the world in pursuing convergence of higher education systems and structures with other regions. Even from the perspective of trade, the North American Free Trade Agreement (NAFTA) and successive bilateral agreements include few implications for higher education (Altbach 2004). This may reflect a North American perception of superiority and dominance in this area, which would seem to be upheld by even those outside the region since much of the higher education convergence activity worldwide is moving in line with established U.S. standards.

Beyond Latin America, the Bologna Process has propelled initiatives similar to Florianopolis in Asia, Africa and elsewhere.

Alongside Bologna Process efforts with the international higher education community to pursue convergence and related quality assurance issues, international organizations have also stepped up their participation in this area. In response to demands by the international community that it take a more proactive role in this regard, UNESCO has led numerous regional and global conferences on the issue in the past couple of decades. From these and related initiatives, the UNESCO/OECD guidelines on quality in cross-border provision of higher education were published (UNESCO 2004). While still a work in progress, this represents the start of a global reference and a new role for UNESCO in the process of higher education convergence.

Economic Forces

While the ideal of convergence has been at the heart of the political forces affecting higher education internationally, the power of technology is what lies behind most of economic trends affecting higher education worldwide. Globalization and information technology (IT) are inextricably connected, with the Internet serving as the primary vehicle for the global dissemination of knowledge and communications (Castells 2000). As a result, IT has serious implications for higher education in relation to online learning; publishing and copyrights; information storage and retrieval; and networking and research and development collaboration.

The increasing importance of technology and the speed with which it propels information transfer has given rise to the evolution of the "knowledge economy," a society more dependent for its economic welfare on the production and management of knowledge than on the production of manufactured goods. This trend is reflected in increasing investments in knowledge industries (including higher education and training) and the expansion of the services sector, particularly those classified as advanced business services—typically, banking and finance, insurance, IT, legal services, real estate, and media and communications (Sassen 2001). With the growing dependence of many economies on knowledge products, highly educated personnel have become critical for continued growth (Altbach and Knight 2006; Friedman 2006). This has had the effect of linking higher education to earning potential, leading to increased demand for higher education (Thomas 2004). It has also led to efforts to include knowledge services in global trade regulation. The Global Agreement on Trade in Services (GATS) is the first multi-lateral agreement on this and seeks to open markets for all service and knowledge products.

This is significant not only because of its potential scope but also for what it indicates about globalization; conceptually, GATS positions knowledge and education as commodities on par with rice and computer chips—an idea that is discomfiting to many. The GATS negotiations also carry implications for relations between developed countries, the chief exporters of education, and developing countries, the main importers. These fuel considerable debate on potential benefits and risks, most of which revolve around issues of quality assurance, professional mobility and recognition of qualifications (Knight 2003).

The rise of technology, knowledge economies and trade-able knowledge services has had an internationalizing effect on higher education worldwide. Institutions can link beyond nations and regions quickly and easily, which means that higher education now corresponds to a global, not national, marketplace. This is evident in the multitude of multinational higher education programs now available. These programs range from co-sponsored "twinning" arrangements linking two or more academic institutions in different countries to franchising agreements to universities in one country setting up branches in another. Online distance learning programs offer yet another means for the multi-nationalization of higher education. While some traditional public higher education institutions have invested in these multinational educational initiatives, the major players have come primarily from the private sector. Nationally and internationally, private higher education suppliers have been far more responsive to increased demand for higher education, have expanded the university offer exponentially around the world, and continue to grow in number. In several Asian countries, nearly 80 percent of university enrollments are at private institutions and in Latin America the figure oscillates between 20 and 40 percent (Altbach 2007). This new public-private mix includes actors beyond universities; unaccredited commercial enterprises that offer a range of post-secondary courses and degrees are becoming increasingly common throughout the world. As these corporate entities are involved in the higher education business primarily for the purpose of earning a profit as opposed to imparting knowledge, they have met with a certain resistance from traditional university operators.

With more post-secondary educational options available on the market, the resulting rise in enrollment has propelled a global "massification" of higher education, particularly in places where demographic trends have inclined toward a larger youth population. This massification is the major force behind recent trends and policy guiding the development of higher education worldwide at every level. The concern about the massification of higher education and its many service providers is linked to the commoditization of learning and the "McDonaldization"[55] of higher education constructive, but generally the application of the fast-food metaphor in this context reflects societal concern for maintaining the university as a liberal institution whose primary mission is the pursuit, generation and dissemination of knowledge. For both sides, questions continue to surface about the capacity and qualifications of the graduates being turned out by the new systems. Issues of quality assurance are paramount (Hayes and Wynyard 2002). Some view this commoditization as potentially moving to the forefront as existing regulatory systems become overwhelmed and ill-equipped to deal with the present array of higher education alternatives (Thomas 2004). And while quality assurance is a major concern within

---

[55]The term "McDonaldization," coined by sociologist George Ritzer in his book *The McDonaldization of Society* (1995), describes how society has taken on many of the characteristics most associated with fast-food restaurants. Ritzer uses McDonaldization to reconceptualize rationalization and emphasizes four principal components of it: efficiency, calculability (the ability to be quantified), predictability (through standardization), and control (often achieved with the implementation of mechanized, instead of human, processes).

countries, it is becoming an even bigger problem internationally. Critics grumble about the low standards of many international higher education programs, but few have proposed specific measures with which to gauge quality (Altbach and Knight 2006; Bello 2003).

Implications for Developing Countries

To complete this review of global trends, it is important to mention the implications for developing countries. Developing countries are the ones that will experience the bulk of the higher education expansion projected to take place in the coming years (Task Force on Higher Education 2000). The topics discussed here—technology, knowledge services, mobility, quality assurance, internationalization—all carry for the developing world repercussions related to issues of center and periphery. The globalization of higher education has the potential to increase the inequality gap, both within the developing countries themselves and between developing and developed countries (Torres Shugurensky 2002; Bello 2003; Garnier 2004). Since developed countries are better able to invest more in higher education and research and development, the major gains and the vast majority of corresponding publication tend to come from the developed world (Altbach 2002, 2004).

Higher education does have the potential to narrow the inequality gap, too, but most developing countries face formidable obstacles with higher education and with utilizing it as a driver of the national economy. With demand for increased access projected to continue, both public and private sectors will likely persist in their attempts to meet the growing demand with a wide range of new higher education alternatives. The result of these efforts, however, is often an accelerated, chaotic expansion—usually with the public sector lacking sufficient capacity for funding, technical expertise, and regulatory oversight and the private sector lacking sufficient facility for establishing quality programs that address requirements beyond short-term, market-driven needs (Task Force on Higher Education 2000). To be able to participate in today's global knowledge economy, developing countries are left with the enormous challenge of simultaneously expanding their higher education systems and improving their quality—all within the context of tightening budgetary constraints. This is proving to be a daunting task for most.

Conceptual Framework

The work done on general global trends in higher education is considerable, but there is still comparatively little theorization focused on the effects of globalization in higher education systems and particular universities. Rather, there is a tendency to read globalization deductively into higher education from more general theories on globalization (Mohamedbhai 2002, Marginson and Sawir 2005).

In order to examine more precisely the higher education trends presented above as they relate to globalization and, in turn, to the changes that are taking place at the national level, several scholars have begun to elaborate frameworks for isolating and analyzing specific factors that may determine how universal, global shifts manifest in the local setting (Vaira 2004, Douglass 2005, Marginson and Sawir 2005, Marginson and van der Wende 2007). Though such frameworks provide considerable potential for developing a better understanding of how global influences affect specific national higher education systems, there are still relatively few. And of the existing frameworks, even fewer have been applied to empirical studies, though global higher education research is beginning to move in this direction and acknowledge the need for the kind of tool that facilitates the interpretation of global change on local environments (Mohamedbhai 2002, Marginson and Sawir 2005, Yoder 2006).

The conceptual framework presented here is original. It is based on an examination of constructs derived from the literature on global higher education developments over the past two decades, as discussed in the previous section. The framework takes its inspiration from existing models, particularly that of Douglass (2005), which offers one of more developed and workable theoretical examples and emphasizes how the effects of globalization on a given university system will be the result of an interactive combination of universal "mega-global" forces and unique local (national) "countervailing" forces. As with the Douglass model, the constructs used here combine factors in the international arena with those in the national environment and can be synthesized broadly as follows:

- **Globalization**, defined as the cross-border economic, political and social forces associated with increased connection worldwide.
- **Global higher education trends and priorities**, most of which tend to fall into two major categories: (1) those associated with worldwide convergence priorities (regulation oriented, politically driven, and aimed at the creation of international standards and quality assurance mechanisms); and (2) those associated with transnational business opportunities (market oriented, economically driven and related to the broadening market for services, the knowledge economy and growth of advanced business services, technology assisted learning, and the recent massification and multi-nationalization of higher education).
- **National economic development**, which examines the macro- and microeconomic drivers for the country in question.
- **National participation in international higher education initiatives**, as indicated by a country's involvement with various bilateral and multilateral international higher education agreements, initiatives and regulatory bodies.
- **Potential business opportunity and political vision** associated with higher education in the country being examined and how the two interact to produce the existing university system.

These different constructs are presented in the diagram of the framework below. In most countries, at both international and national levels, there are the simultaneous influences of economic, market driven forces and political, regulation oriented forces affecting the development of the university systems—both of which incorporate various social forces as well. This conceptual framework attempts to organize and examine the different aspects of these global forces in an effort to determine which appear to be the predominant influences on a country's existing university system.

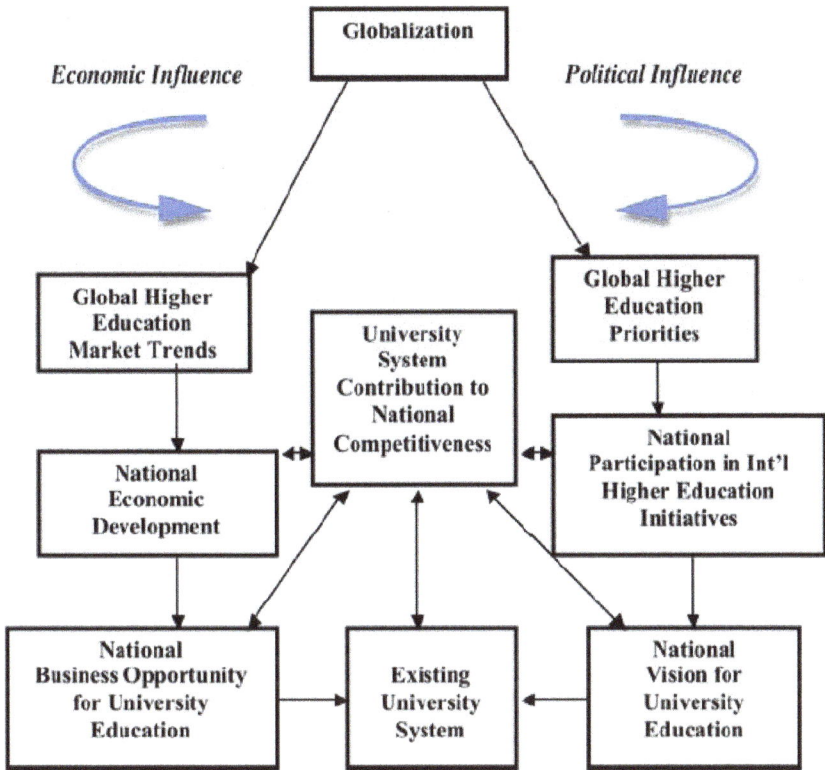

Figure 1: Conceptual Framework the Effects of Globalization on a Country's University System

Given the basic conceptual framework introduced above, the specific research questions that guide the investigation into how global economic and political forces interact with the national environment to affect university system development are as follows:

1. How many and what types of universities are available?
2. What factors have contributed to shaping the regulatory environment of university education?
3. What factors have contributed to making university education an attractive business proposition?
4. How are the regulatory and business factors reflected in the current university offer?

5. What are the current perceptions of business, government, academic and civil society leaders regarding the strengths, weaknesses, opportunities and threats associated with the university offer?
6. What are the implications of these perceptions for national competitiveness?

Methodology and Application to the Case of Panama

The examination of the research questions above in the application of the conceptual framework to the case of the Republic of Panama was carried out within the design of an embedded, single-case study as described by Robert K. Yin (2002).

The research incorporated both qualitative and quantitative data to present a descriptive review of Panama's recent globalization and economic growth, trends in the globalization of higher education and Panama's involvement in this process, the structure and composition of the university system in Panama, and implications for the future. Specific methodologies employed include document and secondary data analyses and semi-structured interviews.

Documents reviewed include public registry data, Ministry of Education and other institutional records related to the university system, national assembly legislation and international accords, newspaper articles, websites, other mass media communication. National and international statistical databases were also consulted.

The semi-structured interviews used non-probability, purposive sampling techniques.

They were conducted with representatives from selected universities, government entities, business associations, and national and international non-governmental organizations.

Though Panama is a small, middle-income country in Central America, its experience in recent years with higher education is similar to that of many countries in the region and in the developing world in general. Panama has historically served as a global crossroads, so its economy, politics and culture have always been subject to the effects of global forces. In the past few decades in which technology and markets have advanced with unprecedented speed, the effects of globalization have been especially impacting--for the economy in general and also for specific sectors. Higher education is one sector that has changed dramatically.

Until the early 1980s there were only two universities in Panama, whereas, the Ministry of Education now officially recognizes 36 institutions and the Public Registry lists as many as 90. Alongside this growth, several independent studies on higher education in Panama have begun to reflect concerns about ambiguous regulatory legislation, lack of evaluation and quality assurance mechanisms, and weak relationships with both government and the productive sector. These reports suggest that existing program quality does not meet with international standards (Bernal 2002, IADB 2003, UNESCO-IESALC 2005) or prepare students for market demand (COSPAE 2007, Goethals 2008). Within this context, Panama's overall competitiveness—which has risen steadily in recent years (WEF 2008)—is now sluggish and at a critical juncture. In connection with this, higher education and human resource capacity has been identified repeatedly as a weak link and the factor that will determine much of future development (UNDP 2002; Euromoney 2006; WEF 2008). Therefore, information on globalization and how it is affecting the university system, capacity development and competitiveness is particularly important for Panama at this moment; however, the fundamentals underlying the importance of the research are similarly applicable to most countries in the region and the developing world.

Summary of Findings

The Existing University System

Skipping directly to the bottom of the model presented in the conceptual framework above and focusing on the existing university system in Panama, a significant finding from this research was the lack of consistent, centrally databased information on universities in the country. There is a general list Ministry of Education recognized institutions, but it represents only around a third of those listed in the Public Registry and does not include much beyond the name of the institution.

Institutional contact data, course and degree offerings, information on faculty and facilities are all difficult to obtain for many of the universities in Panama and nowhere is this general information warehoused in a central database.

There is a broad range of university education now available in Panama; however, the general consensus from the research was that little of it offers a quality learning experience. Grouping findings on institutional dimensions, the table below provides a general overview of characteristics noted in the current university offer.

Table 1: General Characteristics of Universities in Panama 2007

Organizational Structure	
Governance	5 public universities 90 registered private universities
Public Registry	60 public limited companies 16 privately held organizations 3 privately held foundations 11 universities registered under a different entity name
Ownership	Several universities have distinctly foreign connections, Florida State University (FSU), Quality Leadership University (QLU)—representing the University of Louisville and Towson—San Martin and Isthmus of Colombia, and the Laureate and Aden groups, for example, but specific ownership breakdowns are difficult to obtain.
Financial	Non-profit universities include the state universities, the Catholic university USMA, and UNESCPA; the rest are profit generating.
Religious	The only Catholic run university is the USMA; others with a religious affiliation appear to include the Kabbalah and Hosanna universities and the Specialized Christian University. The majority of universities in Panama do not have religious affiliations.
Educational Structure	
Program level	Almost all universities in Panama now offer undergraduate and graduate degrees along with various types of certifications.
Program focus	There are several specialized universities, mostly public institutions—the UMIP (maritime), UNESCPA (public accounting), UTP (science and technology) and UDELAS (special education); the rest offer a varied mix of general programming.
Instructional-Research	Many universities claim to do research, but only the state institutions and the USMA have conducted documented projects, and even then very few. All universities in Panama tend to concentrate on teaching.
Transnational programming-Degree options	FSU, QLU (representing Louisville, Towson and others), San Martin and Isthmus grant degrees in coordination with their affiliate foreign universities; The state technological university UTP, via its FUNIBER virtual PhD program, combines foreign university programming with a local degree; and the rest of the universities offer mainly local programming and local university degrees.
Instruction modality	Many are beginning to experiment with various aspects of online instruction, but only the two distance universities (UNADP and UNEIDPA) and the UTP offer formal online degree programs.
Professors	FSU, QLU, Isthmus and San Martin boast a majority of foreign national professors, but the rest rely principally on Panamanians. Most Panamanian university professors do not hold doctoral degrees and many do not hold Master's degrees.
Infrastructure	
Physical structures	There are no resident university institutions in Panama. Those with traditional structures that include separate library and laboratory structures are limited to the state institutions and a few of the private universities (such as the USMA), with many of the public structures in states of disrepair. An increasing number of universities operate out of converted apartment and office buildings.
Information-technology	Access to journals, databases and virtual libraries is limited, even in the larger, more traditional universities. Access to computers and internet services is improving in the largest of the private universities.
Official Status	
National recognition	36 universities have Ministry of Education permission to operate and University of Panama curricular approval.
International accreditation	FSU and QLU offer programs accredited by U.S. accrediting agencies.

Most of the university sector growth has occurred in the last 15 years, so most schools have been operating for only a decade or less. Private, for-profit institutions account for the majority. There are five public universities, representing about 75% of enrollment, the oldest and largest of which is the University of Panama (UP). The others have evolved more recently from former UP departments or regional centers.

The private sector represents only about 25% of university enrollment, but is the fastest growing segment in terms of numbers. It accounts for all Public Registry institutions and 31 of the 36 Ministry recognized universities. Many of these universities are products of transnational agreements with international providers that involve branch campuses, online programs, "off-shore" degrees, franchising arrangements, or multinational corporations.

International institutions with representation in Panama include Florida State University (FSU), University of Louisville, Towson University, College of Notre Dame of Maryland, Florida International University, Universidad de San Martin of Colombia, McGill University, University of St. Louis, School of International Training (SIT), and ADEN Business School. Only FSU has a full branch campus and market presence that spans decades. The others are recent entries and tend to franchise specific degrees or courses. Several run study-abroad programs for outside students only. Thus, though the international university presence is growing, the overall impact on the sector is still weak. Multinational university corporations include Laureate International Universities and Whitney International University System, both of which own multiple schools and offer programs targeting lower income populations. These have had more impact on numbers enrolled.

Among the legally registered private universities are dozens for which no general information is available. A number of others could be considered "garage universities"—apartments or offices with signs in front that tend to disappear as quickly as they appear. Both of these trends raise concerns of diploma mills and fraudulent business practice, but because Panama does not have a functioning accreditation system, there is little to stop the proliferation of questionable operations.

The Influencing Political and Economic Forces

The description of worldwide trends affecting higher education in recent decades put forth in the second section of this paper dealt with the political and economic influences operating at the global level and shown in the top layers of the conceptual framework presented. Dropping down to the national level of the framework, a host of local political and economic issues mix with the global forces to influence the development of the university system and produce the current offer.

On the political front, like many countries in Latin America, Panama has signed many laws and international accords reflecting its commitment to higher education globalization and objective of moving its universities toward international norms. Chief among these are the 1998 law establishing Panama's City of Knowledge, designed to bring international business, technology, and academia together in a former US military facility; the 2003 accord founding the Central American University Accreditation Council; and the 2006 law creating Panama's National Council for the Evaluation and Accreditation of University Education (CONEAUPA). These last two are a direct consequence of Bologna Process efforts and subsequent European Commission sponsored regional convergence follow-up.

The visionary international accords compete, however, with more firmly established legislation: (1) the 1927 law facilitating creation of corporations for any non-illegal enterprise, including higher education; and (2) the 1972 Constitution, which centralizes university system control and private institutional oversight in the University of Panama (UP), an institution perceived to be seriously deficient academically and highly corrupt. This normative set-up abets university proliferation since it is not difficult to obtain Ministry of Education recognition but complicated for authorities to thwart those who fail to do so. It also provides a business for the UP and impedes establishment of autonomous quality assurance; CONEAUPA, three years after inception, is still not operational.

Economically, Panama has always been a dollar-based service economy that, due to its geographic location, caters to international services. The economy is based primarily on a highly developed services sector that now accounts for three quarters of GDP. Major services include the Panama Canal, the COPA-Continental airline hub, the container ports, the railway, the Colon Free Zone, and banking and insurance. In the past decade, tourism and construction have also become major contributors and the country has been able to attract increasing foreign investment. All of this has begun to push rapid economic growth (Table 2). In spite of this progress, however, a third of the population still lives in poverty, the country's Gini index, which measures income inequality, is among the highest in the region, and unemployment (and informal employment) rates continue to be high.

Table 2: Panama, Selected Statistics: 1990-2006

	1990	2006	Average Annual Growth (%)
Population (millions)	2.4	3.3	2.3
Labor force (millions)	0.9	1.5	4.2
GDP (US $m)	5,313	17,097	13.9
GDP per capita (US$)	2,214	5,970	10.6
GDP composition by sector			
Agriculture	10%	8.0%	-1.3
Industry	15%	19%	1.7
Services	75%	73%	-0.2
Foreign Direct Investment (US $m)	136	2,574	112
Population below poverty line (1997)	--	37.3%	--
Gini index (2003)	--	56.1	--
Inflation rate (consumer prices)	1.1%	7.1%	37.5
Unemployment rate	14.7%	10.3%	-1.9

Source: World Development Indicators 2006, 2008

In addition to the booming service economy and the normative factors mentioned above, certain non-regulatory factors—a large, national pool of low-paid adjunct professors, an increasing demand for skilled labor, and limited vocational education options—further contribute to making university education an attractive business in Panama. These factors also make it profitable for universities to sell short-term modules for generic proficiencies like English, office protocol and computer skills in addition to degree courses.

Implications for Competitiveness

The general consensus in Panama, based on the interviews conducted for this research, is that the content and relevance of most university programs do not coincide with international standards or market demand. Without a solid, operational quality assurance body supported by both public and private sectors, short-term oriented economic forces will continue to dominate the longer-term political vision. The upshot of this is that although higher education may become available to more of the population, the worth of local degrees diminishes. Without immediate implementation of effective quality assurance measures and programs directed toward the country's actual educational needs, the university system will soon be relegated to a position of relative insignificance for Panama's development. This portends an increased reliance on foreign education and labor for Panama to be able to continue its trajectory of growth in the provision of international services, the motor driving the national economy. Evidence of this is already beginning to surface; a recent national study reports that 80% of mid- and high-level management holds degrees from universities outside the country (Goethals 2008).

Panama is well positioned geographically, historically, politically and economically to meet this challenge of developing a more adequate and responsive university system. But it will require considerable changes in the country's current academic power and decision-making structure, as well as the importing of necessary expertise and higher education programming, with sufficient mechanisms for knowledge transfer. More than anything, this will require a shift in thinking; national mentality must move away from equating university development with short-term business opportunity and toward equating it with long-term strategic necessity.

CONCLUSION

The purpose of presenting the conceptual framework put forth in this paper along with an empirical example of its application is to introduce a comprehensive model for analyzing how global forces influence university system development in a given country. It may be applied to any country, but was constructed specifically with developing countries in mind as they are now, for the most part, in a position of serious disadvantage with regard to their university systems. They must react quickly to a shifting global scenario that affects national development and competitiveness— without having the benefit of university systems that are as stable, established, productive and endowed as those of many industrialized countries.

The issue of content and relevance of university programs not corresponding to either international standards or market demand is not unique to Panama. Rather, it is a common problem for developing countries. The framework presented here and the stock-taking exercise it propels is useful not only for Panama but for developing countries everywhere. It is the first step toward taking the decisions and actions necessary for better positioning the university system to contribute to national development. At international and national levels, a collection of forces works to affect the evolution of a country's university sector. These forces can be categorized into two major groupings: economic, market driven forces and political, regulation oriented forces, both of which incorporate multiple social forces as well. Existing studies on globalization and university systems all mention various economic, political and social factors at play in the development of these systems, but none have offered a way to group or classify these factors or forces in an effort to determine where and how the agendas corresponding to these forces may converge or diverge. And this is critical for better understanding and harnessing these forces for application to a country's sustainable development. The framework presented in this study attempts to organize and examine the different components of these economic and political forces and facilitates the application of development oriented analysis and decision-making to national university system policy.

REFERENCES

Altbach, Philip. 2002. The Decline of the Guru: The academic profession in developing and middle-income countries. Chestnut Hill, MA: Boston College.

Altbach, Philip. 2004. "Globalization and the university: Myths and realities in an unequal world." Changes 1-12.

Altbach, Philip. 2007. Tradition and Transition: The International Imperative in Higher Education. Chestnut Hill, MA: Boston College.

Altbach, Philip; Knight, Jane. 2006. "The Internationalization of Higher Education: Motivations and Realities." The NEA 2006 Almanac of Higher Education.

Bello, Maria Eugenia. 2003. Educación y globalización – Los discursoseducativos en Iberoamérica. Barcelona: Anthropos.

Beneitone, Pablo, Cesar Esquetini, Julia Gonzalez, Maida Marty Maleta, Gabriela Siufi and Robert Wagenaar (eds.). 2007. Reflexiones y Perspectivas de la Educación Superior en América Latina: Informe Final Proyecto Tuning América Latina 2004-2007. Bilboa, Spain: Universidad de Deusto.

Bernal, Juan Bosco. 2002. "La educacion superior en Panama: Situacion, problemas y desafios." Universidad Francisco Gavidia, San Salvador.

Birdsall, Nancy. 2005. "Rising Inequality in the New Global Economy." WIDER Angle No. 2.World Institute for Development Economics Research.

Carrington, William J. and Enrica Detragiache, 1998. "How Big Is the Brain Drain?" IMF Working Paper: 98/102.

Castells, Manuel. 2000. The rise of the network society. Oxford: Blackwell.

Charlier, Jean Emile and Sarah Croche. 2004. "The Bologna Process and its Actors." Working Paper no. 8. UniversitadegliStudidi Siena. Retrieved October 30, 2008 (http://www.ntua.gr/posdep/BOLOGNA/2004-Charlier-Croche_wp8.pdf).

City of Knowledge - Ciudad del Saber. 2007. Historical background. Panama City, Panama. Retrieved July 20, 2007 (http://www.cdspanama.org).

Consejo Centroamericano de Acreditación (CCA). "Origin, Objectives, Structure." Retrieved October 1, 2007 (http://www.cca.ucr.ac.cr/concurso.html).

Daniel, John. 1998. Mega-universities and Knowledge Media: Technology Strategies for Higher Education. London: Routledge.

Daniel, John. 2001. "Lessons From the Open University: Low-Tech Learning Often Works Best." The Chronicle of Higher Education. Retrieved December 13, 2007. (http://www.chronicle.com/weekly/v48/i02/02b02401.htm).

Dirección de Estadística y Censo (Department of Statistics and Census, DEC). 2008. Situación Económica: Cuentas Nacionales 2007 (Economic Situation: National Accounts 2007).Panama City, Panama: DEC.

Douglass, John A. 2005. "How All Globalization Is Local: Countervailing Forces and their Influence on Higher Education Markets." Higher Education Policy 18: 445-473.

Euromoney. 2006. "Real Estate and Tourism Investment: Speculative Bubble or Sustainable Growth." Presented in The Euromoney Panama Conference: Hub of the Americas? Panama City, Panama.

European University Association (EUA). 2006. "Europe's New Higher Education Landscape." Brussels: EUA. Retrieved March 20, 2007 (http://www.eua.be/fileadmin/user_upload/files/).

Florida State University (FSU). 2007. Panama Campus. Retrieved December 1, 2007 (http://panama.fsu.edu/).

Friedman, Thomas. 2006. The World is Flat: a brief history of the twenty-first century. New York: Farrar, Straus and Giroux.

Garnier, Leonardo. 2004. "Knowledge and Higher Education in Latin America." in Globalization and Higher Education, edited by J. Odin. Honolulu: University of Hawaii Press.

Global Legal Information Network (GLIN). 2008. Jurisdiction of Panama. Retrieved March 1-23, 2008 (http://www.glin.gov).

Goethals Consulting Corporation. 2008. "Mercado laboral en perspectiva." Panama City, Panama: Goethals Consulting Corp.

Hayes, Dennis and Robin Wynyard. 2002. The McDonaldization of Higher Education. Westport, CT, and London: Bergin and Garvey.

Inter-American Development Bank. 2003. "Enfrentando el Futuro. La Educación Terciaria en Panamá: Desafíosy Oportunidades" Inter-American Development Bank, Washington DC.

International Monetary Fund (IMF). 2008. World Economic Outlook. Washington, DC: IMF.

Knight, Jane. 2003. "GATS, trade and higher education perspective 2003 - Where are we?" The Observatory on Borderless Education, London.

Lundvall, Bengt-Ake. 2007. "Higher Education, Innovation and Economic Development." Paper presented at the World Bank's Regional Bank Conference on Development Economics, Beijing, January 16-17, 2007.

Ministerio de Educación de la República de Panamá (Ministry of Education, MEDUCA). 2007. "Education Statistics." Retrieved March 30, 2008 (http://www.meduca.gob.pa).

Noble, David. 2001. Digital Diploma Mills: The automation of higher education. New York: Monthly Review Press.

Programa de Promoción de la ReformaEducativa en América Latina y el Caribe - Consejo del Sector Privadopara la Asistencia Educacional (PREALCOSPAE). 2007. "Informe de ProgresoEducativo – Panama." Panama City, Panama: COSPAE.

Reichert, Sybille and Christian Tauch. 2005. "Trends IV: European Universities Implementing Bologna." Brussels: European University Association.

Retrieved October 12, 2007 (http://www.bologna-bergen2005.no/Docs/02-EUA/050425_EUA_TrendsIV.pdf).

RegistroPública de Panamá (Public Registry of Panama). 2008. "Online verification of registration." Retrieved November 2007-March 2008 (https://www.registropublico.gob.pa).

Ritzer, George. 1995. The Mcdonaldization of Society. Thousand Oaks: Sage Publications.

Sassen, Saskia. 2001. The Global City. Second edition. New Jersey; Oxford: Princeton University Press.

Task Force on higher education and society. 2000. Higher education in developing countries: Peril and Promise. Washington DC: World Bank.

Thomas, Scott. 2004. "Socioeconomic Mobility." in Globalization and Higher Education, edited by O. Jaishree. Honolulu: Univeristy of Hawaii Press.

Torres, Carlos; Schugurensky, Daniel 2002. "The Political Economy of Higher Education in the Era of Neoliberal Globalization: Latin America in Comparative Perspective." Higher Education 43:429-455.

Tuning America Latina. 2007. Tuning America Latina 2007. Mexico City: Universidad Autonoma de Mexico (UNAM).

UNESCO-IESALC. 2007. Report on Higher Education in Latin America and the Caribbean 2000-2005: The Metamorphosis of Higher Education. Caracas, Venezuela: UNESCO-IESALC.

UNESCO. 2004. UNESCO/OECD Guidelines on Quality Provision In Cross-Border Higher Education. Prepared for Drafting Meeting 2, 14-15 October 2004, Tokyo, Japan. UNESCO Division of Higher Education Section for Reform, Innovation and Quality Assurance (RIQ). Retrieved October 24, 2007 (http://www.oecd.org/dataoecd/43/28/33783530.pdf).

UNESCO. 2005. Guidelines for Quality Provision in Cross-border Higher Education. Paris: UNESCO.

United Nations Development Programme (UNDP). 2002. Informe Nacional de Desarrollo Humano (National Human Development Report). Panama City, Panama: UNDP.

Universidad Católica Santa María La Antigua (USMA). 2007. Introducción. Retrieved December 1, 2007 (http://www.usma.ac.pa).

Universidad de Panamá (University of Panama, UP). 2007. Oferta Academica. Retrieved December 1, 2007 (http://www.up.ac.pa).

Universidad Tecnológica de Panamá (Technological University of Panama, UTP). 2007. Oferta Academica. Retrieved December 1, 2007 (http://www.utp.ac.pa).

World Bank. 2006. "World Development Indicators 2006." Washington, DC: World Bank.

World Bank. 2008. "World Development Indicators 2008." Washington, DC: World Bank.

World Economic Forum. 2008. "Global Competitiveness Index 2008." World Economic Forum, Washington DC.

Yin, Robert K. 2002.Case Study Research Design and Methods, third edition. Thousand Oaks: Sage Publication

CHAPTER 14

Human Capital Development, Technological Capabilities, and National Development

Victor E. Dike

INTRODUCTION

This paper examines forces that have prevented leaders from effectively utilizing the abundant human and natural resources at their disposal in Nigeria to build up the technological base of society and transform the nation into an industrialized country. The population of Nigeria is estimated to be about 154 million, and it is rapidly growing without commensurate economic growth and development to sustain the teeming population (NBS, 2009). The unemployment rate is over 14 percent and public schools lack adequate funding to provide quality education to students; and the few private schools that exist are beyond the reach of the common people (NBS, 2009; Kakwagh and Ikwuba, 2010).

Teachers at all levels of the educational system (primary, secondary, and tertiary) are not properly motivated to effectively perform their duties. For instance, the government is always talking about revamping their annual development training program and investing more in education as well as providing them the same privileges civil servants in other sectors of the economy are enjoying without backing them with actions (Dike, 2002). As a result, they are always on strike to force the government to pay their basic salaries and benefits. Over the years the government has been promising to improve their conditions of services, such as to refocus science and technology education toward better teaching, learning and national development (Offor, 2007), but each time it has failed to honor its promises. The teachers' frequent industrial actions have more often than not disrupted regular academic calendars (NBS, 2009).

Consequently, experienced and high quality teachers who are disgusted and can no longer tolerate the poor conditions of services they find themselves in are departing in droves to neighboring countries with better working conditions. For instance, many of them have died of 'starvation, diseases and out of frustration' (Dike, 2002). These are among the major causes of the dwindling standard of education in Nigeria. Poor investment in human capital development (education and health), and particularly the neglect of technical and vocational education and training (TVET) and science-based technology education, has contributed in no small measure to a lack of highly-skilled technical manpower and the "technological capabilities" (Mahon, 2003) needed to drive the economy and transform Nigeria into an industrialized society and improve the living conditions of the nation's teeming population.

Experts in human capital development, ranging from classical scholars such as Schumpeter (1942) to the contemporary scholars such as Schultz (1993) and Hanushek and Kym (1995), have identified some dimensions of human capital: entrepreneurial skills (or human skills or human skills capital); technological progress and results from Joseph Schumpeter's "creative destructive"; accumulated human knowledge and skills that are as important as physical capital in the production process; and of course social capital (the relationship between the individual-social and institutional capital).   These are some of the positive results of long-term investment in human capital development (education and health) (Piazza-Georgi, 2002).

But poor leadership and governance are integral aspects of the problems facing the nation, as leaders have made investment in human capital development difficult. Economic growth and development are difficult if not impossible in any society that does not seriously invest in human capital development. That is the crux of the matter with oil-rich Nigeria; the majority of political leaders are not working for the wellbeing of the citizenry, but rather for their own selfish purposes. They are known to have diverted public funds allocated for education and other national development programs into their own private bank accounts. Some of them have been "convicted of corruption"; they are living extravagant life style without any other identifiable sources of income (Nossiter, 2013).

In addition to poor investment in human capital development, neglect of infrastructure and institutions that drive the economy in a major concern. Today, these structures are in shambles, leading to an unfriendly business environment. Many business organizations, particularly manufacturing industries, are closing down, leading to rising unemployment and crime. The industries that can afford to are relocating to neighboring countries with more inviting business environments.

It is unquestionably a Herculean task to govern a society, but it becomes much more daunting in a society such as Nigeria with an uncertain sociopolitical and economic environment. The state and fate of Nigeria today is defined by the ineffectiveness of its political leaders, non-functional institutions and dilapidated infrastructure, which has crippled the economy and pauperized the people. Thus, the myriad of sociopolitical and economic problems facing the society today are exerting untold pressures on the people who are utilizing every available opportunity to pour out their anger and frustration. The question is: Can the greedy and "me first" new breed of politicians lead Nigeria to true democracy and toward a true capitalistic system and economic prosperity?

Purpose

The purpose of this paper is to examine the obstacles to Nigeria's quest for national development, from the point of view of investment in human capital development, technological capability, and good governance and leadership. Thus, the paper seeks to discuss the issues in an attempt to suggest some solutions to policymakers. This includes ways and means of providing employment for the growing numbers of jobless youths' and lifting out of poverty the millions of other suffering citizens.

RESEARCH METHODS

The data for this case study were derived from the research and analysis of scholars, analysts and practitioners, government documents and recent newspaper and journal articles as noted in the introduction. The primary method of study was an extensive review of available literature for an in-depth analysis of the problems facing the Nigerian educational system and the economy. Sources of information were carefully verified, evaluated and analyzed to determine their veracity. It has been noted that the educational system of any society is designed to transmit the beliefs, values, attitudes, and norms from one generation to another as well as to train skilled technical manpower to drive and sustain the economy.

PROBLEM STATEMENT

Over the years Nigeria has been investing less in education, infrastructure, and institutions that are critical to building a viable economy. A review of available data on spending (per cent of GDP) on education in Africa shows Nigeria's unimpressive position. For instance, Angola spends about 2.7 of its GDP on education; Mozambique 2.4; Algeria 4.3; Namibia 8.6; Cote d'Ivoire 4.6 while Nigeria spends a paltry of 1.3 percent. Yet political leaders think that Nigeria can be transformed into an industrialized society without these necessary preconditions. The political leaders of Nigeria have not kept their promises with the people; they appear to be working on their behalf and not for the people's welfare. Thus, Nigerians should check their enthusiasm whenever the politicians are making their usual paper promises. Developed countries around the globe could not have become what they are today without investing in human capital development, good governance and leadership, and technological capability.

RESEARCH QUESTIONS

This paper focuses on the following research questions: Can Nigeria become an industrialized society without functional fundamental institutions and infrastructure (i.e. an effective judicial system, stable electricity supply, functional educational system, good network of roads, security, good leadership and governance, etc.). Are Nigerians (leaders and followers) making good efforts to resolve the challenges facing the nation and its quest for national development? Can Nigeria meet its challenges for national development without copious investments in human capital development and technological capabilities? Can the people (the leaders and followers) build the technological base that will transform Nigeria into an industrialized society?

CHALLENGES FACING EDUCATION AND THE NIGERIAN ECONOMY

The next section of this paper discusses the myriad forces that have prevented Nigeria from investing in education and the emerging instructional technologies so as to empower the citizens with employable skills through quality education directed by highly trained and motivated teachers. Human capital development gurus (Schumpeter, 1942; Schultz, 1993; Becker, 1993) have convincingly argued that without investment in human, physical, and social capital, economic growth and development will be difficult if not impossible.

HUMAN CAPITAL DEVELOPMENT

Ancient and contemporary human and social capital thinkers have been confronted by the issue of human capital development for decades because they recognize the critical role human capital and physical capital development play in workers' productive capability, the prosperity of a nation, and the overall living condition of the people (Schumpeter, 1942; Schultz, 1993; Becker, 1993; Hanushek and Kym, 2005; Bell and Pavitt, 1995). However, Becker (1993) who is widely known for his work on human capital development observed that human capital theory tends to draw a distinction between general education and specific training. He observed that the key focus of human capital theory is how education increases human productivity by improving human knowledge and skills and increases an individual worker's productive capacity, future income, and lifetime earnings. Thus, the neglect of this important element has a far-reaching consequence on the welfare of a nation.

According to Becker (1993) general education creates general human capital, while technical and vocational education provides specific human capital. In a human capital framework the economic prosperity and progress of a nation depends precariously on the stock of its physical and human capital (Becker, 1993). This author anchors his work on this perspective because no nation can talk about manpower, planning, growth, development, and the creation of employment opportunities to improve the lives of the citizens without bringing education (formal, non-formal and informal) or learning into the equation (Perkins, et al., 2001). This is because the shortage of manpower (this author emphasizes technical education) has the tendency to impede individual productivity, national productivity, and economic growth. In other words, human resource development has an essential role to play in the economic health of a nation (Perkins, et al., 2001).

Recognizing the importance of education in national development, the UNESCO international experts, declared that "since education is considered the key to effective development strategies, technical and vocational education and training must be the master key that can... improve the quality of life for all and help achieve sustainable development" (UNESCO, October 2004). One of the major problems facing Nigeria and its economy is that the nation, which aspires to transform itself into an advanced economy, is not investing enough in the necessary institutional and infrastructural conditions.

Social thinkers in the field of human capital and social capital theory have observed that a workforce's productivity capability is determined by many variables, including its human skills and ability, health, motivation, and job satisfaction (Judge, May 2001). Experts in this field, as well as social analysts, have also observed that the majority of the sociopolitical and economic issues facing Nigeria can be attributed to its poor investment in human capital and physical capital development, poor governance, and visionless leadership (Dike, April-September, 2010; Ferriss, 2006; Lewis, 2004).

Nigeria's underdevelopment can be traced to poor governance and inept leadership, which breeds the corruption that has become pandemic in Nigerian society (see *San Francisco Chronicle,* 2007; Dike, April-September, 2010). This appears to be the undisputable reason for the lack of investment in institutional and infrastructural structures, human capital development (particularly health, technical and vocational education and training, and science-based technology education) that will enable the nation to develop a highly-skilled technical workforce to drive economic growth and national development and improve the health of the nation (Krueger and Mikael, 2001).

Thus, a lack of long-term investments in human capital and the accumulation of knowledge and human skills and "physical capital development" (or the "stock of equipment and structures that are used to produce goods and services" (Mankiw, 2008)) creates a bottleneck to economic growth and development and prevents the creation of employment opportunities for citizens (Hanushek and Kym 2005; Becker, 1993). Specifically, poor investment in human capital and physical capital development (patchy electricity distribution and potable water supply; bad networks of roads, railways, and airways; congested sea ports, a deficient postal system, *et cetera*) has contributed in no small measure to the poor performance of the economy, and by extension, the dwindling standard of education in Nigeria.

Over the years employers in Nigeria have been complaining that most of the recent university graduates lack employable skills, problem-solving abilities, and other competencies that used to determine an individual worker's productivity capability (Mankiw, 2008; Dike, 2002).Yet Nigeria's educational administrators and policymakers have done very little, if anything, to improve the quality of human capital, which has a direct bearing on workers' productivity (Perkins, et al., 2001).

However, because of the effect of "human skills capital" (HSC) on individual productivity and by extension profit margins, organizations around the globe are said to be spending billions of dollars annually to educate and upgrade their employees' "human skills capital" (Piazza-Georgi, 2002). More often than not workers are rewarded for higher productivity and the high quality of their goods and services, which influences the profit margins of their companies (Clayton, 1995).

Before independence in 1960 the schools in Nigeria were properly funded and managed, students were well behaved, and the quality of graduates was equal to those from advanced nations (Dike, 2002). But today, the schools lack adequate funding to hire quality teachers and purchase the necessary instructional technologies to produce high quality graduates and enhance technological development. Studies show that no nation can make meaningful socioeconomic and political strides without a good pool of skilled technical workers (Hanushek and Kym, 2005) with strong technological abilities (Mohan, 2003; Bell and Pavitt, 1995).

Instead of Nigeria's schools being properly funded and developed into places for high quality research, technological innovation, and good character formation, they have become breeding grounds for cultism and other destructive social behaviors. Today, "values education," good "moral values" and civic responsibility, which shape the character of nations, have become a thing of the past (Dike, 2002).

As Lickona (1992) has aptly observed "respect and responsibility are the two foundational moral values" that a society should teach its citizens. Other admirable qualities include: honesty, fairness, tolerance, prudence, self-discipline, helpfulness, compassion, cooperation, courage (the virtues of Aristotle) among other democratic values. Thus, "taking responsibility for the things we do wrong as well as the things we do right" (Lickona, 1992) is important for national development.

As noted earlier, as the nation's quality of education is rapidly deteriorating so is the economic environment. In its 2010 report on "Doing Business in Nigeria 2010-Through Difficult Times," the World Bank ranked Nigeria 125th out of 182 economies surveyed in its Global Doing Business Report. The report showed that about 90 per cent of Nigerian businesses that operate in the informal sector lack access to credit. In its 2008 Review of World Development, the United Nations Development Programme (UNDP) ranked Nigeria 157th out of 177 in the Human Development Index. Nigeria was also named among the "Least Livable" nations (UNDP-see 2008 Review of World Population).

Some of the problems facing Nigeria today require common sense solutions, but others require a sophisticated framework of ideas and the application of advanced technologies. As Albert Einstein observed decades ago, "the specific problems we face today cannot be solved at the same level of thinking we were at when we created them" (see quote from Albert Einstein, n/d). Thus, for the economy to grow and for businesses to thrive and create employment, Nigeria should employ or elect political leaders with proper skills, knowledge and vision as well as the political courage to adopt and implement policies to meet the challenges facing the nation.

LEADERSHIP AND GOVERNANCE

The role that leadership plays in the direction of organizations and the development of nations has continued to prompt debates as leadership appears to have many meanings (Marquis and Huston, 2012). Although there is no single definition of leadership, it is imperative for this paper to consider some perspectives. Ward (2009) has defined leadership as "the art of motivating a group of people to act towards achieving a common goal" and not a selfish objective. Meanwhile, as Northouse (2007) has aptly noted, leadership "is a process of getting things done through people"; it "means responsibility"— having "passion for the purpose and the mission of the organization" or society that one leads.

However, because of poor leadership or "leadership without a purpose" the state of the polity appears to be rapidly deteriorating. Very few of the leaders of Nigeria, if any, work to improve the living conditions of the citizens. Over the years a wave of reform programs have been undertaken, but society still lacks leaders with the political will and commitment to implement effective policies to transform the economy and tackle the sociopolitical problems facing the nation. Political leaders do not seem to understand that leadership means assuming responsibility for something. They appear good at prescribing solutions to economic problems (Dike, 2003) without providing the institutional and infrastructural framework to help the economy grow (Acemoglu, 2003; Edison, 2003). As noted earlier, they have not provided any practical solutions to problems other than talking about the issues. The government should utilize the rule of law to change the society and build a more productive economy.

More often than not, their policies are hastily put together and poorly executed. The political landscape is littered with the wreckage of unreasoned policies, and those involved in such activities appear to enjoy the nation's underdeveloped status (Dike, 2003). Clearly, the activities of the leaders shape the reality of the nations they lead (UNDP-See its 2008 Review of World Population).

To resolve the leadership challenge facing Nigeria today and transform its organizations into productive entities (Kouzes and Posner, 1995) Nigerians must elect or appoint men and women of proven integrity, drive, and know-how to transform (Burns, 2003) and manage the affairs of the nation. If it fails to meet these ethical and leadership challenges (Johnson, 2005) and improve its organizational effectiveness (Bass and Avolio, 1994), Nigeria may not achieve its objectives. The nation's economic growth and development rests on good leadership and governance. Thus, this author would suggest that for Nigeria to move forward the leaders as well as the followers must clean up their act and invest in the fundamental infrastructure and institutions that will promote technological innovation, transform the economy, and develop the society.

Related to the leadership problem is governance, which has been defined as a system of values, policies, and institutions by which a society manages its economic, social, and political affairs through interactions within the state, civil society and private sector. Essentially, governance comprises the mechanisms and processes for citizens and groups to articulate their interests, to work together and mediate their differences, and exercise their legal rights and obligations with rules, institutions and practices that set limits and provide incentives for individuals, organizations and firms (UNDP-see 2008 Review of World Population).

Thus, good governance-consisting of the three dimensions of governance: political, economic and social governance (Shabbir-Cheema, May 2005)-refers to the question of how a society can organize itself to ensure equality of opportunity and equity (social and economic justice) for all its citizens. Good governance promotes people-centered development; but "bad governance" the opposite of good governance (Shabbir-Cheema, May 2005), is among the major causes of the problems currently facing Nigeria. For instance, the people are not allowed equal economic opportunity and freedom to participate in the political process. This inequality threatens to destabilize the polity and undermine Nigeria's democratization process.

As Sen (1999) observed, "unfreedoms" leave the people with little choice to exercise "their reasoned agency." According to Sen (1999), "Freedoms are not only the primary ends of development, they are also among its primary means." Thus, development, whether social, political and economic, "requires the removal of major sources of unfreedoms" (p. 36-37).

Because of bad governance (and thus corruption) Nigeria's system lacks checks and balances (or mechanisms) to control the autocratic tendencies in government or hold political actors accountable for their actions. The politicians do not practice ethical politics and their actions do not add values to the system. This lack of "ethical politics and values,"-as well as a politics of hate and destruction, has contributed significantly to the economic and political hiccups in society. Corruption (Smith, 2008) is, however, plays a larger role in the problems facing Nigeria, as it leads to the bad governance that has hampered socio-political and economic development.

BRIBERY AND CORRUPTION

Although corruption is a global scourge, Nigeria appears to suffer the most from it because the nation's leaders are pathologically corrupt. Was Nigeria born to be corrupt? Everyone appears to believe that Nigeria has a "culture of corruption" (Smith, 2008). Over the years, Nigeria has earned a lot of revenue from crude oil. However, these profits have plummeted because of rampant political corruption. An articlein the *San Francisco Chronicle*, March 11, 2007, described Nigeria as a rich nation floating on oil wealth, but almost none of it flows to the people." This is evidence that the top public servants are rich because they harbor the mentality that public money belongs to no one (Dike, April-September, 2010; October-March, 2011).

Nigeria is perceived today as a hotbed of corruption; and it seems to be fighting a losing battle over its so-called war against "corruption". Thus, it appears the country has become synonymous with corruption. The majority of the elected officials, appointees, and top members of government are corrupt. They often extract bribes from the citizens (business owners, those seeking to do business with the state, etc.) while performing their official duties. The magnitude of high-profile political corruption in Nigeria (Nossiter, 2013) tends to dwarf any genuine efforts to enhance economic growth and nation development and it diminishes the people's trust in government. National dailies are awash with news of how public officials are acquiring million-dollar homes (within and outside of Nigeria) and stockpiling stolen public money in financial institutions abroad. Thus, corruption scandals are strewn all over the society like a straw hut in a hurricane (*Business Day,* May 14, 2010; May 15, 2010; and April 17, 2012).

There are two sides to every problem; private individuals are also involved in corrupt activities. A spate of studies shows that corruption leads to "poor governance and low growth" and hampers social development (Rose-Ackerman, 2004; Bensinger, 2007). The leaders of Nigeria have demonstrated their unwillingness to reform the society despite the number of top government officials involved in corruption (*BusinessDay,*May 14, 2010; May 15, 2010; and April 17, 2012). For instance, the former governor of Delta State, James Ibori, who eluded the Economic and Financial

Crimes Commission (EFCC), was arrested in Dubai recently (*BusinessDay,* May 14, 2010) on money laundering charges.

Since corruption is anathema to political stability and economic prosperity, this author can hazard to support the assertion that Nigeria's problems are not the result of the "harshness and the niggardliness of nature" (Keynes, May 1932). Rather, corruption has prevented Nigeria from investing in human capital development, particularly the technological capacitation that would drive the economy, create employment, and put the nation's abundant human resources into productive use.

If political leaders want to fight corruption they should start by fixing the economy, since some of the petty corrupt activities are caused by poverty. For instance, some of the roadblocks on the roads and highways in the society are manned by police officers some of whom are thieves in uniform; others get involved in corrupt activities because they are ill-trained and poorly paid (Dike, April-September, 2010; October-March, 2011). In addition, to breathe new life into the nation's ossified economy Nigeria must strengthen its critical institutions and the infrastructure that drives the economy.

INFRASTRUCTURAL AND INSTITUTIONAL CHALLENGES

Ineffective institutions and dilapidated infrastructure (pot-holed roads, erratic power supply, limited access to potable water and basic healthcare, and ineffective regulatory agencies, *et cetera*) are among the serious challenges facing Nigeria and its economy. A plethora of reforms and development policies are ineffective due to shoddy infrastructure and institutional failure (Hoff, Fall 2003). In particular, the electricity supply is poor and expensive, and investors are not impressed. In a country where electricity takes about 40 percent cost of production, improving the electricity supply would lure foreign investors into the society and spur on the sluggish economy (*Daily Sun,* June 7, 2010). The growth and development of the Nigerian economy appears impossible without the necessary critical infrastructure and institutions. Essentially, with functional infrastructure, effective institutions, and high-quality education system, Nigeria could be transformed into the Singapore of West Africa. Singapore is said to have "one of the world's best-educated populations and busiest port" (*The Economist,* February 25, 2012, p. 80).

As economists have observed, building a vibrant economy or restoring growth to an ailing economy takes resources. To ensure long-term growth and prosperity, Nigeria must use its resources wisely and invest in science-based technology education to train a good stock of highly-skilled technical workers to build and maintain the critical institutions and infrastructure without which the economy will be unable to gain the "power of productivity" (Lewis, 2004). A nation enjoys higher standards of living if its workers can produce large quantities of quality goods and services for local consumption and extra for export (Mankiw, 2008). Without technological capabilities, however, the economy will remain in shambles, productivity will remain low, the quality of goods and services will remain poor, and Nigeria will be unable to produce enough food to feed its teeming population and will be unable to compete effectively in the global marketplace.

TECHNOLOGICAL CAPABILITIES

This paper posits that the problems facing the Nigerian economy (including the low capability utilization of domestic industries and firms) hinge precariously on the nation's poor investment in human capital development (education and health) and a lack of long-term investment in education, particularly the science-based technology education and technical and vocational education and training (TVET) that will enable the country to develop a good stock of highly-skilled technical workers to inspire innovation and the technological development and economic growth that will sustain the nation's industrialization process.

Put differently, the "growth tragedy" (Easterly and Levin, April 1997), of the Nigerian economy has its roots in ineffective and inefficient domestic development policy design and implementation, as well as the policymakers' failure to learn from the impressive history of economic growth and development in the East Asian countries that are today branded Asian Tigers. To move forward technologically Nigeria has to invest copiously in technical education and develop "an effective national system of innovation" (Mohan, 2003; Asian Development Bank, 2008; Dike, 2009), which is a precondition for rapid technological development. The pace of technological change in any society is a reflection of the health of its infrastructure and institutions, and of courses its social capital, which will encourage innovative system activities and enhance industrial capital accumulation, technological transformation, and national development (Mohan, 2003).

As in human capital development, physical capital development in the form of technological capabilities and innovation will drive a sagging economy and create employment. Studies show that there is a correlation between a nation's underdeveloped status and soaring unemployment rates and their lack of technological capabilities and the highly-skilled technical workers needed to drive the economy and create employment (Rose, 2009; Mohan, 2003; Sen, 1975; Dike, October-March, 2011).

Thus, because of a lack of investment in science-based technology education and technical and vocational education and training (TVET), Nigeria is suffering from a shortage of highly-skilled technical manpower to build and maintain its critical infrastructure and produce quality goods and services at a low cost and compete effectively in the global marketplace. The on-going global financial and economic crisis that started in 2008 has worsened the already weak Nigerian economy plagued by rising youth unemployment (Kakwagh and Ikwuba, 2010), social crisis and lawlessness (kidnapping for ransom and the *Boko Haram* (a militant Islamic group)) (*Daily Trust*, August 18, 2010; *ThisDay*, January 9, 2012).

Social scientists, especially economists, have aptly noted that modern economy demands technological skills to enhance innovation and to function effectively and efficiently (Rose, 2009; Offor, 2007; Freeman, 1987). In particular, development economists have noted that socio-economic changes or transformations are impossible in any society without several preconditions, one of which is technological capabilities (Webb and Grant, 2003; Soubbotina, 2004). In addition, studies show that no nation has developed without "technological capabilities" (Kim, 1980, 1997; Bell and Pavitt, 1995; Mohan, 2003).

For Kim (1980) "technological capability" is "the ability to make effective use of technological knowledge in efforts to assimilate, use, adapt and change existing technologies" (Kim, 1980, p.254-277). In fact, experts have noted that "technological capability" is an essential component for "sustainable development," which is a "development" that "meets the needs of the present generation without compromising the ability of future generations to meet their own needs" (United Nations, December 11, 1987; Smith and Rees, 1998).

In spite of some development efforts (some people would argue that these efforts are cosmetic or superficial designed to deceive the masses), the economic environment remains very unfriendly, with industries and organizations still facing a huge hurdle. However, because of poor employment opportunities, most of the youth are frustrated and desperate to leave the country. Stories abound of how desperate Nigerians, mostly youth, take extraordinary risks to travel to Europe, the United States and even to other African nations in search of an elusive better life. Some of them have been arrested, tortured, maimed or imprisoned in foreign countries; and some of them have died in the deserts of North Africa in the process of trying to escape economic hardship (Hamoon, May 13, 2006; Fletcher, *BBC News*, December 2007).

CONCLUDING REMARKS: SYSTEM INNOVATION AND TECHNOLOGICAL CAPABILITIES

Does Nigeria possess the skilled technical manpower needed for system innovation and technological transformation? The world economy is rapidly changing and the only countries that are capable of competing effectively in the global marketplace are those that are investing in human capital development and technological innovation. Nigerians are tired of being hungry in the midst of plenty. Investors (both domestic and foreign) are not motivated to invest in the domestic economy because of the unlimited hurdles posed by the shoddy infrastructure and institutions.

It is impossible for Nigeria to meet its technological and systemic challenges, while also moving along with the changing global economy, without investing copiously in technological education and research and development. To transform its economy and effectively compete in the global marketplace of tomorrow Nigeria should begin today to nurture and strengthen the infrastructure and institutions that make technological development possible. Technological innovation will give rise to new entrepreneurs and knowledge-driven industries that will push through the barriers to economic growth and development.

No nation can grow and thrive in the present knowledge-intensive global economy without a long-term investment in human capital development (education and health) and technological innovation. No society can grow and thrive in the present knowledge-driven global economy without copious investment in human capital development (education and health), research and development (R&D), and technological innovation either by developing serious indigenous technological innovation (fresh thinking) or copying and adapting other nations' technological ideas in the cheapest possible means.

China and other serious nations have taken this route to become technological giants. And today, China possesses the technological clout to gain from the power of productivity (*The Economist,* May 26th – June 1st, 2012). To move forward, Nigeria should adopt and adapt the economic policies and technological innovation of successful nations. Nigeria can become an industrialized nation either by developing its indigenous technology or by copying and adapting other nations' technological ideas via the cheapest possible means.

Thus, without creating a hospitable environment to lure investors into the economy; and without ensuring that the Constitution and rule of law is respected and business contracts honored; and without investing in human capital development, particularly technology education Nigeria will continue to dream of being an industrialized nation.

REFERENCES

Acemoglu, D. (2003). "Root Causes: A historical approach to assessing the role of institutions in economic development." Finance and Development, June, 40 (2), p.27-30.

Asian Development Bank (2008). "Education and Skills: Strategies for Accelerated Development in Asia and the Pacific." *Asian Development Bank* (ADB).

Bass, B.M. and Avolio, B.J (1994 editors), *Improving Organizational Effectiveness through Transformational Leadership*; Thousand Oaks, CA: Sage.

Becker, G.S. (1993[1964]), *Human Capital: A Theoretical and Empirical Analysis, with Special Reference to Education* (3rd edition): Chicago, University of Chicago Press.

Bell, M. and Pavitt, K. (1995)."The Development of Technological Capabilities." In Hague, I. U. (editor), *Trade, Technology and International Competitiveness*. Washington, DC: The World Bank.

Bensinger, G. (2007, March 11). "Oil giant that runs on grease of politics." *San Francisco Chronicle.*

Burns, J.M. (2003). *Transforming leadership,* New York: NY: Grove/Atlantic, Inc.

BusinessDay, (2010)."EFCC seeks Ibori's extradition from Dubai." May 14.

BusinessDay (2010). "I resigned to face corruption charges-Ogbulafor," May 15.

BusinessDay(2012). "Ibori jailed for 13 years;" April 17.

Clayton G.E. (1995). *Economics: Principles and Practices*, New York: Glenco, McGraw-Hill; p.23; p.136.

Daily Trust (2010). "Experts Proffer Solution to Collapse of Buildings." August 18.

Daily Sun (2010). "In Nigeria, power is about 40% cost of production – John Aluya, MD, TechnoGlass."June 7.

Dike, V. E. (2002). "The State of Education in Nigeria and the Health of the Nation," *NESG Economic Indicators,* Jan-March, 8 (1), p. 45-50

Dike, V. E. (2003). "Nigeria: Economic Growth and Institutional Factors," *NESG Economic Indicators,* October–December, 9 (4), p. 46-50.

Dike, V.E. (April-September, 2010). "Review of the Challenges facing the Nigerian Economy: What is the Way Forward?" *NESG Economic & Policy Review,* 17(2&3), p. 45-53.

Dike, V.E. (October-March, 2011). "Can Nigeria Build its economic future: Can Nigeria Build its Economic Future?: A Critical Review of Issues Facing the Nation." *Economic and Policy Review,* Vol.17 &18(4&1), p.24-32.

Dike, V.E. (2009). "The Relevance of Technical and Vocational Education in Nigeria's Development Strategy: A New Paradigm for Effective Economic Transformation." *African Journal of Science and Technology, Innovation and Development (AJSTID),*1 (2&3),197-216.

Edison, H. (2003). "Test the Links: How strong is the links between institutional quality and economic performance?" *Finance and Development*, June, 40(2), p.35-37.

Easterly, W. and Levin, R (April 1997)."Africa's Growth Tragedy: Policies and Ethic Divisions."   Retrieved   from

http://williameasterly.files.wordpress.com/2010/08/17_
   easterly_levine_africasgrowthtragedy_prp.pdfon February 17, 2012.
Einstein, A. (Quote, n/d). Online: http://www.quotedb.com/quotes/11. Retrieved,
   March 28, 2011.
Ferriss, A.L. (2006). "A Theory of Social Structure and the Quality of Life," *Applied
   Research in Quality of Life,* May, 1(1), p. 117-123.
Fletcher, P. (2007). "Mirage of rich Europe Lures Job-Hungry Africa;" *BBC News-
   online,* December 5.
Freeman, C. (1987). *Technology and Economic Performance: Lessons from Japan.*
   London: Pinter.
Hamoon, S. (2006). *Africa Transit Migration through Libya to Europe: the Human
   Cost.* May 13, Cairo: FMRS/AUC.
Hanushek, E. and Kym, D. (2005). Schooling Labour Forces Quality and Economic
   Growth. NBER Working Paper 5399. MA: Cambridge.
Hoff, K. (2003). "Paths of Institutional Development: A view from Economic
   History." *The World Bank Research Observer,* Fall, 18(2), p. 205-226.
Judge T.A;Thoresen, C.J; Bono, J.E.; and Patton, G.K. (May 2001). "The job
   satisfaction–job Performance relationship: A qualitative and quantitative
   review." *Psychological Bulletin,* 127(3), p. 376-407.
Johnson, C.E. (2005). Meeting ethical challenges of leadership (2nd edition).
   Thousand Oaks, VA: Sage.
Kakwagh, V.V. and Ikwuba, A. (2010). "Unemployment in Nigeria: Causes and
   Related Issues." *Canadian Social Science,* 6(4), p. 61-67.
Keynes, J.M. (1932). "The World's Economic Outlook." *The Atlantic, May.* Retrieved
   from   http://www.theatlantic.com/unbound/flashbks/budget/keynesf.htm,
   December 4, 2006.
Kim, L. (1980). "Stages of Development in Industrial technology in a Developing
   Country," *Research Policy,* 9(3), p. 254-277.
Kim, L. (1997). *From Imitation to Innovation: The dynamics of Korea's
   Technological Learning.* Boston, MA: Harvard Business School Press.
Kouzes, J.M. and Posner, B.Z (1995). *The Leadership Challenge: How to keep getting
   extraordinary things done in Organizations.* San Francisco: Jose-Bass.
Krueger, A.B. and Mikael, L. (2001). "Education for Growth, Why and for
   Whom?"*Journal of Economic Literature,* 39(4), p. 1101–136.
Lewis, W.W. (2004). *The Power of Productivity: Wealth, Poverty, and the Threat to
   Global Stability.* Chicago: University of Chicago Press.
Lickona, T. (1992, October). *Educating for Character: How Our Schools can Teach
   Respect and Responsibility.* New York: Bantman Books.
Mankiw, N. G. (2008). *Essentials Of Economics* (5th edition). South-Western:
   CENGAGE Learning: Australia.
Marquis, B.L. and Huston, C.J. (2012). *Leadership Roles and Management Functions
   in Nursing.* New Delhi: Wolters Kluwer, Lippincott Williams and Wilkins.
Mohan R. (2003), *Facets of the Indian Economy: The NCAER Golden Jubilee
   Lectures.* New Delhi, India: Oxford University Press.
National Bureau of Statistics (NBS). Federal Government of Nigeria-Statistical Fact
   Sheet on Economic and Social Development. Nigeria: Abuja, 2009.

Northouse, G. (2007). *Leadership theory and practice* (3rd edition). Thousand Oak, London, New Delhi: Sage Publications (see p. 3).

Nossiter, A. (2013). "U.S. Embassy criticizes pardons in Nigerian corruption cases." *The New York Times*, March 15.

Offor, E.N. (2007). "Refocusing Science and Technology Education toward National Development." *Knowledge Review: A Multidiciplinary Journal of NAFAK*, 15 (6), p.53-55

Perkins, D.H., Radelet, S., Snowgrass, D.R., Gillis, M., and Roemer, M. (2001). *Economic Development* (5th edition). W.W. Norton Company. See in particular Chapters 8 and 9.

Piazza-Georgi, B. (2002). "The role of human and social capital in growth: extending our understanding." *Cambridge Journal of Economics,* 26, p.461-479.

Rose-Ackerman, S. (2004). "Governance and Corruption." Lomborg, B. (ed.), *Global Crises, Global Solutions.* Cambridge: Cambridge University Press.

Rose, K. (2009). "Enhancing Innovation in Developing Country Systems: A Synthesis of Case Studies and Lesson from Uganda." *African Journal of Science and Technology, Innovation and Development,* 1(2&3), p. 89-114.

Schumpeter, J.A. (1942). *Capitalism, Socialism and Democracy.* Harper (reprinted by Harper Colophon, 1975).

Schultz, T.W. (1993). *Origins of Increasing Returns,* Oxford, Blackwell.

Sen, A. (1975). *Employment, Technology and Development*; Oxford: Clarendon.

Sen A. (1999). *Development as Freedom*; New York: Anchor Books (see Chapters 1-3), p.36-37.

ShabbirCheema, G. (2004). "From public administration to governance: the paradigm shift in the link between government and citizens." Paper presented at the 6th Global Forum on Reinventing Government, with a theme, Towards Participatory and Transparent Governance, 24-May 27, 2005.

Smith, C. and Rees, G. (1998). *Economic Development* (2nd edition). Basingstoke: Macmillan.

Smith, D.J. (2008). *A Culture of Corruption.* Princeton and Oxford: Princeton University Press.

Soubbotina, T.P. (2004). *Beyond Economic Growth: An Introduction to Sustainable Development* (2nd edition). World Bank Publications.

The Economist (February 25, 2012). see 'Business in Rwanda'-"Africa's Singapore?" p.80.

The Economist (May 26 - June 1, 2012). "How strong is China's economy?" (p. 11).

ThisDay (2012). "Jonathan-Boko Haram Has Sympathizers in Govt." January 9.

United Nations (1987). "Report of the World Commission on Environment and Development."

General Assembly Resolution 42/187, December 11. Retrieved from http://www.un-documents.net/a42r187.htm_on September 6, 2010.

UNESCO: Learning for Work, Citizenship and Sustainability. Final report: UNESCO International Experts Meeting: Bonn, Germany, 25-28 October 2004:107.

UNDP: see the 2008 Review of World Population.

Ward, S. (2009). Leadership. About.com. Canada: Small Business; retrieved from http://sbinfocanada.about.com/od/leadership/g/leadership.htm on March 18, 2012.

Webb, C. J. and Grant, C. (2003). Economic Transformation: An Implementation Framework. Tertiary Education Commission Research Paper. Wellington: Tertiary Education Commission.

www.ingramcontent.com/pod-product-compliance
Lightning Source LLC
Chambersburg PA
CBHW041935260326
41914CB00010B/1311